Ontotheological Turnings?

SUNY series in Theology and Continental Thought

Douglas L. Donkel, editor

Ontotheological Turnings?

The Decentering of the Modern Subject in Recent French Phenomenology

JOERI SCHRIJVERS

Published by State University of New York Press, Albany

© 2011 State University of New York

For information, contact State University of New York Press, Albany, NY
www.sunypress.edu

Production by Eileen Meehan
Marketing by Anne M. Valentine

Library of Congress Cataloging-in-Publication Data

Schrijvers, Joeri.
 Ontotheological turnings? : the decentering of the modern subject in recent French phenomenology / Joeri Schrijvers.
     p. cm. — (SUNY series in theology and Continental thought)
 Includes bibliographical references (p.) and index.
 ISBN 978-1-4384-3893-1 (hardcover : alk. paper)
 ISBN 978-1-4384-3894-8 (pbk. : alk. paper)
 1. Phenomenological theology. 2. Marion, Jean-Luc, 1946– 3. Lacoste, Jean-Yves. 4. Lévinas, Emmanuel. I. Title.

 BT40.S365 2011
 230.01—dc22   2011003138

To the memory of Saskia Vermeulen

Contents

Acknowledgments

I should like to offer my gratitude to my promoter, Lieven Boeve, who supported this work in a manifold of generous ways. A word of thanks also to Jean-Yves Lacoste and Kevin Hart who were so kind as to participate in the jury and commented upon earlier versions of this text.

This work has benefited much from the encouragement of and conversations with my colleagues. I would like to thank the members of the research group Theology in a Postmodern Context for the inspiring environment from which this work sprang and for the friendship they have given me. Special mention also to Michael Funk Deckard for taking so much care with the text. Finally, my gratitude to FWO-Flanders, for granting me the scholarship that enabled me to write this work. Thanks also to Nancy, Eileen, Anne, and Doug at SUNY for the smooth cooperation with this volume.

Chapter 1, "Some Notes on a French Debate," is a revised and extended version of *New Blackfriars* 87 (2006), pp. 302–14, "On Doing Theology 'after' Ontotheology: Notes on a French Debate."

Chapter 2 is a revised and extended version of two articles that have appeared earlier: "Phenomenology, Liturgy, and Metaphysics: The Thought of Jean-Yves Lacoste," in *God in France: Eight Contemporary French Thinkers on God*, eds. P. Jonkers and R. Welten (Leuven: Peeters, 2005), pp. 207–25, and "Jean-Yves Lacoste: A Phenomenology of the Liturgy," *Heythrop Journal* 46 (2005), pp. 314–33.

Portions of chapters 4 and 6 are taken from "Ontotheological Turnings? Marion, Lacoste, and Levinas on the Decentering of the Modern Subject," in *Modern Theology* 22 (2006), pp. 221–53, and "Marion on Miracles: Of Insufficient Reason and a New Enlightenment," in *Faith in the Enlightenment? The Critique of the Enlightenment Revisited* ed. Lieven Boeve, Joeri Schrijvers, Wessel Stoker and Henk Vroom (Amsterdam: Rodopi, 2006).

Chapter 7 is a corrected version of "'And There Shall Be No More Boredom' Problems with Overcoming Metaphysics (Heidegger, Levinas, Marion)," in C. Cunningham and P. Candler (eds.), *Transcendence and Phenomenology* (London: SCM Press, 2007).

Abbreviations

Levinas

OB   *Otherwise than Being, or Beyond Essence* (Pittsburgh: Duquesne University Press, 2002), trans. A. Lingis

AqE   *Autrement qu'être, ou au-delà de l'essence* (The Hague: Martinus Nijhoff, 1974)

TI   *Totality and Infinity: An Essay on Exteriority* (Pittsburgh: Duquesne University Press, 2002), trans. A. Lingis

TeI   *Totalité et infini: Essai sur l'extériorité* (The Hague: Martinus Nijhoff, 1961)

BPW   *Basic Philosophical Writings* (Bloomington/Indianapolis: Indiana University Press, 1996), eds. A. Peperzak, S. Critchley, and R. Bernasconi

GDT   *God, Death, and Time* (Stanford: Stanford University Press, 2000), trans. B. Bergo

DMT   *Dieu, la mort et le temps* (Paris: Grasset, 1993)

GP   "God and Philosophy," in E. Levinas, *Of God Who Comes to Mind* (Stanford: Stanford University Press, 1998), trans. B. Bergo. Pp. 55–78

HAM   *Humanism of the Other* (Urbana/Chicago: University of Illinois Press, 2003), trans. N. Poller

Marion

BG   *Being Given: Toward a Phenomenology of Givenness* (Stanford: Stanford University Press, 2002), trans. J. Kosky

ED   *Étant Donné: Essai d'une phenomenologie de la donation* (Paris: PUF, 1998)

IE   *In Excess: Studies of Saturated Phenomena* (New York: Fordham University Press, 2002), trans. R. Horner and V. Berraud

DS   *De surcroît: Essai sur les phénomènes saturés* (Paris: PUF, 2001)

GWB   *God without Being: Hors-Texte* (Chicago and London: University of Chicago Press, 1991), trans. T. A. Carlson

DsE   *Dieu sans l'être* (Paris: PUF, 2002)

RG   *Reduction and Givenness: Investigations of Husserl, Heidegger, and Phenomenology* (Evanston: Northwestern University Press, 1998), trans. T. A. Carlson

RD   *Réduction et donation: Recherches sur Husserl, Heidegger et la phénoménologie* (Paris: PUF, 1989)

EP   *The Erotic Phenomenon* (Chicago and London: University of Chicago Press, 2007), trans. S. E. Lewis

DMP   *On Descartes' Metaphysical Prism: The Constitution and the Limits of Onto-Theology in Cartesian Thought* (Chicago/London: University of Chicago Press, 1999), trans. J. L. Kosky

ID   *The Idol and Distance: Five Studies* (New York: Fordham University Press, 2001), trans. T. A. Carlson

IeD   *L'idole et la distance: Cinq études* (Paris: Grasset, 1991)

CV   *The Crossing of the Visible* (Stanford: Stanford University Press, 2004), trans. J. K. A. Smith

CdV   *La croisée du visible* (Paris: Ed. De la Différence, 1991)

VR   *The Visible and the Revealed* (New York: Fordham University Press, 2008), trans. C. Gschwandtner

VeR   *Le visible et le révélé* (Paris: CERF, 2005)

Lacoste

EA   *Experience and the Absolute: Disputed Questions on the Humanity of Man* (New York: Fordham University Press, 2004), trans. M. Raftery-Skehan

EeA   *Expérience et absolu: Questions disputées sur l'humanité de l'homme*
          (Paris: PUF, 1994)

NT   *Note sur le temps: Essai sur les raisons de la mémoire et de l'espérance*
          (Paris: PUF, 1990)

MO   *Le monde et l'absence de l'œuvre et autres études* (Paris: PUF,
          2000)

PP   *Présence et Parousie* (Genève: Ad Solem, 2006)

Carmel   "De la phénoménologie de l'Esprit à la montée du Carmel,"
          Revue Thomiste 89 (1989), pp. 5–39, 569–98

BHP   "Batîr, habiter, prier," in *Revue Thomiste* 87 (1987), pp. 357–90,
          547–78

All references will be to the English editions, although translations have occasionally been modified. Unless otherwise noted, all italics are mine. For the works in French of these authors of which no translation is available, I have provided my own.

Introduction

This book is launched from one simple thesis that it then, somewhat tirelessly, explores: that which Marion, Lacoste, and Levinas present as a 'decentering of the subject' is, for reasons that I hope will become obvious, in fact, no such decentering, for their accounts of the decentering of the subject seems simply to reverse the subject-object dichotomy. If the subject may not see any object, then the best thing to do is to look for one or the other instance that takes on the contours of a subject—the candidates are 'God,' 'givenness,' and 'the Other'—that turns us, the human being, into an object. We will see, then, that for Lacoste the I "becomes the object of God's intention," that for Marion the I "becomes the object and objective of givenness," and that the I, for Levinas, stands "without secrets"—somewhat like an object indeed—before this or that other.

Some readers might be surprised by the decidedly nonchronological way of presenting the authors in this work. Such a chronology would have been easy: Levinas influenced Marion, Marion influenced Lacoste, and so on. There would have been, if you like, a story-line. But, in fact, this nonchronological way of presenting Lacoste, Marion, and Levinas suits the purposes of this book very well: the problem toward which it tries to point might be present in these thinkers precisely because it is, in a certain way, 'ahistorical' in the sense that it concerns everyone at all times and all places. For, if ontotheology will turn out to be inevitable, the eternal recurrence of the subject, and of the subject-object distinction, comes as no surprise. In effect, what I will advance, with Levinas and Heidegger, is that ontotheology, and thus the subject-object distinction, is part and parcel of our ontological make-up, and therefore its recurrence cannot be avoided.

The understanding of ontotheology and metaphysics here is fueled by a reading of Heidegger, and of course by Marion's, Lacoste's, and Levinas' reading of him. First, if the subject-object distinction and representational thinking are part of the metaphysical tradition, because the subject, as some sort of highest being would, accounts for and justifies all there would be to the object to such an extent that the object would be defined clearly and distinctly and in such a transparent manner that the object would yield its essence and perhaps even its 'unknown,' then such a subject is indeed to be avoided. Now, if that which is supposed to avoid such a subject takes on the form of precisely such a subject by robbing immanence and finitude of its mute mysteriousness by considering it as merely an object that could in principle be determined in a transparent manner—*all* I am is for the Other, *all* I am is given to me, *all* I am, I am before God—then it seems justified to take into account a return of the subject and thus also of ontotheology. Second, if such a reversal at times even extends (phenomenological) intentionality to God—as Marion and Lacoste sometimes do—then this returning toward the most classical form of ontotheology, where the (infinite) being of God is thought in the very same, univocal, manner as (finite) beings are thought, is so glaring that it would have been impossible not to speak of a return of ontotheology. I will contend, then, that it is precisely such an ontotheological turn that I perceive in my sparring partners' works and that any, proclaimed or not, overcoming of ontotheology has not yet succeeded. In fact, it is my contention that ontotheology cannot be overcome and that this is the best explanation to be inferred from the residues of and contaminations with ontotheological modes of procedures that can be found in the works of Levinas, Marion, and Lacoste.

Chapter 1 may function somewhat as an overview of and introduction to the main themes of this work. It tries to present the argument of this book in a clear and short way and at the same time introduces the questions that will be posed in the rest of the work. In chapters 2 through 5, I present the thought of Lacoste, Marion, and Levinas respectively. These presentations offer concise surveys of the most important insights of the authors under discussion in order to make their questions available to readers not already acquainted with them.

In chapter 6, I question what seems to be the axiom of much of contemporary philosophy, namely, that immanence is and needs to be portrayed as an "egg in its shell" (Levinas) and a "visual prison" (Marion) without windows and doors or even that "Dasein is without God in the world" (Lacoste). Therefore, from chapter 6 onward, the question concerning ontotheology again comes into focus. In these chapters, I tried to propagate the inevitability of ontotheology as a more viable hypothesis to explain the recurrence of metaphysical structures in the thought of Levinas, Lacoste, and Marion. One can argue that, seen from the viewpoint of ontotheology's inevitability, the recurrence of metaphysical modes of procedure loses its initial strangeness and at least becomes somewhat intelligible.

In chapter 7 I hope to offer some insight in the ontotheological turns of Marion, Lacoste, and Levinas by explaining some of the reasons why I think ontotheology is still present in Levinas and Marion (and in Heidegger as well). For, if we are to affirm, with Heidegger, that "the reversal of a metaphysical statement remains a metaphysical statement," then we have yet to understand *why* the reversal of a metaphysical statement still is a metaphysical statement. If indeed a reversal of the subject-object distinction is at issue, in that in one way or another human beings turn into the 'object and the objective' of an autonomous instance (whether it is God, givenness, or the Other), then one should ponder to what extent these metaphysical residues point us in a different direction than a fair amount of authors on the theme of 'overcoming ontotheology' have taken. Indeed, this 'overcoming' of ontotheology takes place under the *assumption* that an escape from ontotheology *is* possible. I will conclude that 'overcoming' metaphysics only makes sense if, in one way or another, a metaphysical mode of procedure is presupposed.

In chapter 8, I turn to Marion's historical account of metaphysics and try to understand why the reversal of the subject-object distinction is still inscribed within a metaphysical logic. Here I will also consider Levinas' interest in the problem of ontotheology and ask to what extent and if it is possible for Levinas at all to think "God outside of onto-theo-logy." The guiding line of this chapter will be what seems to be an undecided issue in contemporary philosophy, namely, that "if there is such a thing as ontotheology, [and] if this concept has a precise sense (non-ideological, not vague), when did it start to operate and how far does its concept extend?" (Marion). I try to point, moreover, to the problem that any solely historical assessment of the problem of ontotheology risks substituting the problem of ontotheology itself for a concept of ontotheology. According to such a concept, then, we would be able to point to what counts for ontotheology and what does not, which thinker is 'ontotheological' and which one is not. Approaching ontotheology in this way, however, remains stuck in the problem of conceptual representation that originated this enquiry in the first place. The purely historical assessment of the problem of ontotheology must therefore always be accompanied by a proper philosophical understanding of its stakes.

Finally, in the conclusion, I rehearse the major arguments of this work and restate some of my key questions. Furthermore, I will suggest that

Heidegger's understanding of the difference between the presencing of beings and their simple presence might bring to bear some prospects for helping us understand more clearly the ever-present temptation of ontotheology. It is for this reason that I tried to sketch how a phenomenology of the presencing of the invisible might counter the contemporary addiction to visible and comprehensible objects and to what kind of theology it may lead.

Chapter 1

Some Notes on a French Debate

Introducing Ontotheology

Thinkers such as Levinas, Marion, and Lacoste are all trying to understand what the word *God* might mean in the contemporary world once that which was understood by this term previously has been proclaimed dead. Indeed, it seems that the God that passed away is brought to life again in what has been called "the theological turn of French phenomenology."[1] Lacoste, Marion, and Levinas, then, try to think God as other than the 'God' of ontotheology.

Although the term *ontotheology* was first used by Kant, the concept and the problem thereof stems from Heidegger. According to Heidegger, ontotheology first and foremost concerns philosophy. Broadly speaking, Heidegger criticized philosophy's tendency to talk about God too hastily and too easily. Philosophy's task is to think 'being' and not God. For Heidegger, ontotheology and metaphysics are essentially a forgetting of being, concerned merely with beings. Therefore, philosophy cannot open up to the 'ontological difference' between being and beings; it prefers controllable, foreseeable, and 'present-at-hand' objects. Objects lend themselves easily to the reckoning and calculations required for technology's mastery over being. It is in this sense that we encounter in our God talk the same, univocal primacy of beings or objects. In general, the ontotheological endeavor seeks an ultimate reason that can account for the totality of beings. Its point of departure—beings—forbids that ontotheology encounters anything *other*, at the end of the chain of beings, than *a* being. Proceeding from the finite to the infinite, ontotheology's obsession with objects decides in advance how God will enter the philosophical discourse. This 'God' is often modeled after causal theories—as much as each house requires an architect as its cause, the

5

totality of beings requires a '*prima causa*,' a *First* Being. God is an instrument used, by philosophy, to found finitude, to give reasons for the totality of beings. God, in the ontotheological way of thinking, *must* be a foundation or the explanation of the totality of beings. God cannot be anything else than that instance that saves the finite system from its own contingency and incoherency. And yes, *this is what we all call "God"* or, rather, this is what we used to call God.

The modern subject is, if not the instigator then at least the heir of all ontotheologies. Marion, Lacoste, and Levinas all frame their thought around that which might counter the subject's reckoning with beings and objects (respectively 'givenness' for Marion, 'liturgy' for Lacoste, and 'the other' for Levinas). The 'modern' subject, mainly identified in the works of Descartes, Kant, Hegel, and Husserl proclaims itself to be—or at least that is the way it came to be perceived—the center of the world, the 'master and possessor of nature.' Human beings, in modernity, were thought of as free, autonomous, and active agents. To be sure, such an Enlightenment was a liberation in a manifold of ways, but it is not my task to repeat those here. The fact remains that many philosophers criticize this portrayal of the human being as an autonomous agent, since such autonomy is deemed to be responsible for many problems contemporary societies are facing. I will offer some indications as to the kinds of problems these might be in the next section. All of the authors I have chosen as this work's privileged interlocutors—Levinas, Marion, Lacoste, and, through them, Heidegger— insist on giving an account of the human being as a more passive, affective instance. Heidegger, for instance, criticizes the 'world-less ego' as it comes to us from the philosophical tradition starting with Descartes. Human beings, according to Heidegger, are already in a world. It is this fact of finding oneself in a world with others that is the proper topic of philosophical reflection. Levinas and Marion, for reasons which will become obvious shortly, primarily target the transcendental '*Ich denke*' of Kant. '*Le Je pense transcendental*,' Levinas says, does not speak; it is the word of, really, no one.[2] The human being is not to be found in this way. Marion, then, contends that it would be better to substitute the '*Ich denke*' for an 'I feel' ('*je sens*'), and Lacoste will outline the human being as a radically passive being.

The decentering of subjectivity is thus for the most part a confrontation with transcendental and idealist philosophy. That is why much of the debate has turned upon the critique of 'representation.' The ego cogito of Descartes indeed *represents* itself as a thinking substance, and Kant is famous for, among many other things of course, the '*Ich Denke muss alle Vorstellungen begeleiten*.' But why, precisely, critique *representations*? Because, in the very epistemological operation of the subject representing an object, this object is put under the guard of the subject and is submitted to the subject's power to know and represent in the manner it thinks appropriate. For Heidegger, this means that the subject-object distinction rages through our contemporary technological cultures to such an extent that human beings tend to lose the ability to encounter being and beings in another way than as a represented object.[3] Levinas would agree but considers the main victim of such a violent reduction the other human being, who, when represented through a subject, loses his or her uniqueness and becomes merely 'one amongst many,' a genus of a species. Marion sees in this reduction to object-ness an alienation of the phenomenon itself and tries to liberate phenomenality from its representational constraints by evoking the possibility of a phenomenon showing itself of itself. Lacoste's liturgical experience seeks, first and foremost, to liberate our experience of God from all of these 'modern' constraints.

All of these authors thus agree that the power of this autonomous subject must be broken. However, on closer inspection, we find these thinkers time and again returning to the subject-object distinction. The question of this work, then, is whether a simple reversal of the subject-object distinction suffices to break out of the ontotheological scheme.

The Present and Our Obsession with Objects

Heidegger, in his commentary on Aristotle's *Physics*, spoke of "the spell of modern man's way of Being," which, for him, was an "addict[ion] to thinking of beings as *objects* and allowing the being of beings to be exhausted in the objectivity of the object."[4] In *Being and Time*, Heidegger refused a long-standing tradition that saw beings merely as representations or as objects. Our being-in-the-world, Heidegger says, hardly encounters objects at all. For this reason he draws a distinction between objects, which are *present-at-hand*, and tools or equipment, which are *ready-to-hand*. Although Heidegger uses a hammer as an example of equipment that is ready-to-hand, beings which are ready-to-hand cannot be reduced to what we usually see as a tool.[5] The distinction between *ready-to-hand* and *present-at-hand* is simple: When one is playing the guitar, one doesn't reflect on the chords and on the corresponding finger settings. Heidegger would say that while playing the guitar, one is involved in a caring relationship toward things that are ready-to-hand. The guitar only becomes an object—present-at-hand—when one, while playing, reflects on these settings. However, if one does this—and this is Heidegger's point—one can no longer play the guitar: the guitar has become an object, present-at-hand, and loses the self-evident character that is intended for things ready-to-hand.

Many of Levinas' own themes echo those of Heidegger. Levinas was mainly concerned with the problem of encountering *the other as other*. However, every other I meet in the public space is an other that I need and use as a means to my own ends. When I buy my train ticket, I do not see the other as other, I see him or her as the one who is going to give me the ticket that I need to get on the train. Levinas says that in this way, the other person is reduced to my representation of him or her, to that which he or she can do and mean for me. Every representation, every image, is, according to Levinas, instrumental and only an expression of humanity's will to power.

Both for Heidegger and Levinas, the question is how to escape the self-evident manner with which knowledge proceeds. Whereas Heidegger asks how we can trace the being of beings (and so re-open the question of being), Levinas wonders if an encounter with the other as other, and not merely with the other as what he or she can mean 'for me,' is possible at all. Marion expresses a similar concern but does so with regard to our knowledge of God. In his book *God without Being*, he distinguishes between the idol and the icon (GWB, 7–24). The first is very close to what I am describing here as an object. The idol is, according to Marion, an *image* of God. God is reduced to that which human beings can know, represent, or experience of God. God is, in this case, modeled after our own image and, in and through this image, tied to finite conditions of appearing. However, if God is truly God, Marion argues, the mode of God's epiphany should be unconditional and thus not restricted to the limits set forward by any mode of (human) knowledge whatsoever.

But, what precisely is an object? Consider the following example. When I look at a dinner table, I evidently see only one side of it. That I, however, still see the table as a table, that is, as consisting of a plateau with four legs, arises from the fact that I constitute the table. *Constitution* is Husserl's term and refers to a mental act that somehow adds to the perception of one leg the three others in order to secure the unity of the table. Constitution occurs with almost every object human beings perceive. (Think of a cube, the dark side of the moon, etc.). However, suppose that I walk around the table and discover that what I constituted as a brown table is, in fact, partially green. One of the legs can be, for instance, colored green. This does not alter my constitution of the table as a table in a significant way. Marion concludes that our knowledge, experience, and representations are, in one way or another, exercising a will to power, or, in his terms: the unseen of an object—the green leg of the table—always has the rank of a preseen (BG, 186; IE, 35–36). Though I may not have seen that the table has one green leg, I still constitute the table as a plateau with four legs. An object therefore can only be unknown, not unknowable. Everything that one wants to know of an object can be known, and it is in this sense that, once again, knowledge is power. Objects are transparent; they have no secrets.

How, then, can we encounter the unknowable? And how, if everything that we see is always 'preseen,' can we see (or experience or know) the invisible God? How, turning to Levinas again, can we see the other as other, and not only as what he or she can mean 'for me'? Or, to use Heidegger's terminology, how do we know being if we only encounter beings? How can we experience God if, as Marion tells us, every (idolatrous) experience of God is like an invisible mirror (GWB, 11–14)? For Marion indeed, human experience of God is like a *mirror* in that human beings want to experience or see God but, in fact, see only the image they themselves have made of God. Human experience of God is then also like an *invisible* mirror in that people like to forget that the God they worship is only a God made after their own likeness. Let us have a brief look at the answers these French philosophers provide.

Jean-Yves Lacoste: The Experience of Faith

One can interpret Lacoste's work as expounding a common belief: the church is one of the few places where one can recover one's breath, a place of peace and quiet amidst the rat race of modern society. For Lacoste, modernity is characterized by the expansion of technology to the point of (the possibility) of the destruction of the world: modernity and technology are essentially a logic of appropriation. Technology's appropriation of the world is knowledge put to the service of power.[6] Lacoste proposes to advance 'liturgy' or faith to counter technology's threat to the world. For liturgy transgresses the world and offers to the realms of the means and ends of technology, the excess and surplus of a preoccupation with God that serves, at least in the world that is ours, no direct end: over and against the utility and the costs and benefit analyses of the world stands the gratuity and the uselessness of liturgy, a place where one can learn anew that not all things are at the service of

and available to the logic of appropriation, productivity, and efficacy of the
modern world.

Lacoste tries to give a philosophical description of the weal and the
woe of an ordinary believer who is liturgically in the midst of the world. A
believer, Lacoste argues, has to reckon with a nonexperience. One has to
take this nonexperience quite literally. When a believer directs his attention
to God in prayer or by participating in the Eucharist, it seems that nothing
is happening. Indeed, neither ecstasy nor the blinding spiritual force of a
celestine prophecy usually occurs. While believers express a desire to know
God or to dwell in God's kingdom, they find themselves in an often tiresome
church. If nothing happens, faith is first and foremost a nonexperience.

Lacoste conceives of this nonexperience as a passive encounter with
God in which the believer imitates Christ's passivity and obedience toward
the will of God. Therefore, the nonexperience of faith is ascetic in that the
believer must renounce every desire to appropriate God, to experience God
at will (cf. Lk. 22:42). However, Lacoste goes on to describe this ascetic
passivity of the believer in terms of object-ness or objectivity, an objectivity,
moreover, that is akin to that of the thing; one can say that the believer is in
the hands of God as clay is in the hands of the potter (*EA*, 156). Catherine
Pickstock therefore rightly remarks: "For Lacoste, our bodiedness is a sign of
our fundamental objectivity in relation to God, more important than any
notion of subjective desire, which implies that *undergoing* a relationship with
God is more fundamental than desiring it."[7]

But if Lacoste's answer to our age's obsessions with objects is to reverse
the terms of subject-object—if, in other words, human beings no longer
see God as the object of their own imagination, but if it is God who turns
human beings into objects—are we then not once again caught in the web
of the problem that we want to resolve? Is not this God in turn, who treats
believers as mere things, a bit too much *like* the subject that can only deal
with that which it encounters as objects?

Jean-Luc Marion: Experiencing the Given

A striking parallel to this reversal of the subject-object distinction can be
observed in the works of Marion. In *Being Given*, Marion tries to develop an
account of the phenomenon as it gives itself by and of itself, without any
interference from a human agent. With its intentions and desires, the modern
subject, Marion argues, distorts that which gives itself. One can understand

this interpretation of subjectivity in the way in which an accused criminal would narrate the story of the crime he or she has committed. Indeed, it is unlikely that the criminal will relate his or her offence as it really happened. On the contrary, the criminal will distort what happened in order to tell the event of the crime to his own benefit. One cannot expect that the narrative of the crime, related by the criminal, gives an account of the crime as it was in and by itself. The criminal will most often reduce the crime to such an extent that it makes him or her, in one way or another, look good.

To avoid such an interference, Marion tries to describe phenomena as they give themselves, or in his terms, as their 'selves,' to human beings. However, to receive such a givenness, Marion argues, the modern subject is turned into the "clerk" (*IE*, 26) or recorder of that which is given. All intentions and desires of the subject must be subordinated to the gift of the phenomena. How is this possible? How does one encounter the given as it gives itself or its self? Marion's answer is that the phenomena already give themselves *before* any perturbation or interference of a subject can occur. This gift is an appeal one cannot not hear, in the same way that the crime has already been committed when the criminal starts to look for excuses. Marion distinguishes his account of the given both from objects and from beings. Whereas an object is determined within the classical scheme of 'adequation,' meaning that the table is nothing more nor less than an adequate mental representation of a plateau with four legs, beings are determined within an account of finality. The guitar is there *to* play, the pen *to* write, and so on. This finality stems from human beings: they will determine both what is an adequate representation of an object and what use a being has. The given, on the contrary, is given regardless of its actual reception (by human beings). Marion develops an interpretation of reality that no longer relies on man as its measure. 'Givenness' determines every phenomenon without exception. This does not mean, however, that everything is also received: this is so because people's ability to receive is always hindered by desires and intentions, which reduce the capacity to receive; human capacity to receive is reduced to that which we already know or are used to seeing: our intention reduces that which we encounter to that which we can adequately represent of this encounter.

One can elucidate Marion's thinking as follows: given that the crime occurred, an account of it as it was in and by itself is possible; the crime is (a) perfectly given, but the reception of that given (by the criminal, witness, victim) always deforms the account of the crime as it was in itself. It is what Lars von Trier called, in his film *Dogville*, the most difficult thing for human beings: to receive. Grace is given to us, whether or not we receive it; however, the effects of Grace also depend on our willingness to receive. In this world, as in the film *Dogville*, Grace is often raped, deformed, or not recognized: "He was in the world, but the world did not recognize him" (John 1:10).

How can anything give itself regardless of whether or not it is received? Marion's answer is very similar to the one of Lacoste. The gift is perfectly given, neither because we aim at it (as we aim at an object) nor because we determine its finality, but because it aims at us. Hence the rather unsettling parallel: "intentionality is inverted: I become the objective of the object" (BG, 146).[8] This seems to be Marion's solution, from his earlier theological works to his later philosophical argumentations. Givenness aims at us; it points to us as its receiver whether we actually receive or not, just as Christ's gaze looks at us through the visible wood of the icon even if human beings do not always pay attention to Christ's presence therein. All that human beings have to do is to record and to register this event as accurately as possible.

Emmanuel Levinas: The Other's Otherness

Thus, for Lacoste, human beings are the object of a divine intention. For Marion, human beings are the object and the objective of givenness. The active and autonomous subject is replaced by a passive instance in that the subject's will to power (over object and beings) is reversed and turned into the "will to powerlessness" (EA, 163) of a clerk. However, if this is the case, is the problem of subjectivity and its supposed mastery over reality really solved? Have we not simply replaced this problem with another by, on the one hand, postulating of God as the (modern) subject or, on the other hand, by granting givenness the contours of subjectivity if only through seeing its gift as a supposed "insubstituable selfhood" (BG, 165)? It is here that one finds the overarching question of this work, for such a simple reversal of the subject-object distinction makes one wonder whether Lacoste and Marion succeed in overcoming metaphysics, since one could say, following Heidegger in this regard: "the reversal of a metaphysical statement remains a metaphysical statement."[9]

At first sight, such a reversal is precisely what Levinas wants to avoid, for one of his fundamental questions is surely how we can avoid seeing the relation between, for instance, human beings and God as a relation between antithetical terms, that is, between "terms that complete one another and consequently are reciprocally lacking to one another" (*TI*, 103). How should I avoid seeing myself as a subject that aims at the other to determine what use this other can have for me, or, in another manner of speaking, how do I avoid seeing the other as the subject that determines me as his or her object? Levinas' answer is the following: the relation between the other and I is not a relation between antithetical terms, but rather a relation between "terms that suffice to themselves" (ibid.). This means that the subject cannot be understood *in relation to* an object and that human beings cannot be understood in relation to God but rather that in order to understand the relation of human beings to God, one must first interpret human beings *as* human beings, that is, as beings that stand on their own, sufficient to themselves, and who are not in need of God to know what it is to be human and finite. Levinas therefore says that human beings must be "capable of atheism" (*TI*, 58). The finite does not point to the infinite as its fulfillment, and neither does the infinite offer the satisfaction of the supposedly inferior finite creature's desire.

This 'relation without relation' indeed discards the traditional account of the creature as a diminution of the transcendent creator. Such an account is the result of a theoretical approach toward transcendence. Such a conscious thematization of this relation will inevitably see God as a term of this relationship. But, according to Levinas, transcendence is not a theoretical affair. God is not the answer to the problems that finitude poses. If God were the answer to the problems of finitude, then God would be not only the term of the relationship but also its terminus. For example, the problem of death is in Christian theology often answered with reference to the promise of eternal life—the finite is supposed to point to, to aim at, this eternal life as its term. But such a solution obviously entails the danger of terminating transcendence and so also terminating human beings' involvement in it. Indeed, all too often, the promise of eternal life has blinded human beings to their ethical duties in the here and now.

According to Levinas, a theoretical account of transcendence overlooks the finite creature's positive role in its relation to transcendence. To put this in Levinas' own terms, the atheism of the creature—and thus its freedom to relate to God—is "a great glory for the creator" (ibid.). Levinas is looking for a more existential involvement with transcendence, not the abstract glance of the scientist that terminates transcendence by only thinking of it. For Levinas, "the dimension of the divine opens forth from the human face" (*TI*, 78); It is only through the face of the other that we might be able to speak of God again. This is the positive role to be played by the finite being: the creature must attend to the neighbor in an ethical way. 'God' is at stake in our ethical response toward the other. Amidst (post) modern relativism, there is one instance that utters an absolute appeal: the other. This other is the one thing that cannot be theorized, since he or she is always more (or less) than that which I can represent of him or her. Therefore, the other *exceeds* the subject's will to power, but not because he or she is more powerful than I am (which would be to fall back again in an antithetical relation), but because he or she as other is at the same time more and less than I am. He or she is more in the sense that his or her appeal is absolute, and I cannot therefore *not* hear it. But the other is less in the sense that the other's appeal towards me implies that I have the means to respond to it and to help him or her in their destitution. The other does not deprive me of my power and knowledge, but he or she appeals to my power and knowledge precisely to alter their orientation: I do not need them for my own sake, but for that of the other. Levinas says: "I did not know myself so rich, but I have no longer any right to keep anything."[10]

Theology 'after' Ontotheology

The recurrence of the metaphysical subject-object distinction in the works of Lacoste and Marion is surprising. In both cases, human beings are reduced to a fundamental object-ness (over and against God or givenness, which then takes on the contours of subjectivity). The finite is taken to be an obstacle for people's relation to God. Rather than focusing on our embodiment, Lacoste prefers an objectness toward God like a thing is in the hands of the potter. Rather than allowing any involvement of the human being in his or her relation to God, Marion wants the human being to be the mere clerk of that history. For Levinas, only the other's appeal overcomes the subject's adherence to being and ties the subject solely to ethics. This move redefines the subject's adherence to being as a decentering that is 'not contaminated' by or without "remainder"—as Marion has it (BG, 309)—of being or immanence. It is precisely this desire for a single, univocal approach to immanence and finitude, that is, the phenomenological and/or ethical redescription of it without 'contamination' or 'remainder,' that we need to question, for it might be just here that metaphysical residues remain in the works of Marion, Lacoste, and even Levinas. Such approaches entail that transcendence (whether one names it God or the Other, it matters little) signals itself in a transparent manner and, in doing so, finitude is yet again made to signify *completely*, as if it were part and parcel of an infinite register.

Consider, for instance, the ontotheological manner in which, traditionally, the problem of evil has been taken into account. When someone close to you is sick or dies, the question is posed to God *why* he or she got sick or *why* bad things happen to good people. However, this often implies that God knows the ultimate reason of this sickness or, who knows, might have even *caused* it. 'God' is used to give reasons for the human condition. That sickness or death might not have a single, univocal signification is not taken into account. The same thing occurs in Levinas' works. The human condition and its ambiguities are replaced, yet again, with the "total transparence" (*TI*, 182) of the encounter with the other. Death, for instance, is made to signify for the other: my death ceases to be meaningless, since I can now die for the other, and, in fact, I must, for "nothing can dispense me from the response to which I am held *passively*. The tomb is not a refuge; it is not a pardon. The debt remains" (*GP*, 200 n. 29). I cannot hold anything back, I am completely for-the-other: a finite and separate being "without secrets" (*OB*, 138)—an object(ive) for the Other?

What would happen indeed if immanence cannot totally receive its signification from transcendence? What if, to leap ahead to one of the main theses of this work, immanence cannot be taken as one monolithic block *next to* which one posits one or the other transcendent instance? Such an incarnational approach to transcendence—incarnational, since it encounters transcendence only *through* and *in* immanence, not *despite* or *next to* immanence—is what the conclusion of this book, aiming at a phenomenology of the invisible from *within* this immanent world of ours, sets out to do.

To give but one example: what would the difference be between the objectivity without secrets with regard to God, as we have seen in Marion, Lacoste, and Levinas, and an incarnational approach? Is not this 'God' who turns me into an object when confronted with his gaze or who makes me the object and objective of a gift not once again the Sartrean God/other who cannot do anything but objectify me? Do we not encounter once again the terrible God who knows 'more of Lucien than Lucien did of himself,' as Sartre wrote in *Le mur*? The incarnational approach avoids an identity without secrets by the simple fact that finitude is not fully signified by an otherwise than being. The secret and the sting of finitude remain. The finite I is not only an enigma for itself, but even for God—there is no transparent encounter. This is why the encounter between human beings and God must be construed as an encounter of two singular freedoms. Incarnation entails both God's freedom to appear and the freedom of human beings with regard to God. God's freedom is certain in the sense that the encounter with transcendence is confined neither to ethics nor to liturgy. God is able to appear anew wherever God wills: in objects, sacraments, persons, or nature. The freedom of human beings to relate to God is safeguarded in the sense that the secret and the sting of their finitude are not made transparent, neither to the other nor to God. Unlike Jonah, to be able to escape God *here* is at the same time to be able to relate freely to God in the decision to pray or in the decision to attend to the neighbor. In this way, one comes close to at least one instance of the biblical encounter with God: "Here I am! I stand at the door and knock. If anyone hears my voice and opens the door, I will come in and eat with him, and he with me" (Rev 3:20).

It is to such a decentered subject that this work tries to point, although it develops this idea from a philosophical perspective, that is, by keeping a close watch on the mystery but also on the muteness of finitude and immanence. In this way, an enquiry into ontotheology (and into the ontotheologies of our era) operates a decentering of the subject that no longer succumbs to the temptation of a 'pure' encounter with its other— and that thereby would differentiate between pure and impure encounters. This approach, as the one of James Smith, indeed avoids these attempts to "demarcate the rigid boundaries of the community."[11]

To develop such an approach taking finitude seriously, I propose to explore the problem of ontotheology in detail. Ontotheology seems to be an intellectual abracadabra. It is used both to justify the disdain against any form of God talk whatsoever and to introduce over against philosophy's tendency toward idolization, the claim of a revelation prior to reason. I will not give a detailed exegesis of Heidegger's texts on ontotheology here (which, by the way, are not many) but I will, with broad strokes, introduce what Heidegger meant by metaphysics.

The Question concerning Ontotheology

Derrida once said that "perhaps onto-theology for Heidegger is not simply a critique of theology, not simply academic discourse, but a real culture."[12] It is indeed one of the main goals of this work to show in what ways the problem of ontotheology is not confined to the philosopher's desk. For theologians as well as philosophers, ontotheology should be, at the very least, disturbing. For if ontotheology is not confined to academic discourse, it might have found its way into our cultures as well. If so, the problem is perhaps not to try to eradicate all the forms of but only to make us at least aware of the problem and its possible consequences.

For Heidegger, as we have seen, metaphysics is essentially a forgetting of being. Thought, and in consequence thereof science, is concerned merely with beings and therefore does not open up to the 'ontological difference.' Heidegger contends that 'being' unfolds historically and takes on different postures in the course of time. Being unfolds in and through beings. Heidegger writes that "the revealing that rules in modern technology is a challenging [Herausfordern], which puts to nature the unreasonable demand that it supply energy."[13] And that this challenging-forth, to which the world can *only* appear as "an area of his own representing" and as "an object of research," is "no mere handiwork of man."[14] This "challenging claim which gathers man thither to order the self-revealing as standing-reserve"[15] is rather the result of the subject-object divide that roves through Western philosophy since Descartes. Our era or 'epoch,' Heidegger contends, is thus, and whether we have chosen it to be so or not, a technological one, and perhaps therefore 'the age of the world-picture.' As such, a 'world-picture' results from the view that anyone or anything can have a 'picture' of the world both in general and as it is in itself. Such a view, therefore, presupposes a subject that first extricates itself from the world from out of which it thinks—a worldless ego—and then reduces the world (and its own being-in-the-world) to that which can be represented of it. One should thus note that, for Heidegger, technology is not without philosophical presuppositions. On the contrary: the domination of technology in contemporary societies might simply be an extension of the Cartesian position. For, just as Descartes "prescribes for the world its 'real' Being"[16] in making beings appear as present-at-hand, no longer permitting them to present their being themselves (as, for instance, ready-to-hand), so too "the revealing that rules in modern technology is a challenging [Herausfordern]," which reduces the self-revealing to a standing reserve. The representation of a being thus gets the upperhand over against our everyday encounter with beings ready-to-hand. An example: water is represented (defined, categorized) as H_2O, but, in fact, in the world, we never drink H_2O; the piece of wax we see lying on the table is in our factical being-in-the-world almost never a mere extended thing (*res extensa*); we rather, and simply, refer to it as being a candle.[17] This means, among other things, that in and through the 'representation' of the being of water as H_2O, the being that we are and have to be with water (if you like: our *sein-bei* water)[18] goes unnoticed and is, in a certain sense, forgotten. Nevertheless, Heidegger's point is that the representation of water as H_2O is derived from or secondary to being-in-the-world with others or with entities within-the-world (as water and stones). Whereas for Descartes, the world was to be conceived of mathematically to such an extent that the medieval *ordo* of the hierarchy of beings was to be replaced by the rationality of geometry, such that no point in the universe differs qualitatively from another, Heidegger points out that, in our everyday world, "the objective distances of things present-at-hand do not coincide with the remoteness and closeness of what is ready-to-hand."[19] This is why, for instance, "a pathway which is long 'objectively' can be much shorter than one which is 'objectively' shorter still but which is perhaps 'hard going' and comes before us as interminably long"[20] or why time flies when you are having fun, and so on.

In this sense, Heidegger's retrieval of the question of being was a retrieval of those things that are closest to us. But that which is closest, he often says, is at the same time that which is furthest, that is, what we usually do not see or notice. This is where phenomenology comes in: as a method to make those things appear that usually do not appear. It might even be that, because of the ontotheological constitution of Western metaphysics, philosophy has not been able to take into account those instances that are closest to us, namely, beings as such, and that it therefore only now can begin to reflect on what it means to exist in a determinate world. One could argue that the technological understanding of 'being' obfuscates men and women's being-in-the-world and that Heidegger envisioned a sort of domination of and by the technological understanding of being. Things are no longer 'ready-to-hand' nor 'present-at-hand,' but, if you will, out of hand. The 'supreme danger' for Heidegger, so it seems, would consist in the fact that the human being, though 'lord of the earth,' "comes to the point where he himself will have to be taken as standing-reserve."[21] A human being will encounter mere technological constructs to the point of conceiving him-or herself as such a construct. Iain Thomson comments: "[W]e late moderns come to treat even ourselves in the nihilistic terms that underlie our technological refashioning of the world: no longer as conscious subjects standing over against an objective world [. . .], but merely as one more intrinsically meaningless resource to be optimized, ordered, and enhanced with maximal efficiency"[22] It is to such an 'objectification of the subject' that I will relate the thoughts of Lacoste, Levinas, and Marion. It is not that these three authors consider the human being as merely one more resource to be optimized, however; it is rather that the metaphors and the methods they use in the larger bulk of their work point toward a *complete* (if not one that can be represented adequately) determination and identification of the being of the human being. Consequently, the human being is treated *as if* it were an object that in principle could be robbed of its mystery and uniqueness.

Unsurprisingly, in our God talk, we encounter the same sort of primacy of beings and objects. For Heidegger indeed has warned us that in our epoch "even God can [. . .] lose all that is holy and exalted, the mysteriousness of his distance. [God] can sink to the level of a cause, of *causa efficiens*. He then becomes, even in theology, the god of the philosophers."[23] The God that enters philosophical discourse is consequently a highly determinate concept of God. Iain Thomson notes that a particular understanding of the being of beings also bears on the question of God: "[I]n so far as metaphysics—as theology—is not satisfied with striving to identify the highest or supreme being (the question of God), but asks further about the mode of God's existence, metaphysics seeks to understand the being of God (that is, the sense in which God 'is,' or the kind of being which God has)."[24] Thus, not only does metaphysics treat 'God' as *a* being among all the others, but it also feels no particular reluctance to enquire into the being of God. At this point, we must make mention of Smith's astonishment about modern rational theology: "[T]he *Westminster Catechism* (1647) [is] completely comfortable asking the question, 'what is God?' and provide an answer—with straight face and no apology: 'God is . . .'"[25] It is such a rational theology that for Levinas would be the accomplice of the "destruction of transcendence" (*GP*, 56) that characterizes Western philosophy. Therefore, just as human beings are the object of the human sciences because human beings show themselves *as* objects to these sciences (e.g., *GDT*, 150), so too in theo-logy God is reduced to an object, of which theology, as an "*intellection* of the biblical God" (*GP*, 56), does not hesitate to determine both its essence and its existence. One can think here, of course, on those abstract debates on the compatibility of God's all-powerfulness with God's goodness. In such a theology, Levinas would argue, belief in God is almost automatically reduced to a set of propositions in which God is 'grasped.'[26] No doubt a catechism would be nothing less than a blasphemy for Levinas!

It seems as if we silently equate the end of metaphysics with the end of all religion, as if God talk is no longer possible because philosophy has, since the discovery of the problem of ontotheology, resigned from thinking something like God. In the wake of Nietzsche, 'metaphysics' has been interpreted as a flight into otherworldliness, a realm of suprasensible entities (whether it is the 'God' of the Christian religion or the 'Ideas' of Platonism), which is opposed to this sensible and material world. This supersensible world, as Heidegger noted, was considered to be "the true and genuinely real world."[27] The end of metaphysics thus coincides with the awareness "that the suprasensory world is without effective power."[28] The appraisal of historical progress that in the aftermath of Nietzsche's groundbreaking work has had the upper-hand—consider, for instance, Marx' utopia—and that simply replaced the *ordo* established on divine decree by the tribunal of reason, could not break the spell of the 'critical reserve' that reached us through Nietzsche's philosophy. Ironically, quite the opposite seemed to be the case. Despite the laughing and dancing of Nietzsche's mad men struggling against the will to power, it seems that we are witnessing the appearance of a haunting nihilism: we find ourselves in a world without god(s), without any orienting guidelines—a world for which there is no manual. Both Heidegger and Levinas observed this loss of orientation. Heidegger realized that after the downfall of God as the goal of earthly life, "nothing more remains to which man can cling and by which he can orient himself." Therefore, "the thinking through of Nietzsche's metaphysics becomes a reflection on the situation and the place of contemporary man."[29] Levinas, as we have seen, argues that the attending to the other human being provides the orientation that is lacking in this "new epoch, marked by the death of God" (GDT, 124). In *Humanism of the Other*, Levinas decries the disorientation accompanying the "antiplatonism of contemporary philosophy" (cf. HAM, 18). This disorientation is, according to Levinas, the consequence of the relativism and the historicism that underlie an ontology hailing multivocity and pluralism and that lacks "the sense of the senses" (HAM, 24) and the "absolute orientation" (HAM, 27) inflected upon us by the other human being. Such an ontology would no longer be able to differentiate between what matters and what does not matter.

Nevertheless, we must keep in mind that an ontotheological procedure is an effective means to hold back "the flood-waters of ontological historicity for a time—the time of an epoch"[30] and in so doing provides a ground for our existence *ohne warum*. For Heidegger, however, metaphysics is not just a philosophical doctrine among others. On the contrary, it is a structural phenomenon: "Heidegger's claim is that by giving shape to our historical understanding of 'what *is*,' metaphysics determines the most basic presuppositions of what *anything* is, including ourselves."[31] Metaphysics is therefore an underlying structure or horizon out of which whatever appears can appear. Metaphysics asks what a being is and answers this question by giving an account of the being of these beings: "To establish an answer to the question 'What is an entity?' metaphysics makes a claim about what (and how) entities are, and thus about the *being* of those entities."[32]

Common to all metaphysical systems is that this question of the being of a being is always understood in a double manner: as ontological and theological. As ontology, it looks for the essence of beings from which all beings have something in common. 'Onto-logik' is the discipline that "thinks of beings with respect to the ground that is common to all beings as such." At the same time, however, metaphysics is theological. This occurs when it not only asks for what the different and diverse empirical beings have in common but also when it "thinks of beings as such as a whole, that is, with respect to the highest being which accounts for everything."[33] Metaphysics thinks beings, says Heidegger, "in a twofold manner: in the first place, the totality of beings as such with an eye to their most universal traits [. . .] but at the same time also the totality of beings as such in the sense of the highest and therefore divine being. In the former mode it is ontology; in the latter, theology."[34] In this sense, the question of the being of a being is always and already answered from out of one (particular) being. Therefore, Levinas' understanding of 'being otherwise' as an infinite regress seems to give a lucid account of what is at stake in Heidegger's understanding of ontotheology. In this work, I will indeed try to forge a connection between that which Levinas understands as the 'bad infinite' of being otherwise, which consists in the negation of the finite in order to obtain an infinite instance, and Heidegger's understanding of ontotheology. The 'bad infinite' leads to what Jean-Marc Narbonne has depicted as the "regression *ad infinitum* of a being which explains a being which explains a being."[35] In this way, the bad infinite that Levinas distinguishes from the transcendence of the illeity would be similar to what has been called the "ontic reduction of ontotheology," namely, the reduction to a being (whether it be the highest or not).[36]

To make matters more concrete: the 'essence' of a table, for instance, is that it is 'a plateau with four legs.' It is this essence that will come to determine the existence of particular tables (and even to what extent a particular table can be said to exist). This essence, then, is understood from what diverse particular tables have in common. The essence of the table is that it is a plateau with four legs, in that all empirical tables *share* this property. This 'Ontologik' will yield to 'Theologik' when a leap is made from this 'essence' to someone or something that determines the essence of this thing in advance of the existence of a particular table. Indeed, the essence or 'whatness' retains a reference to the empirical being of the table: it is from diverse tables that 'essence' is abstracted. To avoid this reference to particularity (immanence, thatness, etc.) metaphysics leaps into a 'transcendent' being, which is supposed to have the 'Idea' of this essence eternally *without* any empirical 'instantiation' or 'actualization' of the essence. This is where the infinite regress is at issue. In the words of Heidegger, when beings come to be determined from out of their essence, and insofar as this essence still clings onto the ontic existence of beings and "thus in a certain way is something that is (*on*), the [essence], as such a being, demands *in turn* the determination of its being."[37] One can think here of the Platonic ideas or the 'God' of medieval theology, as the one who, supposedly unfounded or founded in and through Godself, grounds the essence of beings by just thinking them, or by creating these imperfect beings of which God is said to eternally have the perfect idea. If this is correct, one might say that the 'end of metaphysics' is the end of speaking of anything or anyone *in general*. I will show below that it is in this direction that Levinas, Marion, and to a certain extent Lacoste too will take Heidegger's understanding of ontotheology. Ontotheology's point of departure—beings—forbids that it encounters anything *other* at the end of the chain of beings, than *a* being. In this sense, it is close to the bad infinite. Ontotheology proclaims that a being is what it is only insofar as its contingent mode of being *corresponds*, and is thereby grounded, to the essence of this particular being. 'God' can thus only appear here in the light of a correspondence theory, as that being, albeit the highest, who assures a perfect fit between the essence or the 'being' of a being and the empirical being itself.

Ontotheology's obsession with objects decides in advance how God will enter the philosophical discourse. For, as such, the problem of ontotheology is not that it invokes God too easily, but it is rather that, through its preoccupations with beings, it will also think or use God in a particular manner, namely, as a function that outwits the endless referral of beings to other contingent beings. Ontotheology will think God in the very same manner as it thinks beings. "To think beings instead of being [. . .] is to think what is revealed, what comes to presence, rather than to think the mystery of the unconcealment, the coming to presence."[38] To come back to our example of the table: when the table is determined and defined as a 'plateau with four legs,' this essence is abstracted not only from what all tables have in common but also from that which is presented by every particular table we encounter. What the different tables have in common will be configured as that which is 'most present' or 'most being-full' in the table. This 'ideal' essence, which can be held in thought, is what is 'actualized' or 'incarnated' in every particular table. However, since this essence is considered to be 'more real' than any particular table, every particular appearance of a table will, accordingly, be considered only to be an inferior instantiation of the essence of a table, as when one compares a table missing one leg to the 'idea' of a table with four legs. In the same way, 'God' will be thought as that being that perfectly instantiates the imperfections of the material world.

God will be thought of as either the creator who creates an inferior world, a conception which we have already seen Levinas lamenting, or as the one who lies ahead of us as the one whose perfection has already been realized.[39] It is precisely the appearance of such a cleft "between the merely apparent being here below and the real being somewhere up there" that Heidegger will identify as metaphysics, and that, at least according to Heidegger, arose with Plato and is rehearsed by Christianity through "reinterpreting the Below as the created and the Above as the Creator."[40]

Next to its shuddering before contingency and its craving for unity and univocity, metaphysics conceives of the being of beings always with an eye to its foundation or ground. It is here that one needs to understand that ontotheology is not primarily a theological question, or, as Mabille puts it, a bad theological response to a good philosophical question.[41] Yet this is exactly how the problem of ontotheology is most often perceived. Westphal, for instance, distinguishes between theology and the language of prayer and praise in order to at least safeguard the latter from the accusation of ontotheology. Westphal notes that the critique of ontotheology concerns the 'how' rather than the 'what' of our God-talk. In this sense, for Westphal, the critique of ontotheology is directed more to the primacy of theory rather than to the practice of praise. *Here* we have a bad theological response to a good philosophical question, in that it lets a kind of fideism emerge at the expense of all rationality and the seeking of reasons for the Christian faith.[42]

Thus, the highest being need not be divine, but consists only in *a determinate function*, namely, "to render the whole of reality intelligible for philosophical reflection" by proclaiming one or the other Supreme Being "in relation to which all beings must be understood," whether through historical progress or through the reference to another being, albeit divine.[43] Since ontotheology has different postures, it is for this reason that one must ask if and to what extent ontotheology has made its way into Christian theology and into its language of praise as well. Indeed, no flight to a suprasensory world is needed to find a highest being. One might therefore say that while not all metaphysics is ontotheological (here in the sense of evoking the name of God), all ontotheology is metaphysical. This is already obvious in Heidegger's account of Nietzsche. Commenting upon the latter, with a phrasing that reminds one of Derrida's theory of a 'transcendental signifier,' Heidegger writes:

> To be sure, something else can still be attempted in face of the tottering of the dominion of prior values. That is, if God in the sense of the Christian god has disappeared from his authoritative

position in the suprasensory world, then *this authoritative place itself is always preserved*, even though as that which has become empty. The now-empty authoritative realm of the suprasensory and the ideal world can still be adhered to. What is more, *the empty place demands to be occupied anew* and to have the god now vanished from it replaced by something else.[44]

To sum up, if we affirm here Heidegger's statement that a reversal of a metaphysical statement remains a metaphysical statement, then we have yet to understand *why* the reversal of a metaphysical statement remains metaphysical indeed. If, as we have seen in the authors under discussion, a reversal of the subject-object distinction is at issue, in that in one way or another human beings turn into the 'object and the objective' of an autonomous instance (whether it is God, givenness, or the Other), then one should ponder to what extent these metaphysical residues point us in a different direction than a fair amount of authors on the theme of 'overcoming ontotheology' have taken. The guiding question of this book is consonant with one of Marion's questions: "[I]f there is such a thing as ontotheology, [and] if this concept has a precise sense (non-ideological, not vague), when did it start to operate and how far does its concept extend?"[45]

Chapter 2

Phenomenology, Liturgy, and Metaphysics

Jean-Yves Lacoste

From his earlier to his later works, Lacoste engages in a thorough discussion with Heidegger. One could even say that Lacoste is somewhat suspicious of the German philosopher's overwhelming presence in contemporary philosophical and theological circles. This suspicion only becomes fully manifest in Lacoste's recent book, *Le monde et l'absence d'œuvre* (2000). However, one must trace the germs of these questions concerning Heidegger back to his earlier books *Note sur le temps* (1990) and *Expérience et Absolu* (1994).

"En marge du monde et de la terre: l'aise," a chapter in his 2000 book, opens with a discussion on the *historical* nature of Heidegger's 'being-in-the-world,' a nature, we must keep in mind, that Heidegger has never denied. It is thus perhaps no coincidence that in the interbellum 'anxiety' is proclaimed to be Dasein's most fundamental mood.[1] Lacoste asks whether we *must* assume that 'being-in-the-world' and its corresponding anxiety are the most original and fundamental characteristics of human existence? What about friendship, love, and the experience of the work of art?

The Heidegger of *Being and Time* would be inclined to rank these experiences and their corresponding primacy of the present as derivatives (of, for example, *MitDasein*) and consider them to be vulgar, ontologically of no importance. Since a 'primacy of the present' forgets the temporal structure of 'being-in-the-world' as care (*Sorge*), which is always open to the future, the experiences of friendship and love for Heidegger probably would fall under "the they" (*Das Man*), where people live 'from day-to-day' and, in this way, refuse to recognize their finitude. Since love and friendship essentially consist in a joy- and restful present, one can hardly doubt that Heidegger would interpret these phenomena primarily as instances of *Das Man*, for could it not also be in this way that "'the They' provides a constant tranquillization about death"?[2] Lacoste, however, who is as much influenced by Husserl as he is by Heidegger, maintains that these phenomena *do* tell us something of what it means to be human and could be even more fundamental than Heidegger's *Angst*: "If joy, love etc. don't need to enter the brute and naked logic of being-in-the-world, does this immediately mean that these phenomena have to be qualified as not original?" and "Must one infer from the fact that the time of joy and that of analogous phenomena precariously supersede care, that these phenomena are absent from the map of the original?" (MO, 82 and 83). It is in the *margins* of the Heideggerian 'world' that experiences such as these open the human being onto an 'other-than-world.'

Lacoste is a phenomenologist. His works aim to explore the human *aptitude to experience*.[3] That capability could be greater than the Heideggerian figures—'world' and 'earth'—would allow for, and might even incorporate a religious or 'liturgical experience'—note that liturgy, for Lacoste, is defined not only as the celebration of the Mass but also, more generally, as the relation of human beings to God (EA, 2; 22). Lacoste gives a phenomenological account of that which happens (or does not happen) when the believer prays and praises.

Lacoste versus Heidegger: Ontological Differences

For Lacoste, Heidegger outlined the two basic experiences of human beings at the end of the millennium: on the one hand, the atheistic world, in which angst, death, and care prevail; on the other hand, the experience of serenity while dwelling upon the earth (EA, 7–27). Lacoste opens *Experience and the Absolute* therefore by questioning Heidegger's introduction of the concept of 'earth' (EA, 7–22). Indeed this concept yields some remarkable consequences: where *Dasein* is considered to be *Unzuhause*, people are now allowed to dwell upon the earth. Where *Being and Time* analyze angst as the most original affect, people are now capable of serenity and can understand their dwelling on earth as peaceful. Heidegger's turn,[4] according to Lacoste, amounts to a reenchantment of the world: if *Dasein* was without God in the world, the mortals now experience a certain familiarity with the sacred.

How should we understand this turn? To avoid simply taking sides between these two options, Lacoste proposes a dialectical bond between these Heideggerian concepts. Both 'world' and 'earth' are possibilities that appear before our *place* ('lieu,' 'avoir lieu'). In consequence of our corporeality, 'being-in-the-world' and 'dwelling on the earth' presuppose the reality of our place. 'World' and 'earth' are, Lacoste contends, possibilities offered to our 'placedness.' This topology does not want to judge which concept is the most original but does solely affirm that our relation to being is always and already dependent on our corporeality.[5] This placedness is in Lacoste's work conceived of both in a Husserlian and in a Heideggerian manner: Heideggerian, in that the life of the mind is dependent upon an affective and temporal encounter with reality, and Husserlian, in that this placedness allows for a constitution of a present and, in this sense, admits of a plurality of worlds. So the 'world of fatigue'[6] entails a different relation to our placedness than the world of liturgy. It pertains to phenomenology to describe this variety of affective encounters.

There is, according to Lacoste, a certain freedom toward these transcendental figures of world and earth. Lacoste coins this freedom as *memory* and *project* (NT, 27). Both concepts are important to understand the liturgical experience correctly. Lacoste distinguishes between the Heideggerian care and the project. Whereas care means, according to Lacoste, the transcendental-existential relation to the future, the project aims at appropriating this future. Since being-in-the-world as care relates itself to an uncertain future, the present cannot be the only sphere of sense and meaning. To the contrary, precisely because of this openness toward the future, the present cannot be conceived of as a singular moment; it must always be seen and interpreted in its relation to both the past and the future. The project, on the other hand, brings an active decision at the heart of every present. By doing so, the project aims at a certain mastery over the future. It appropriates the future (or the past) as its own. The project, in this sense, opens up a space where one can regard the future as one's own. My future becomes *mine* and, in this way, a genuine human possibility. Take for instance the preparation of a meal for some friends. If I want to invite some guests and welcome them to my dinner table, I will have to buy the necessary ingredients today. Today, the present thus becomes an area of signification. The project masters the possible threat of the future by opening a place where one can *anticipate* the future.

Thereby, however, at once the aporia from which the project suffers is exposed. The project wants to empower itself of that which, by definition, exceeds human powers—the future. The paradigm for our powerlessness is, in Lacoste's opinion, death. Heidegger interpreted death as that which enables

Dasein to take up its existence in an authentic manner. The confrontation
with its finitude is the occasion for *Dasein* to take up its being in its ownmost
way. Lacoste, however, and analogous to the early Levinas, considers death
to be too great an enigma to give any signification to it. The death of
the other (*NT*, 57–58) serves as a guide to understand this fundamental
powerlessness. As embodied beings, we are involved with one another. The
death of a partner affects all previously shared projects. Every meaning that
I anticipated with him or her is destroyed by the death of one of us. The
meaning of death is revealed only by the death of the other: death is that
frontier which annihilates every relation that the other and I might have.
Lacoste thus points out that every (worldly) relation must be characterised
by *incompleteness*. The death of the other only confirms this *ontological
poverty*. Death is that which interrupts every (intersubjective) relation and
puts even the meaning of 'being' in question. With the certainty of death's
dispossession looming over every relationship, all possession is a mere illusion,
and it is such a poverty that according to Lacoste might very well be an
ontological trait of human beings (*NT*, 102; *EA*, 170–72). All projects suffer
this aporia: they tend to confuse the anticipation of the future with the
future *an sich*, in such a way that the future is, mistakenly, understood as a
project. Divertissement (*NT*, 39) consists in the improper appropriation of
signification as something that I give to myself and therefore in the refusal
to see signification as a *given*.

Yet the project encounters something like signification. We enjoy a meal
with our friends, the beauty of a work of art, or the relation with the ones we
love, even though these experiences do not answer the meaning of being in
a definite way. Our projects are like a beginning ('*commencement*,' *NT*, 44):
they hint at a signification of and in being that makes the future appear not
only as a threat but also as an existential and existentiel possibility. Already
in *Note sur le temps*, Lacoste points to this double structure in and of being:

> Why are there beings and rather not nothing? The question
> speaks to us about us: we are the ones who equally could not
> have been. In anxiety, which makes manifest the threat of the
> nothing over being, in wonder, which finds the fact that there
> is being beautiful and good, we learn that we are not exterior
> to that which is questionable to us. Contingency is our fact
> as much as it is the fact of things. And before finitude takes
> on the face of our death, it has the visage of our coming into

being. The sense of the becoming [of a thing] is in the thing
that becomes. (NT, 47)

The Liturgical Experience

The liturgical experience is related to such a sense of wonder, for this
experience is just such a project.[7] In the same way that I can decide to
prepare a meal for my friends, I can decide to direct my attention to
God in prayer or by attending Mass. However, as a project, distinct from
Heideggerian care, liturgy involves a *transgression* of our being-in-the-world.
Liturgy is a desire to see and experience God and to anticipate the future
God prepared for us. In this sense, liturgy is an anticipation of the Kingdom
of God. However, just as the project of preparing a meal is, here and now,
experienced as a "realized anticipation" of that future, liturgy will in a similar
manner anticipate and realize God's proximity.

I will interpret the liturgical experience along three structural moments:
first, an *exodus* out of the (Heideggerian) world; second, the *conversion* to
the image of Christ, and third, the ethical *mission* toward the other.

Exodus: Being Exposed to a Nonexperience

One must understand liturgy as a transgression of and rupture with the
Heideggerian being-in-the-world. This rupture does not and cannot, however,
complete a total rupture with this world. A necessary, though not sufficient,
condition for this interruption is (Augustinian) restlessness. Lacoste defines
this restlessness as that "mark of the humanity of man which removes man
from every satisfaction to which world and earth hold the key" (EA, 198
n. 20). Restlessness involves the refusal to be our being as *Dasein* or as a
'mortal.' Thus, this restlessness aptly describes our dissatisfaction and boredom
with and about being. Unrest is in this sense the desire of something beyond
being and beyond the world.

Such a restlessness appears as a specific kind of project. The project
tried to neutralise the threat of the future by anticipating this future. Since
the future never lives up to our expectations, restlessness awakens. "The
eschatological restlessness is not related extrinsically to our worldliness.
The world, which manifests itself at every moment and in every place of
our being, lures us into questioning and the corresponding restlessness."[8]

Restlessness is therefore correlative to being-in-the-world. The believer's free choice to expose himself or herself to a being-before-God, which Lacoste calls 'exposition' (EA, 40–42), is not completely distinct from this restlessness but does establish a discontinuity with 'world' and 'earth.' While restlessness is "a desire that does not know what it really desires" (EA, 41), liturgy is an explicit choice for God. Theologically, one must understand this as follows: while restlessness is the condition needed to *receive* the Word of God,[9] liturgy and exposition are those acts that, through praying, *answer* to and praise that Word.

The liturgical transgression places the 'world' and the 'earth' between brackets. Prayer displays a different relation to the reality of our place: it opens a *nonplace* (EA, 27) that is determined by neither the angst of and for our being-in-the-world nor by the sacrality of the earth. Answering to the Word of God demands that one leave the world *as* world, where *Dasein* is without God, behind (EA, 23–32).

Liturgy therefore desires to see and know God. In this respect, our answer to the Word of God in praise and prayer is an anticipation of the absolute future—the coming of God, God's kingdom. Lacoste is convinced of the fact that not one prayer is without God's proximity. This proximity, however, needs to be distinguished from God's presence, even though the liturgy initially confuses presence and proximity in a "parousiacal moment" (EA, 59). The nonplace of prayer and liturgy opened up, we recall, a space wherein that which keeps us at a distance from God's coming—the 'world' and 'history'—is temporarily put between brackets. It should not go unnoticed that Lacoste understands this putting between brackets of world, earth, and history in a manner similar to the phenomenological reduction: just as the phenomenological reduction brackets for an instance the existence of a thing in order to make the thing itself appear *as* it appears to consciousness, so too the liturgical or theological reduction (EA, 175; NT, 122) puts the world and earth between parentheses in order to gain sight of the weal and the woe of the ones existing *coram Deo*. Since prayer interrupts the dialectic that governs history, liturgy installs, along with the nonplace, the *kairos* and opportunity of a *nontime* (EA, 83). To make this phenomenologically more concrete, Lacoste not only points to the figures of the pilgrim and the hermit (EA, 23–32) but also expounds on the possibility that the (Hegelian) master and slave pray together. Indeed, my foes are not refused entrance to the church where I am praying. The nonplace and nontime of the liturgical experience therefore suggest that one sojourns in eschatological peace and unity (EA, 51). The distance between the liturgical experience and the world makes room for a fragile anticipation and realization of the eschatological good. The proximity of God in prayer gives the religious a present that knows no shortcomings (*EA*, 59) one wherein the desire of God is temporarily appeased. That is why one prays as if God's proximity therein coincides with God's presence.

The liturgical nontime and nonplace of prayer is however threatened by the weal and the woe of every project. Faith and prayer risk interrupting being-in-the-world and losing the self completely in the enthusiastic vision of God's kingdom. The liturgical project, as every project, thus aims at more than is in its power. The believer tries to appropriate the absolute future. Lacoste claims, however, that the liturgical experience is prevented from being merely a distraction, since the fact that people present themselves to God does not mean that God 'presents' Godself to them. I present myself to God in prayer and confess to be at God's disposal, but God does not present Godself 'in person,' if you like. Therefore, the liturgy has to reckon with a *nonexperience* (*EA*, 40–54). This nonexperience will interrupt the liturgical project and, by doing so, initiates a conversion.

The Nocturnal Nonexperience as Locus of the Gift and of Conversion

We need to understand this nonexperience phenomenologically as follows: the liturgical project is eager to appropriate its object, the absolute future of God, and therefore a space is opened wherein God's proximity is no longer differentiated from God's presence. But God is in this nonplace, this *being-in-the-Church* (*NT*, 190), absent to both perception and to affectivity. While the believer desires to dwell in the kingdom, (s)he stays, under guidance of the spirit, in the church and this only 'for a moment,' *kairologically* (*NT*, 187–202; *EA*, 131). The plenitude of the eschatological enters this world unnoticed and does so always in a fragile tension with a worldly phenomenon (*NT*, 198; *EA*, 92). Between the believer and God there is the materiality of the provisional: the bread that is broken and the wine that is shed. The desire is sobered and summoned to patiencce by this worldly appearance of the Absolute. The world(ly) again draws a veil between God and man (e.g. *EA*, 50).

Lacoste proposes to think this nonexperience as a *night* (Cf. John of the Cross). The nocturnal nonexperience is a brutal and violent confrontation with the liturgical experience's own aporia: the intention to anticipate God's coming does not suffice to appropriate one's own absolute future. Where the believer sees himself or herself as *consciously* desiring God, he or she stands before his or her God as a *soul*. According to Lacoste, this nonexperience is, in the first place, a frustrating terror that ultimately leaves the believer exhausted (*EA*, 188). It is a crisis of intentionality: nothing happens. Only faith can save us now: *sola fide* (*EA*, 146). This faith, however, is fueled by the knowledge of the church, which, according to Lacoste, safeguards the memory of the divine self-communication because of the theological reduction in which it operates. In this sense, the night is "the pure affirmation of this knowledge, or of the pure reiteration of consent" (*EA*, 146). The liturgical experience manifests itself at the margins of our being-there: *Dasein* relates to the liturgical being-there, this *ecce homo* of the religious person, as acting relates to nonacting, sensing to nonsensing, and experiencing to nonexperiencing. Liturgy is in this sense "a transgression of every capacity for experience that consciousness can avail itself of" (*EA*, 152). The effusion of the eschatological in the historical brings consciousness and thus the autonomy of the project to its limits. The liturgy dismantles and disorients the transcendental constitution of subjectivity and suggests that the carnal dimension of existence serves as a more appropriate paradigm, both for intersubjective relations as for the *coram Deo* relation (*EA*, 156). We are exposed to God and the other in our corporeality and not primarily as 'thinking things.'

It is through this crisis of the nonexperience that God operates a liberating decentering of the (autonomous) subject. When the eschatological enters into the world, under the disguise of the bread and the wine of the Eucharist, it interrupts the liturgical project and alerts this project of its limits. The desire of God is sobered precisely because of this refusal of its satisfaction: the believer desires God's coming but is confronted with the bread and the wine of the Eucharist. It is this confrontation that will protect the liturgical anticipation against *divertissement* in which the project would no longer be aware of its precarious nature and would understand itself as an autonomous affair. The consequences of such a nonexperience are, therefore, twofold. On the one hand, the desire to see and 'experience' God, in other words the desire for something beyond being, is sobered by this worldly appearance of the Absolute, by God's appearing *in* being. It is this that, according to Lacoste, appeals to the believer's *patience*: God will come, but not *because* you and I are praying (cf. Matt. 24, 36). On the other hand, this nonexperience summons the believer, precisely because of this worldly appearance, not to ignore his or her worldly *responsibilities*. The liturgical experience therefore takes on an ethical form as well. Liturgy is prevented from being a distraction, not only because of the appeal to the believer's patience but also because of the fact that this logic of the church and of the nonexperience is essentially a "constant reminder of our historiality" (EA, 92, also NT, 193). The believer's desire to experience God and the corresponding risk of losing oneself in enthusiastic contemplation of the kingdom is countered by the reference to the neighbor and to our historical responsibilities toward him or her: "[N]o one can participate in the logic [of the liturgy] without being instructed that our neighbour too possesses a sacramental dignity" (NT, 213).[10]

The night thus reduces the liturgical project to its essence: liturgy is putting oneself at the disposal of God (EA 151 mod.), a desire to deliver my being into God's hands (EA, 156). By turning to the believer, God dispossesses the religious person of his dazzling desire for his (absolute) future by revealing being as a *gift*. In praying the believer manifests a visibly impoverished existence. He lives in an *empty present* and a *dead time* (EA, 148). Thereby the liturgy enjoys the fruit of a being that no longer can be characterized as a being that has to be its being. Lacoste conceives of the being of the religious person as a being that neither desires nor acts and thereby is forced into a 'position' where (s)he can only receive. Thus, the nonexperience is according to Lacoste best conceived of as a *kairos* that allows the liturgy to be, instead of a distraction, a *conversion*. It is precisely this discrepancy between the believer's intention to experience God and the liturgical nonexperience (or God's refusal to satisfy the desire) that alerts the believer to the limits of the liturgical project. Later Lacoste explains that though God may be said to be present in the earthly realities of bread and wine, the believer must acknowledge that "God's phenomenality cannot be understood if we do not understand that God transcends his phenomenality [. . .] I suggest that love only understands, first that presence is presence, then that presence is *only* presence."[11] The project, be it liturgical or otherwise, resembles modern, autonomous subjectivity. As divertissement, it refuses to open itself to that which gives itself; it is no longer aware of its precarious nature and understands itself as an autonomous affair. The project of modern subjectivity consists in the refusal to see signification as a gift or as given. It is important to understand that this nonexperience serves to distinguish the liturgical experience from the concept of 'religious experience' that has dominated theology since Schleiermacher. According to Lacoste, God is not primarily present to a lived experience of consciousness. However, this is not to "preclude the idea that the Absolute can enter into the field of experience, or that the contents of consciousness can bear truthful witness to its descension" but rather "that all experience that takes place within the immediate sphere of consciousness is necessarily bound up within a still greater inexperience" (EA, 48–49).

Over and against modern subjectivity, prayer and the liturgical celebration *incarnate* a passivity that precedes every conscious act, *creation*. But affirming being as the gift of creation, we recall, requires the ascetic exodus from the Heideggerian world. This gift is a *confirmation* of the liturgical exodus. The liturgical experience, in which the believer resists every autonomous act of signification, is therefore put into a position where signification can *only* be received. Indeed, this impoverished existence has as its reverse the admission of the fact that being truly is "being-in-relation" (NT, 180), in other words, that signification is always dependent upon another, whether it be God or a fellow human being. It is in relation to the other and in relation with God that the signification of being is decided.

Lacoste's phenomenology of *boredom* elucidates well the conversion that is the nonexperience (EA, 148–49; Carmel, 588–93). The liturgical person restlessly anticipates the coming of God. But when he or she realizes that this liturgical project does not oblige God to respond either visibly or experientially, the liturgical person might become bored with prayer. It is precisely this boredom that Lacoste indicates as the 'experience' of the gift. One learns what giving means when there is hardly anything given back; true giving does not demand reciprocation. The one who prays patiently gives his time and thereby him- or herself to God. This abandoning of self teaches man about the essence of giving. In liturgical experience, human beings turn over their lives to God in order to receive God's Word. What it is to be human is then entirely in God's hands. Only God can *confirm* the being of the believer at this stage. Only when the other restores one's being does one begin to understand the meaning of being. The humanity of man is a question that only an other, namely God, can answer. Being-bored-before-God is a modality of the-putting-oneself-at-the-disposal-of: "The I here wants to be the You pronounced by the other" (Carmel, 589). It is exactly this abandoning of the self that is *confirmed* through and *incarnated* before the Word of God one hears in the Eucharist: "[B]efore being self-same, man is in the first place this other than God in whom God finds a you" (EA, 152). This confirmation and incarnation is, in the eyes of Lacoste, the *eschatological* truth of our being-there. The truth of one's being is one's kenotic emptying of one's self for an other. Only an other can speak words of confirmation over one's being. Theologically speaking, that other obviously is Christ. It is Christ who offers us the eschatological mode of our being-there. Prayer and church are those instances where God, by turning to human beings, gives human beings their being as a vocation (NT, 117,

169; EA, 147). The believer is revealed to himself or herself as the being
that is called and promised to a being such as (the being of) Christ. In the
liturgical experience the whole of existence, including death, is interpreted
as a promise.

The nonexperience that affects prayer is thus a conversion to the image
of (the suffering) Christ in spite of the human tendency to understand one's
self autonomously. But Lacoste also distinguishes a more active moment in
this movement of conversion called "abnegation" (de Bérulle's term) (EA,
160–63). This abnegation is the aptitude to live the liturgical experience
not as a tragedy but as reconciliation. Abnegation is a gesture in which the
believer *consents* to the authentic being-there as did Christ and thereby marks
the point where the passive 'being converted' is turned into an active 'letting
oneself be converted.' The abnegation is not the end of the project or desire
but indicates its modification: the project wants and desires nothing other
than imitating the will of Christ, while the erroneous attempt to appropriate
one's own absolute future is left behind. Lacoste again points to the Christian
images of the errant, the hermit, and the fool to understand the logic of
the liturgy as a logic of imitation of Christ. This foolishness might not be
a universal demand, but it confers to liturgy a visibility without which its
transgression would not really be a transgression (EA, 178). The fool thus
makes visible that which is present in every faithful confrontation with
the Absolute. In this way, the liturgy is a logic of *imitation*. The liturgical
experience turns the believer into an imitator of Christ's death on the cross.
Christ's cross is for Lacoste the climax of nonexperience (EA, 191). The
foolishness of the faithful thus isolates the foolishness of the cross. Only
theology can duly account for this experience. Indeed theology will say that
"the only donation of meaning in this case comes from beyond, and that
in the fool's humiliated humanity [. . .] we actually recognize the image of
the humiliated humanity of God himself" (EA, 190, mod.). The one who
patiently endures this nonexperience will share in and receive the *joy* of
Easter, knowing that death is the final fact of our lives but not the final
word. Lacoste interprets the fool as the one who knows how to live the
events of Good Friday with reference to Easter and who therefore knows
that true joy follows humiliation.[12]

Mission and Ethics

Is the one who in this way incarnates kenotic existence able at all to call
others to incarnate their most proper existence? Is the believer, 'after' his
or her exodus, sent back to the world to operate there as an illuminating

example for others? Such a moment of mission is indeed present in Lacoste's works. The fool stirs up *restlessness* because of his frightening alterity (*EA* 190).[13] The poor appearance of the fool exposes the interpretations in which humanity usually lives and moves—for instance, the interpretation of human beings as 'animal rationale' (*EA*, 185–89). The prayer of the believer and the extreme ascesis of the fool remind one of the scandal of the cross. Precisely in this way, the ontological restlessness of others, who desire something beyond this world but do not know exactly what they desire, can be awakened and called forward to the most proper possibility: an existence that empties itself of itself in the name of Christ. Furthermore, the ascesis of the fool corelates to the ontological poverty that Lacoste, already in *Note sur le temps*, discerned as the most fundamental trait of the human beings' humanity. It is this ontological poverty that might function as a sort of philosophical mediation that can bridge the gap between liturgical existence before God and atheistic being-in-the-world.[14] According to Lacoste, "whoever desires poverty [. . .] wants nothing other than to accede to the truth of his being and to exist according to this truth" (*EA*, 173, mod.). This choice of voluntary poverty therefore "proves [. . .] that fundamental ontology can be translated into ways of being [. . .], into concrete gestures that break with every kind of divertissement" (ibid.) and to which liturgical poverty can align itself. It is in this sense that the strangeness of the fool (and, a fortiori, of the believer) might serve as a visible sign for, and awaken in, (post)modern people the desire for God by which the liturgical experience is driven. In Lacoste's words: "[T]he ascetic does, in fact, act on behalf of everyone and as everyone's proxy" (*EA*, 178).

Mission must, on the other hand, incorporate an ethical element as well. If the believer can call others to "a more genuine experience of the world and of oneself" (*EA*, 175), then this awakening must also entail a love of the good. At the time of *Experience and the Absolute*, the modern subject is decentered only by the liturgical experience, as illustrated well by the relation between ethics and liturgy. According to Lacoste, the ethical endeavor *does* encounter, in this world, an absolute imperative—the appeal to do good everywhere and always (*NT*, 49–55; *EA*, 66–76). However, this appeal, discovered in and through being-in-the-world, needs the interruption of the liturgical experience with the world to interpret the ethical exigencies correctly. One could object, of course, that one need not be liturgical in order to be ethical. But, according to Lacoste, this would miss the point of decentering the subject as intended by the liturgical experience. Left to itself, ethics can only respond to the absolute appeal in its own way; in its claim to know how one should respond to the absolute appeal, it would construct the signification of this appeal autonomously and so refuse to incorporate other points of view.

Ethics, for Lacoste, becomes a "second liturgy" (*EA*, 74 mod.). However, the relation between ethics and liturgy remains somewhat ambiguous. For we know that the subordination of ethics to a liturgical experience can amount to a terror of the religious itself. In Lacoste's words, the believer must always counter the suspicion that he or she "is incapable of existing in the world humanely" (*EA*, 68–69). Therefore, ethics is not only a second liturgy but also liturgy's first critic (e.g., *EA*, 56).

There is also a theological element to this ethical conversion. With this in mind, Lacoste distinguishes between the 'beginning' of the liturgy, such as the possibility of the master and the slave praying together, and the "desire for a new beginning" (*BHP*, 573) that is aroused *in* liturgy. The believer asks God for a liberation of his freedom, a freedom that is in the world always seduced by evil and sin. It comes as no surprise that Lacoste labels 'being-in-the-world' as sinful more than once (*EA*, 31, 94). Ethical reconciliation between the master and the slave, wherein they give one another a new beginning, cannot liberate them from their pasts, where both, by doing evil, have rendered themselves evil. The confessed sin is not only something that one *did* but also something that one *is*. Sin is an ontological determination of human beings (*BHP*, 572). The believer turns away from the world to ask God for a future that one cannot give to oneself. The believer desires, then, a 'new beginning' in which only God liberates him or her from sin.

Hence prayer is a symbolic place where God turns to women and men to give them a new future and beginning: the nocturnal liturgical experience is, at one and the same time, a new dawn. Only a confrontation with the Absolute can free human beings of their attachments to evil. The believer is sent back to the world to dwell there as a new human being who, hopefully, will never again deny the exigencies of ethics (*EA*, 73).

The liturgical experience is, however, not the only experience—other than the Heideggerian *Dasein* or *mortal* experience—that Lacoste indicates as a possible way of 'being there.' The publication of *Experience and the Absolute* was soon followed by investigations into the experience of resting and the experience of a work of art as a possible "opening to a philosophy of liturgy."[15] This is surprising because the liturgical experience, with its emphasis on the distance between experiences of the world and liturgy. seems to exclude this more 'worldly' interpretation of liturgy.

The Experience of Resting and of the Work of Art

The liturgical experience can be seen as analogous to, on the one hand, the experience of 'resting,' and on the other hand, the experience of the art work, because of the appeasement that these experiences have in common. "En marge du monde et de la terre: l'aise" refers to the question that, even in *Experience and the Absolute*, points to a theology of the world: are there not experiences in the world, other than liturgical ones, that can suggest the *eschaton* (EA, 97)? In *Experience and the Absolute*, however, this question is answered mostly negatively: only for a saint does the liturgical experience *permanently* determine his or her 'being-in-the-world.'

In the article just mentioned Lacoste does offer a positive answer to the question raised in *Experience and the Absolute*. The liturgy is not the only experience in which human beings break with the 'world' and the 'earth.' There is, for instance, also the *pause* we take from our work. This interruption, however, does not mean that I am no longer 'there.' It does mean, however, that my 'being there' is no longer determined by the Heideggerian world and earth, even though I rest in the world and on the earth. Instead, a certain calmness and joy determines my 'being there,' which Lacoste calls the "well-being-there" ('*bien-être-là*,' MO, 19). I know that this pause cannot last forever and that I soon have to be concerned with my work once again. During such an interruption, Lacoste states, I am content but in no means satisfied (ibid.). I still have to *care* about my work or my life, but these concerns are temporarily set aside. The pause is simply the quiet enjoyment of a between (world and earth). What is at stake in this 'resting' experience is the real, albeit fragile, unconcerned-ness wherein world and earth are kept at a distance. My place of resting is the place where I dwell. Therefore, *Daseins's Unzuhause* does not come into question here. But neither does my resting place remind me of my origins or rootedness. Thus, the experience of resting must be conceived of as an excess and transgression of the transcendental expressions of our being human, *Dasein*, and mortals. Lacoste nevertheless insists on interpreting this interval theologically by calling it a *sabbathic experience* (MO, 21).[16]

Very similar is the experience of *a work of art* (MO, 68–72). A work of art liberates human beings from their involvement with world and earth because it puts the appearance of every phenomenon other than itself between brackets. The work of art calls for our undivided attention, and its appearance is to be understood with reference to the *joy* and the *rest* that it produces. Art promises and delivers an unconcerned present. Over and against care for the future, a work of art offers a joyful constitution of the present.

Note that Lacoste pointed out four aptitudes of experience: being-in-the-world, the earth, liturgy, and sabbathic experience. All of this necessitates the further questioning of the affective nature of our placedness. It is on the basis of this questioning that Lacoste will give full ontological weight to these experiences that the Heidegger of *Being and Time* would probably have qualified as divertissement.

Ontology and Affectivity

One can already identify Lacoste's questions concerning affectivity in his description of the differences between Heidegger and Husserl: "There is between the Husserlian and the Heideggerian descriptions a distance which distinguishes the 'seeing' (the 'appearing') from the 'letting see' (the 'making appear,' 'the bringing to light')" (MO, 81). Being-in-the-world for instance is not a visible and objective being for an intentional ego but more like a horizon without which beings would not even appear. For this reason, Heidegger reserves, in *Being and Time*, an affective *Grundbefindlichkeit* (*Angst*) to indicate *Dasein*'s being-in-the-world.

The 'earth' is also more like a horizon than an objective 'being.' So, for example, in "The Origin of the Work of Art," it is not what the work of art shows, that is, the 'shoes' in Van Gogh's painting, but what the work of art makes appear that is important. One cannot exclude, however, that Heidegger could have fallen into the well-known trap of the interpreter who, by wanting to show certain things, always risks disregarding others. Lacoste's question concerns once again the relation between the concepts of 'world' and 'earth,' the latter making its first appearance in Heidegger's famous tract on art.

To retrieve Lacoste's answer, let us return to the relation between the perception of the work of art and the (rural) interpretation Heidegger gave of it. Indeed, in his tract on the work of art, Heidegger does not tell us *how* we can know the 'world' or 'earth.' Certainly it is not merely perception that informs us about their existence, otherwise a look at the painting would have sufficed. Instructed by the lessons of *Being and Time*, Lacoste proposes that, to understand Heidegger's lecture on art correctly, one must return to Heidegger's insight that it is only by way of affectivity that we know what it is to be or that we know what being is.[17]

This, however, raises another problem: is it *necessary* that our affective response to Van Gogh's painting instructs us about what it is to dwell on 'earth'? How can Heidegger's philosophical description of the 'earth' be reconciled with the affective response to the work of art?[18] Is it not the case, Lacoste asks, that this response is plural and, therefore, more ambiguous than Heidegger allowed for? Recall that, for Lacoste, art's mode of appearing is that of captivation: every other phenomenon than the work of art itself is put between brackets. The affective tonality appropriate to this captivation is *joy*, which is (almost) absent from Heidegger's *Being and Time*.[19] Hence Lacoste's thesis is that the work of art distracts from being-in-the-world or at least from that which *Being and Time* considered to be most original.

Lacoste proceeds by asking what would happen if Heidegger would be mistaken in his interpretation of Van Gogh's work? And indeed, according to Derrida, Heidegger was mistaken: the shoes on the painting of Van Gogh turned out to be, not the shoes of a peasant, as Heidegger argued, but, on the contrary, those of a city-dweller.[20] Therefore, Heidegger's rather rural description of the earth, in fact, was the consequence of some over-interpretation on his part. Interpretation always entails the risk of saying too much or too little. According to Lacoste, Heidegger exposes himself to both.

On the other hand, nothing forbids Heidegger's interpretation. Just as one cannot condemn someone for not seeing the work of art as a work of art, one cannot judge Heidegger for not giving a 'correct' interpretation of that which this particular work of art represents. It is precisely this diversity of affective answers that needs to be taken into account. Lacoste's hypothesis is that on the relation between interpretation and affectivity Heidegger might not have said enough.

This 'too much and too little' admits, according to Lacoste, of a first conclusion: since the 'earth' does not *necessarily* arise from the perception of the pair of shoes of Van Gogh, one should try to determine in what sort of a realm or horizon the work of art ravishes us. From the fact that Heidegger's interpretation is not necessary follows the thesis that other descriptions are equally possible: one could be reminded of the angst for and of being-in-the-world.[21] From the fact that Heidegger's 'earth' is nevertheless a possible determination of Van Gogh's painting, Lacoste infers that there can never be a 'pure' assessment of that 'earth' and that every interpretative determination of the affective answer to the work of art is always only partial.

It is, finally, this partiality that needs to be thought. Lacoste agrees with Heidegger in that the work of art offers an excessive presence; he disagrees with him in that it is not primarily the 'earth' that the work of art discloses. According to Lacoste, there is inevitably a discrepancy between the excessive presence offered by the work of art itself and that which is encountered only affectively and the interpretation given of it. Therefore, to evoke the pure presence of the earth, Lacoste contends, is to err about the logic of affectivity. Rather, one should speak of a "fundamental duplicity" between world and earth and dare to say that this "ambiguity can be the truth."[22] The meaning of being thus lies, according to Lacoste, in the ambiguous, but perpetual "double presence"[23] of world and earth. Every affective answer always prepares an only partial determination of the excessive presence. The problem then is, for Lacoste, that affectivity is *older* than, or, at least "more rich than the constitutions in which it takes its form" (MO, 101). The attraction of the artwork interrupts the Heideggerian being-in-the-world and delivers us into "the moving outline of an [affective, JS] field"[24] where free affective constitutions, deconstitutions, and reconstitutions succeed one another without deciding which constitution is the most original and wherein world and earth appear only as possibilities. Of course the world and its all too apparent finitude is inevitable, and of course one is always rooted in the 'earth' in one way or another. But since these determinations are to be considered as only partial and thus do not preclude a joyous sojourning, it is easy to imagine not only how the liturgical experience gains a legitimate place in this ontology of affectivity but also how experiences such as friendship and love, as in the work of art, presuppose a joyful constitution of the present and become ontologically significant.

Lacoste thus acknowledges in his later works that the liturgical experience is not the only experience that can manifest a rupture with being-in-the-world. The believer can effectively elucidate his existence to, for instance, nonbelievers, by pointing to those analogous experiences of resting and enjoying a work of art. Resting and the experience of a work of art, too, show a certain freedom over and against the transcendental expressions of being human. It is precisely with this 'worldly' between that the liturgical between can align itself. One can therefore hardly be surprised when *Le monde et l'absence d'œuvre* concludes with the very same words with which *Experience and the Absolute* opens: "[O]ur aptitudes to experience in fact exceed our aptitude to experience the world" (MO, 101).

Conclusion and Critical Remarks

Phenomenology and Theology

One could wonder, of course, if such a phenomenology of liturgy is still phenomenology or, rather, whether one must sweep away attempts like these, since they entail a 'theological turn of French phenomenology.' According to this latter statement, phenomenology of the kind Lacoste proposes is, in one way or another, unfaithful to the basic atheistic presuppositions of the phenomenology Husserl envisioned. Jean Greisch has expressed some hesitation about Lacoste's project: Is a phenomenology of the liturgy capable of describing what happens when consciousness is stripped of its basic characteristic, when there is no longer a lived experience to be described?[25]

But one could just as well take attempts such as those of Lacoste at face value, that is, as a theologian who elaborates on faith in a phenomenological manner? One needs neither faith nor theology to see that in the church nothing happens. The faithful leave the church unchanged.[26] Furthermore, Lacoste would admit that, from a strictly philosophical point of view, this nonexperience is an atheistic experience (EA, 147; 150). A phenomenology of the liturgy results from the confrontation of the phenomenological gaze with the being-there of the believer. It is in this sense that a phenomenology of the liturgy does not markedly differ from a phenomenology of labor or any other phenomenology one might imagine.

It is true, however, that Lacoste not only envisages this nonexperience from a philosophical point of view. To interpret this nonexperience as an *imitatio Christi* is surely to invoke theological reasoning. However, if one takes the *phenomenology* of the liturgy seriously, that is, as the confrontation of the phenomenological gaze with the life of the believer, are we not in a better position to evaluate the phenomenological accomplishments of Lacoste's endeavor? After all, one should pay close attention to the relation between the world, which can be approached phenomenologically, and the liturgical experience, which is, according to some of its critics, theological and therefore not phenomenologically accessible. The liturgical experience, according to Lacoste, is not a flight into otherworldliness; it is an experience in which the presence of the world is felt more vividly than ever (e.g. EA, 73). The liturgical experience is affected by the condition in which it arises: "Even the eucharistic gift, in which the Absolute takes place here and now, is conditioned by the interposition of the world. Saying that this presence is 'real,' does not make it diaphanic or theophanic. This interposition is obvious in an ontic manner: it must be detected in the materiality of bread and wine. But these ontic realities carry with them the ontological density of the world" (EA, 112).

This is neither an 'otherwise than being' (Levinas) nor a "God without being" (Marion); this is the beyond of being thought *from within* being. Believers celebrate in the world, and the liturgical experience never stops reminding them precisely of this world. More than Marion, Lacoste is willing to incorporate the "tension between being-in-fact and being-in-vocation" (*EA*, 157), between God and being. God's condescension to the world and to immanence is always and already affected by the condition in which it arises. Whereas for Marion, for the invisible to appear *as* invisible, the visible is to be "deduced [. . .] from itself" (*GWB*, 17) so as to make the visible refer only to the invisible (*GWB*, 23), Lacoste would point to the limits of such an enterprise, for the liturgical experience "gives itself first as a manner of being-in-the-world. [Liturgy] is a way of being-in-the-world" (*PP*, 156). Just as the bread and the wine of the Eucharist are not rendered theophanic, so Lacoste would point out to Marion that, from a phenomenological point of view, the wood and the paint of the icon admit of no 'spiritualization' and therefore, do not allow for a transparent crossing of the visible and the invisible.[27] In the nonexperience of prayer and of the church, the believer is not allowed to forget his or her presence in the world. This faithfulness toward the believer's presence in the world is the reason why this liturgical experience can be depicted phenomenologically. For Lacoste, and to paraphrase the text *La connaissance silencieuse*, it is as beings of flesh and blood that we approach the Absolute. As beings of flesh and blood, it is our body, praying with the hands crossed, kneeled down, or with the palms of the hands wide open to receive the *sancta*, that phenomenalizes the relation *coram*.[28] What happens in church and in the liturgical experience is, as Greisch argues correctly, "the projection of a different light on the phenomena of the world, an invitation to envisage them differently."[29] Such a change of perspective need not be irrational. On the contrary, it is an 'other thinking' ("*pensée autre*") that interprets its ties to a particular tradition in a rational way.[30]

It is this interpretation that severs itself from phenomenology, not the liturgical experience as such, for faith, in the liturgical experience, amounts to just such a change of perspective, and Lacoste's later works all try to describe just how such a change of horizon can be effectuated. It is, therefore, within this horizon of faith that believers discover their ineradicable attachment to being. And it is here that opinions differ. According to Lacoste, this embeddedness causes one to wonder to what extent the change of horizons effected in faith hints at a truth prior to the decision to believe. Indeed, theologically faith must be considered as a gift or as a grace—it is a transgression of the transcendental conditions of being human which, therefore, may not be reduced to these conditions (e.g. *EA*, 20–22) and the recognition that my auto-conversion (my decision to believe) might

point to a hetero-conversion (faith as gift of God). This, one could say, is
the temporal mode of procedure in faith: it is through faith that the subject
comes to believe in a God who first gave me to be, in God as Creator.[31]
This insight only subsequently throws a different light upon being. Only now
being appears to be, in Lacoste's words, "pre-eschatological" (*EA*, 139). The
term already indicates that it awaits its fulfilment: being and its projects are
only sketches of signification. They do not know that of which they are a
sketch (*NT*, 84). This presupposes, of course, both that the attachment to
being can be overcome and that theology knows how this is to be done.
The liturgical experience, therefore, remains trapped in what it wanted
to reject: the desire to see and experience God. Indeed, this desire for a
full-presence of God is never left altogether; it is only postponed: *patience*
is the liturgical virtue par excellence (*EA*, 91). Thus, there might be in
Lacoste a certain metaphysical nostalgia toward God's full presence and an
immediate experience thereof. From the perspective of deconstructionist
thinking, however, the attachment to being cannot be subordinated to a
time or a place in which this attachment (to being, to materiality, to the
body) would be undone. One might object to Lacoste, therefore, that it is
not at all sure whether our projects are to be conceived of as *sketches* of
a signification that will reveal, give, and present itself more fully. From a
Heideggerian perspective, one could object that it is uncertain whether these
sketches are sketches of a *signification* at all, for behind every signification
stands the mute fact of being thrown into the world.

The Différend between the World and Creation

Although Lacoste somewhat corrects Marion's search of transparency between
invisibility and visibility, Lacoste's stress on the visibility of the world is
most often accompanied by a negative evaluation of the world's visibility.
If the world draws a veil between God and the human being and hinders
the liturgical relation more than it helps it, this is so because the liturgical
experience is caught up in a logic of creation. The leave we can take of the
'world' in liturgy reminds one of our status as created beings, and the passivity
of this experience is older than any autonomous intentionality and confirms
the fundamental passivity issuing from creation. According to Lacoste, there
exists a différend between the (Heideggerian) world and creation (*EA*, 94;
NT, 89–91), and though this différend seems somewhat softened in his later
works, one still needs to question the structural move Lacoste undertakes
to justify this distinction, for it is precisely this différend that accounts for

the gap that exists between the liturgical being-in-the-world and existence *coram Deo*. One recalls that the liturgical experience originates in the project, wherein one, by reflexively appropriating the Heideggerian 'care,' encounters 'signification' *in* this world of finitude. It is therefore clearly stated by Lacoste that one can encounter 'signification' in a philosophical account of facticity. The problem here is that Lacoste *immediately* qualifies these experiences and the similar experiences of well-being-there as creation. In this way, the world is *immediately* forced into a difference with creation: if everything that is good and meaningful must be conceived of as creation, all that there is to the world can only be the negativity of death and sin. This *negative evaluation of the world*[32] means, of course, that Lacoste never really takes into account our 'being-in-the-world' as such. Though philosophy is able to detect signification in our worldly projects, only the theological concept of creation removes the discrepancy between signification and facticity, between the excess of signification with regard to its condition of possibility (*NT*, 101; 201), for instance between the ethical appeal to do good always and everywhere and 'being-in-the-world.' Hence Lacoste's presupposition that the distance theology takes from (philosophical) facticity and the world is "necessary for a true vantage point" (*EA*, 73–74). Note in passing that a similar objection can be raised against Marion, who tells us that the liberation of and from being can only occur through a view "instituted at and in a certain distance" (*GWB*, 84). Such axiomatic reasoning of course has as a result that facticity cannot interpret itself (*NT*, 84). In the words of Lacoste: "If one does not even know what the sketch wants to be a sketch [of], one cannot even perceive the sketch as such" (*NT*, 84). Every encounter with signification in the world is a sketch of something to which philosophy is not granted access. Philosophy understands neither the sketch of signification as such nor the encounter with signification as a sketch. One could object that this is the point where a phenomenology of liturgy leaps into metaphysics: it is no longer the description of the life of the believer, celebrating in a world that matters, it is its overcoming that ought to be the ultimate goal of this relation to God. Whilst it need not be problematic to believe in God's coming, it remains to be considered whether this coming can and must be inscribed as the *telos* of the relationship between humankind and God. Surely, if this goal is defined as that which, ultimately, surpasses the worldly conditions of faith, then, of course, such a goal could only be achieved at the expense of precisely those conditions. Thus, within the liturgical experience, a metaphysical move must be detected: the reinscription of an otherworldliness as the *telos* of faith professed in a world.

The difference between the world and creation ultimately gives way to a similar mechanism of exclusion in the relation between philosophy and theology. What is at stake here is that the philosophical enterprise, and perhaps not just that of Heidegger, is being *misused* as a preparation for theological discourse. Philosophy serves theology, but only to see its realizations crossed by theology. Consider for instance the following analogies between the formal structure of the liturgical experience and Heidegger's *Being and Time*. Where *Being and Time*'s 'being-in-the-world' consists in existentials that have their antidotes in existentieIexistential modes, Lacoste's 'being-in-the-Church' is constituted in the same formal way: it has existentials (e.g., ontological restlessness) and its modes (e.g., mission, imitation). The analogy not only holds at this formal level but also at the liturgical level. Where in *Being and Time* the confrontation with one's own death is the occasion to assume one's authenticity, in the liturgical one experiences the confrontation with the events surrounding the death of Christ as the *kairos* in which authentic being human begins to appear. Where in *Being and Time* the confrontation with finitude takes place in angst, the liturgical person has to reckon with the terror of the nonexperience. Where in *Being and Time* this anxious relation to death singularizes *Dasein*, the believer experiences a solipsism analogous to Heidegger's 'existential solipsism,' when in the liturgical nonexperience one remains alone with one's faith. Where in *Being and Time* death discloses *Dasein*'s temporality, the liturgical person's historicality, that is, history's grip on human existence, is revealed (*EA*, 62; 153). When Heidegger's book repeatedly states that 'the They' interposes itself between *Dasein* and its authenticity, this structural element also found its way into the liturgical experience, albeit that therein the world interposes itself between God and man. Finally, where in *Being and Time* angst removes the veils with which 'the They' covers up *Dasein* and leaves *Dasein* with the naked fact that it has to be its being, there seems to be little difference with Lacoste's liturgical experience in which God kairologically removes all masks with which human beings cover themselves up to leave them with the humiliation of their nudity and poverty.

Decentering the Subject?

It is important to note that the negative evaluation of being-in-the-world and philosophy that we perceived in Lacoste's work also bears on his description of the liturgical decentering of modern subjectivity. There are two instances in which he elaborates on this decentering. Whereas, at first, Lacoste states that the liturgical experience suggests that, for the relation 'coram Deo,' our carnal presence serves as a more appropriate paradigm (EA, 156), he immediately goes on to say that of this liturgical passivity before God, "it would be by no means aberrant to say that [its] objectivity is, then, yet more radical than that of the flesh, and is similar to the objectivity of the thing—to say, therefore, that [one] is in God's hands as clay [. . .] is in the hands of the potter" (EA, 156).[33] If one wants to speak of intentionality in the case of the liturgical experience one should say that the believer in this experience becomes the object of God's intention.

Thus, the negative light thrown upon being, suspected to be a hindrance for the relation to God, finds its pendant in a negative light thrown upon our embodiment: the body must be detached from itself to become an object. Far from being a genuine decentering of modern subjectivity, the liturgical experience turns out to be a simple inversion of the terms that constitute this subjectivity. This inversion of intentionality, of course, remains trapped in that which it tried to overcome: whereas the project's divertissement consisted in the refusal to see signification as given, a refusal that results in seeing the future as the (controllable) object of my intention, the solution Lacoste proposes yet again adheres to the problem it wanted to resolve: God's gaze upon human beings is equivalent to the projective gaze of human beings towards objects. It may no longer be people that exercise power and control over objects; it is God who, like a modern subject, encounters nothing other than objectivity and makes us the object of God's intention (EA, 150).[34] Lacoste seems to align himself here once again with Marion, who, as we will later see, almost literally repeats Lacoste's phrasing (or vice versa)

A Different Différend between the World and Creation

To conclude this chapter I will try to sketch a different relation between the world and creation. There are a few instances in which Lacoste seems to abandon the strictly negative appraisal of being-in-the-world. First, in Note sur le temps Lacoste comments on the death of Christ on the Cross. When God appears in being, God necessarily takes on the contours of the historical and the provisional. At this stage, however, God's appearance in history seems to benefit from precisely this appearance in that the appearance of God in history as a human being adds to the being of God, for "it is not really certain whether we have to learn from God how to die—this is rather something that God has learned from human beings" (NT, 182). It is this death of God on the Cross that instructs us, second, that "agony has a place in the Absolute itself" (ibid.) and that, in Christ's abandonment on the Cross, "God undergoes the distance that constitutes the historical and mundane mode with which human beings live their distance to God" (*NT*, 193). Consider also the fact that, in both *Note sur le temps* and *Experience and the Absolute*, one finds the idea that "in resurrecting the Crucified, God also puts himself in *a position of debt* to whoever has reconciled himself through his Cross" (*EA*, 138–39; *NT*, 209). It is this position of debt that deserves our attention here, for wherever there is a debtor, there is correspondingly a creditor. But if the world can appear as a *creditor* over and against the Absolute, should one not at the same time admit that the world can interpret itself as a *demand* for a beyond of being? Is such a demand, as Lacoste suggests, only the demand of satisfaction of the promise of a resurrection, or is it likewise the demand of the one that, confronted with the radicality of evil or the brutality of one's own nonexperience, can no longer be satisfied with a call to patience?

To conceive of such a demand, one should perhaps recontextualize the relation between the eschatological blessings already granted and the eschatological blessings that still remain within the economy of the promise (cf. *EA*, 139). Lacoste envisions this relation between these blessings somewhat as an adequation, in that the already lived reconciliation in this world will be accompanied with the perennial joy of beatitude in the life to come, so as to make the liturgical experience instead of being solely "a veritable tragedy for consciousness" (*EA*, 143), an instance of joy and hope. However, one should perhaps question this adequation between the grace already received and the grace still to come on the christological basis Lacoste himself advances, for it is not at all sure whether the life to come or beatitude is to be conceived of as a *verification* of the knowledge of faith.[35] It is in this thought of an adequation of the grace received and the grace to come that one might suspect not only a form of ontotheology at the heart of theology but also, from the perspective of theology itself, a form of *hybris*—in the sense of an appropriation of the divine. Therefore, one might want to cling onto a different liturgical experience than the one Lacoste has in mind by pointing, not to the verification of faith's knowledge, but rather to the ever-present possibility of its *falsification*. It is in this sense that one might apply Lacoste's description of "an ignorance proper to the Messiah" (*NT*, 174). Christ's cry on the cross indeed constitutes the climax of the nonexperience. Its radical nonexperience should, however, not be interpreted in an antitheological fashion, for, as Lacoste argues, one does not speak to someone who does not exist (*NT*, 182; *EA*, 191). It is nevertheless important to note that, for a liturgical experience that wants to be an *imitatio Christi*, this ignorance could be instructive, for it is, as Lacoste suggests, precisely an ignorance of the exact nature of God's coming (*parousia*): "he expected the apocalypse, but the history of the world continued; he expected the Kingdom, and it is the Church that has come" (*NT*, 174). Such a falsification, of course, is not without consequences for the question of salvation, for if one avoids the (ontotheological) adequation of the grace received and the grace to come, one could understand the demand that arises from out of the world, not as something still standing out towards its fulfilment, but rather as an unredeemedness sui generis—as if something in man resists redemption.

Chapter Three

From the Subject to the 'Adonné'

Jean-Luc Marion

In this chapter, I will present Marion's concept of 'subjectivity'—summed up in his term *adonné*. It may be clear that Marion's thinking of givenness requires something other than a transcendental subject, since this subject, prior to all reality as it is, constitutes this reality and determines which sense to be given to it (cf. Husserl's '*Sinngebung*'). The *adonné* is no spectator as is the transcendental subject, quietly constituting its phenomena. If phenomena give themselves from their selves as their selves—a conception of the 'given phenomenon' that I will explain in the next section—then the subject is turned into the witness of this phenomenon: the *adonné* does not appear, as was the case with the transcendental subject, before the phenomenon has given itself. On the contrary, the *adonné* only appears *after* the phenomenon's appearance.

It is, however, only in the last book of *Being Given* that Marion develops this figure of the '*adonné*' in full and that one finds the following programmatic statement:

> To have done with the "subject," it is therefore necessary not to destroy it, but to reverse it—to overturn it. It is posited as a center: this will not be contested, but I will contest its mode of occupying and exercising the center to which it lays claim—with the title of a (thinking, constituting, resolute) "I." I will contest the claim that it occupies this center as an origin, an ego or first person, in transcendental "mineness." I will oppose to it the claim that it does not hold this center but is instead

held there as a recipient where what gives itself shows itself, and
that it discloses itself given to and as a pole of givenness, where
all the givens come forward incessantly. At the center stands no
"subject," but a gifted [. . .] whose privilege is confined to the
fact that he himself is received from what he receives. (BG, 322)

In order to explain this conception of subjectivity, I will first have a
look at just what decenters the subject, namely, the given as it gives itself
to what will be called the "*adonné*."

The Given Phenomenon, the Gift, and the Third Reduction

Givenness, for Marion, determines every phenomenon without exception.
Marion will therefore need to show not only how the third reduction to the
given phenomenon surpasses the two 'previous' reductions (to objects and
to beings) but also how the third reduction encompasses these reductions,
for according to Marion it is not a matter of "a relation of exclusion or
juxtaposition" between the given phenomenon and the other realms of
phenomenality, but of the variation by degrees that givenness deploys (cf.
BG, 177–78).

For this, Marion uses the example of an ordinary work of art (BG,
39ff). We *can* consider the work of art as an ordinary object, when we, for
instance, are cleaning its surface or move it around when redecorating our
living room. But in this way, the work of art does not appear as precisely a
work of art. We *can* also consider the work of art as ready-to-hand (Heidegger's
zuhanden), for instance, when we go to a gallery with the intention of buying
one of the artworks. However, in this way, again the work of art is not seen
as a work of art. When the work appears as ready-to-hand, its phenomenality
owes everything to the network of finalities in which it appears. The work
of art, in this case, shows up in relation to its price, to the one who sells
it, and so on, but never in its own right. When the work of art appears
as a work of art, it does appear on its own terms and demands to be seen,
not as an object or as a being among others, but added to these views is
"the event of its apparition in person [. . .] To the ontic visibility of the
painting is added as a super-visibility, ontically indescribable—its upsurge.
This exceptional visibility adds nothing real to the ordinary visibility, but
it imposes it as such, no longer to my representational sight, but to me,
in the flesh, in person, without screen. [It] is no longer a matter of seeing

what is, but of seeing its coming up into visibility—a coming up that has nothing ontic about it" (BG, 47–48). The work of art thus occurs as an event. Its visibility distinguishes itself from the visibility of an object or a being, because of its "effect" (BG, 49) on me. This effect, which attracts me to the appearing of the work of art as a work of art, "attests that a meaning [. . .] autonomous and irreducible, imposes itself, designating the very depths from which the visible surges up, as if from a self" (BG, 49). This upsurging indicates that the painting (or anything that gives itself) arises "independently of its beingness" (BG, 46), for "to see it as a painting in its own phenomenality of the beautiful, I must of course apprehend it as a thing (subsisting, ready-to-hand), but it is precisely not this that opens it to me as beautiful; it is that I "live" its meaning, namely its beautiful appearing, which has nothing thinglike to it, since it cannot be described as the property of a thing, demonstrated by reasons" (ibid.). In this way, it "appears as given in the effect that it gives. Thus is defined the essential invisibility of the painting" (BG, 51–52). Although the effect is what allows the work of art to be seen as a work of art, the effect itself is not seen, only felt. It is in this sense that Marion is doing phenomenology: Marion is not describing this or that object or being, as before with the phenomenologies of Husserl and Heidegger. Instead, Marion is depicting the lived experiences of the 'subject' when confronted with something that imposes itself to consciousness, in this case the work of art.

The example of the work of art provides the occasion to elucidate the characteristics of the *being given* or the given phenomenon. Take, for instance, a visit to a museum. We see one or two paintings without paying much attention to them. Suddenly, and it seems for no particular reason, we stop at a painting to have a close look. What happens? The happening of the work of art that gives itself to be seen in the effect we experience of it. Marion denotes such an event as "the ultimate determination of the given phenomenon" (BG, 177). To describe the contingent character of what appears in this way, Marion uses the concept of *'arrivage,'* translated as 'unpredictable landing' (BG, 131). Indeed, when walking through a museum the painting, if it shows up at all, shows up in a contingent manner: it is equally possible that we spend our afternoon in the museum without seeing any painting as a painting at all. Hence its contingency: I cannot foresee that I will be attracted by one of the paintings at all. It happens to me for no reason in particular, and when it happens, I must admit that it, equally, could not have happened. When I am attracted to this particular painting, therefore, I must admit that it shows up in visibility as arriving to me "by affecting me; that is to say, we can describe it inasmuch as it is a gift to receive" (BG, 174). Similarly, when visiting the museum at another time, there is no guarantee that I will be struck by the same painting. Moreover, even when this is the case, Marion states, we are confronted with another given, "for the same phenomenon given in another moment, therefore to other interlocutors and with other interferences, will definitely not remain the same. The given remains the same only for the moment of its happening" (BG, 139). There is not only no guarantee that I will see the same painting, but also there is no guarantee that, when seeing the same painting, I will still be the same and, therefore, struck by the same peculiarities. Each time the painting (or anything else) arises as a given, it arises as a singular phenomenon, demanding to be seen as it shows itself of itself at this particular point in time and space. In Marion's terms: the phenomenon, in this case the work of art, "shows itself necessarily as non-necessity of showing itself" (BG, 138). *Facticity*, then, no longer only determines *Dasein*; it pertains to the given phenomenon as well: "[F]acticity [consists] in exposing me to the fact, which can thus be accomplished only by weighing upon me, no longer as a detached observer but as an engaged actor" (BG, 146). The work of art shows itself, here and now in its effect on consciousness, at this particular point in time and space, as a fact to be dealt with. This particular given, finally, "comes upon me in such a way that it consists of nothing other than this [. . .] coming upon" (BG, 151). This is what Marion calls the "incident": the artwork as artwork shows nothing else than the effect in which it gives itself to me. That the work of art is also an object or determined by beingness is something that can only be determined afterward. The point is that, when experiencing the work of art as a work of art, I do not consider it as an object or as a being; when I consider it as an object, on the contrary, I do not consider it any longer as a work of art. Thus the work of art is reduced to a pure given in the effect we experience of it, an effect that does not have the character of a being or an object: "In the end, for every reduced being, all that remains is the effect, such that in it the visible is given, is reduced to a given. The painting is not visible; it makes visible. It makes visible in a gesture that remains by definition invisible—the effect, the upsurge, the advance of givenness. To be given requires being reduced [. . .] to this invisible effect which alone makes visible" (BG, 52).

It is important to note that the characteristics of the given phenomenon all serve to acknowledge the irrevocable givenness of the phenomenon in phenomenality. It is here that Marion immanentizes his earlier thought of distance.[1] Whereas a gift was, in the history of philosophy, defined as "what we have from elsewhere," thereby invoking one or the other transcendent instance, Marion attempts "to conceive even this "having from elsewhere, *aliunde habere*" as a determination intrinsic to the given phenomenon, that is, determining it in a strictly phenomenological mode" (*BG*, 122). This "elsewhere," then, does not denote a transcendent origin of the given but "highlights the intrinsic character of what gives itself to us without depending on or referring to us, indeed by coming upon us despite us [. . .] independently of our exchange, our efficiency, and our foresight" (*BG*, 123). The phenomenon "crosses the distance that leads it to assume form, according to an immanent axis, which in each case summons an I/me [. . .] to a precise phenomenological point" (*BG*, 131).

Indeed, the given phenomenon gives itself to someone. The question is just how to receive the event that gives itself of itself and as its self. The given gives itself to be seen according to what Marion calls *"anamorphosis."* The term *anamorphosis* stems from aesthetics and renders that specific procedure where the spectator of a work of art has to put himself or herself in a certain position to perceive a determinate form on a surface seemingly without form. Just as such a work of art demands that the perceiver adjust him- or herself to the work of art, so the 'I,' when confronted with the given phenomenon, has to align him- or herself to its appearance. Anamorphosis can be compared to looking at a horizon from a beach: whereas at first, one sees nothing in particular, suddenly one's gaze is attracted by a boat (or something else). In this case, a leap is made from seeing, as it were, everything to seeing one phenomenon in particular: "[T]his second-level form does not merely make the phenomenon visible; above all, it distinguishes the phenomenon from others by detaching it from them as if from the depths. [T]he ana-morphosis of the phenomenon insofar as it is given, thus designates its property of rising from the first to the second form" (*BG*, 124). To accede to this second form, however, the gaze must "know how to submit to the demands of the figure to be seen: find the unique point of view from which the second level form will appear [. . .] in short, renounce organizing visibility on the basis of free choice or the proper site of a disengaged spectator, in favor of letting visibility be dictated by the phenomenon itself, in itself" (ibid.). The happening of the phenomenon thus operates a decentering of the modern subject. Contrary to transcendental accounts of subjectivity, the subject now finds itself submitted to that which appears "from elsewhere," from itself and of itself.

Marion's analysis of the gift as such adds an important element to the analysis of the given phenomenon. The former resides, just as the latter, in the effect it has on consciousness—in consciousness' lived experiences.

The gift and a fortiori the given phenomenon, Marion claims, have to do, not with the actual giving or receiving of an object or a being, but reside in the immaterial decision to give or to receive. An example: suppose that I walk through the city looking for Christmas presents. I do not have any idea what to buy for my loved one and walk indifferently from one shop to another. Suddenly, my gaze is attracted by one or the other object, and I realize immediately that it is this object that I need to give to her. What has happened? I have seen the object, but I have experienced it in a particular way: the object is not seen or experienced as an object, but rather as 'giveable' (BG, 106ff). Perhaps I have seen this particular object a dozen times, walked by it uninterested, but now, and although the object is the same as it was before, it gives itself to me as a gift to be given to someone. In the lived experience of 'giveability,' therefore, the I must attest to the fact that it owes something to someone, and its autarchy is broken (cf. BG, 108). In Marion's words: "If the gift [. . .] becomes giveable, it does not owe this to any real predicate [. . .] The object remains the same [. . .]. But to the degree that giveability strikes it or not, [. . .] its phenomenality will be modified" (BG, 107). The object appears therefore as giveable, which means that the object appears in a different light and that the gaze receives the impact of the phenomenon to be given.

In a similar vein, the gift is not accomplished by the actual reception of an object or a being but in the recognition and the lived experience of this or that object as acceptable (BG, 108ff). The gift, then, seduces the receiver by imposing on him or her the very fact of being acceptable. With this, the receiver, seduced by the glamor of the receivability, renounces his or her autarchy as well and confesses that, in the receiving of this lived experience of acceptability, he or she owes something to someone (BG, 109). The gift accomplishes itself in the very decision to see this or that object or being as giveable or acceptable.

One must note, however, that the (potential) giver *receives* the glamor of giveability as well.[2] In both cases, then, the decision to receive is absolutely paramount: one has to decide on the gift. This decision to receive and to see, therefore, the visible phenomenon as given, is, according to Marion, "essentially aporetic" (BG, 111). Not only because one has to receive also that which one did not expect or did not even want but also because "to decide to receive a gift therefore demands [. . .] receiving at the same time as this gift the knowledge and the acknowledgement of a debt" (BG, 112). Considering the fact that the reduction to the given does not evoke a transcendent (or otherwise) giver to be indebted to, Marion configures this recognition of a debt as a debt toward the gift itself. One is, therefore, in this reception of the gift as a gift "obliged by the gift" (ibid.). Since the gift gives *itself* in the lived experience of either giveability or acceptability as nothing else than this giving itself of itself, it is therefore not the 'I' who gives the lived experience of acceptability to itself, but, on the contrary, the lived experience of acceptability gives itself to consciousness as that which gives itself of itself. Therefore, the gift occurs to consciousness independently of consciousness' tendency to constitution and can decide itself, through this very movement of giving itself of itself, "its acceptance by deciding (for) its givee" (BG, 112).

The gift thus makes a plea for its own acceptability, and Marion adds: "[T]o thus recognize the gift implies a strict and particular phenomenological gaze: "that which faced with the fact, sees it as a gift" (ibid.). Horner therefore comments: "[T]he decision would be nothing other than a way of seeing something."[3] Marion is willing to concede that this decision involves a certain hermeneutics or an interpretation—deciding to see the visible *as* given—but as before in the case of a work of art, it is a "hermeneutic that does not so much give a meaning as receive it and then understand a gift. Less a gift of meaning than a meaning of the gift" (BG, 112).

It falls, then, to the subject to give itself over to the phenomenon as it gives its self as a gift. It is this 'self' of the phenomenon that will be circumscribed by its character as an event. This 'self' is not the "in itself of the object or the thing" (BG, 159), but rather that which makes itself known by "the pressure that it exerts over the gaze (ibid.). The subject thus undergoes the shock of the phenomenon that enacts by itself the act of giving itself: the initiative to appear belongs entirely to the phenomenon itself. What we have here, therefore, in the phenomenon that gives itself from itself is again *a reversal of intentionality*. For the pressure that the phenomenon exerts on consciousness is "not [made] by me, but at my expense. It is a fact made on my account; by it, I am made. Along the same line intentionality is inverted: I become the objective of the object" (BG, 146). Or: "rendering itself apparent by itself and at my expense, to the point of redirecting intentionality so that it goes from it toward me" (BG, 174). This 'self' of the phenomenon "attest[s] itself [. . .] by appropriating the gravitational center of phenomenality, therefore by assuming the origin of its own event" (BG, 248).

Since "this movement of imposing itself on me [. . .] is just enough to detect a certain givenness" (BG, 63), I will now have a brief look at the relation between the given phenomenon and givenness and how Marion regards phenomenology to be able to overcome metaphysics.

Reduction, Givenness, and Metaphysics

The reduction to the given, according to Marion, acquires an "immanent phenomenality, without transcendence outside consciousness" (BG, 115). To understand this, it is necessary to dwell briefly on Marion's pick of the discipline of phenomenology. Phenomenology, Marion maintains, is a peculiar science: "[I]n the phenomenological realm it [is] a question of letting apparition show itself in its appearance according to its appearing"; it is, in other words, a question of manifestation (BG, 8). But this "is not so self-evident. For a fundamental reason: because knowledge always comes from me, manifestation is never evident by itself. Or rather, it is not so self-evident that it can run its own course, coming from itself, through itself, starting from itself, in short, that it can manifest its self" (BG, 9). The phenomenological method is therefore self-effacing: it approaches the phenomenon only to let the phenomenon approach of itself. In this sense, the reduction "does nothing; it lets manifestation manifest *itself*; it takes initiative (of considering seriously what is lived by consciousness) only in order to offer it to what manifests itself" (BG, 10). Phenomenology does not distinguish, as metaphysics does, between on the one hand the thing in itself and on the other the ways in which it appears. Whereas, in metaphysics, what appears of a thing is always conceived as a mere appearance over and against the thing 'in itself,' in phenomenology the thing coincides with the manner in which it appears—the thing 'is' its manner of appearing.

Marion notes that the famous slogan 'to the things themselves' "does not imply any pre-critical realism, but the reduction of the transcendent to lived experiences such as they give themselves to consciousness" (BG, 16). In the same vein, the reduction to the given "suspends and brackets all that, in appearance, does not succeed in giving itself or is merely added to the given as its parasite. The reduction separates what appears from what does not appear. [The] reduction leads appearing to itself only by limiting it strictly to what it gives to be seen" (ibid.). Marion's conclusion is that "the reduction, by leading apparition back to the conscious I and to appearing itself, leads [the apparition] back to its pure given" (ibid.). This pure given, then, "is defined without necessarily having recourse to any intermediary whatsoever that would be different from it. In particular the pure given giving itself depends, once reduced, only on itself" (BG, 16–17).

What is distinctive of the reduction to the given, and what distinguishes it from the other reductions (to objects or to beings) is this: "it intervenes *after* the manifestation of appearing [. . .] for the sole purpose of sanctioning a posteriori by reduction what, in appearing, truly deserves the title given phenomenon" (*BG*, 18). The reduction does not give the given to itself; rather it records in appearing that which gives itself of itself. That which gives itself in this way points of itself toward its givenness.

But what precisely is being given to the reducing consciousness? "'Self-givenness, *Selbstgebung, donation de soi*' indicates that the phenomenon is given in person but also [. . .] that it is given of itself and starting from itself. Only this givenness, having originated in itself, can give the self of the phenomenon" (*BG*, 20). Givenness, therefore, is that instance that separates what appears only subjectively to consciousness from that which is effectively given. Indeed, in phenomenology, it is always possible that that which gives itself to consciousness is a mere subjective impression.

Marion therefore develops what he considers to be Husserl's breakthrough, commenting upon "the "essential correlation" between appearing and that which appears" (*BG*, 21).[4] In consequence of this correlation, *Reduction and Givenness* notes that "appearing [. . .] no longer counts as a datum for the single conscious subject, but first as the givenness of what thus appears: the appearing [. . .] *gives* that which appears [l'apparaître *donne* l'apparaissant]" (*RG*, 32; *RD*, 52, Marion's italics). It is here, Marion argues, that "phenomenology begins," because "thought sees that which appears appear in appearance [la pensée voit apparaître l'apparaisant dans l'apparition]; it manages to do this only by conceiving the appearing itself no longer as a 'given *of* consciousness,' but indeed as the givenness *to* consciousness [. . .] of the thing itself" (*RG*, 32; *RD*, 53, Marion's italics). The essential correlation of appearing and that which appears opens unto the givenness of both the appearing and that which appears. It is this correlation that intimates that the 'appearing of appearing' is not dependent on any subject whatsoever. Rather the fact that there 'is' this appearing testifies to the fact that the subject is always and already instituted 'after the fact,' a posteriori.

Though Husserl already envisioned such a correlation, Marion differs from Husserl by asking whether that which appears has to correspond to the contours of an object "or if it can be understood within the immense possibilities of what shows itself" (*BG*, 13). Indeed, Husserl allowed for the object's transcendence toward the lived experiences of the subject, in that the object is always more than the perception and the adumbrations one can make of it at one particular point in time. Could there not be other transcendences as well?

Whereas metaphysics maintained a cleft between the appearing of a thing and the thing as it is in itself, in that a thing 'is' without even appearing to someone (realism), and modern philosophy distinguished between subjective impressions of a thing and the thing in itself (transcendentalism), phenomenology succeeds in bridging this cleft, in that the appearance of a thing in and through its various modes of appearing gives *the thing itself* to consciousness. Only in phenomenology "appearances no longer mask what appears" (*BG*, 25), because givenness allows for the appearing and that which appears to arise at the very same moment: "[G]ivenness breaks out because the appearing of appearance becomes the apparition *of* what appears [l'apparaître de l'apparence se fait l'apparaître *de* l'apparaissant]" (*BG*, 25; *ED*, 39, Marion's italics). "And this is indeed *the* givenness: that of transcendence in immanence" (ibid.). In this way, it is givenness that liberates phenomenology from being merely a narration of subjective lived experiences. Phenomenology needs "to give more than a state or lived experience of consciousness" (*BG*, 20). For this, it is necessary "that on its screen [of consciousness, JS] there be projected and come forward something other than it—the unevident, the phenomenon itself" (ibid.). It is for this reason that "a new term has to be introduced—givenness" (ibid.). Phenomenology, according to Marion, begins when consciousness realizes that its lived experiences are "the place of givenness [. . .] not its origin but rather its point of arrival" (ibid.). It is on the screen of consciousness that the phenomenon gives itself of itself and as its self, that is, as the other of consciousness. But, and this is Marion's point, what is other than consciousness is always and already given. And every given bears the mark of that through which it can rise to appearing, givenness.[5]

Here Marion makes a remarkable rapprochement between the indubitability of the cogito and that of givenness. In effect, the appearing of the self of the phenomenon on the screen of consciousness testifies to "the fact that the lived experience arrives to and over consciousness [as] an indubitability in fact, of the very fact that the lived experience arrives incessantly" (*BG*, 125–26). It is in this 'arrival' that "the givenness of every being and nonbeing" (*BG*, 60) is attested and, therefore, that "no one can doubt that givenness has always already given for him (if not to him) and gives to him continually, just as every ego knows that it is inasmuch as it is thinking and as long as it does not stop thinking" (*BG*, 59, mod.). Givenness, therefore, gives itself in the given or, rather, is what allows the given to give itself of itself. As such, givenness remains withdrawn, is "dissimulated by its given" (ibid.). That a given phenomenon can give itself of itself is due to "the power of givenness," (*BG*, 112), but this givenness does not itself appear in that which it gives, namely, the given phenomenon.

This 'fold of the given' is not without reminiscences of Heidegger's portrayal of the ontological difference: as much as being retreats in what it nevertheless unfolds, namely, beings, so givenness holds itself back in that which it gives.[6] But since phenomenology's phenomenon, according to Marion and Husserl, arises from out of the simultaneous givenness of the appearing *and* that which appears (such that 'the appearing of appearance becomes the apparition *of* what appears), this means not only that—in the case of Husserl—the givenness of appearing becomes the givenness of the object (as the other of and transcendent to consciousness) but also that—in Marion's case—, and since the givenness of appearing "is one with givenness as the arising of what gives itself" (BG, 69), the appearing of appearance also becomes one with the apparition of what gives itself of itself. Here "it is indeed a matter of the fold of givenness" (ibid.). It is here that we encounter Marion's claim that givenness determines every phenomenon without exception: "one can legitimately hold that the fold of givenness extends to all regions of phenomenality" (BG, 176–77). Even the object or a being gives itself according to this fold of the given, but the givenness of the object and the givenness of the being gives itself to a lesser extent, articulates the fold of givenness only to a lesser degree or, as Marion puts it, is merely a "weakened variant" (BG, 227), therefore marking less "the givenness from which it comes" (ibid.).

In the case of the given phenomenon, then, the phenomenon gives itself to consciousness, "as such, and not as the appearance of something else more essential to it than itself, in short it can appear without the lack implied by an in-itself or the withdrawal implied by a noumenon [. . .]. Appearing must thus remove itself (if not always contradict) from the imperial rule of the a priori conditions of knowledge by requiring that what appears [*l'apparaissant*] force its entry onto the scene of the world without a [. . .] double, [. . .] abandoned to the world" (BG, 69; ED, 101). The pure given is thus the phenomenon giving itself of itself and as its self. It is this self, pertaining to the phenomenon, that Marion tries to elucidate.

We have seen that Marion considers an immanent phenomenality without, however, leaving the intentional immanence of consciousness. This immanence, however, is capable of receiving that which is other to it, not in some precritical realist vein, but precisely on the basis of that which gives itself of itself to consciousness, namely, the (given) phenomenon. The phenomenon can attest itself of itself to consciousness: just as, for Husserl, the transcendence of the object is attested to in the intentional immanence of consciousness, so Marion will contend that within "the given lived experiences" (BG, 116), thus within the immanence of consciousness, the transcendence of the given is attested.

Such a consciousness, which undergoes the lived experiences of a given phenomenon, is no longer the stable, everpresent a priori of a transcendental I; rather it assumes the position of one that is forced into receiving the experience of that which gives itself of itself. The gift and the given phenomenon are attested to in nothing other than the lived experience of 'something' that does not any longer have the status of a thing. This giving itself of itself, though it concerns every 'thing' without exception, is for each 'thing' nevertheless each time different: Marion tries to think the human being's encounter with phenomena as a *singular* encounter, new at each moment in time, for "the same phenomenon given in another moment [. . .] will definitely not remain the same. The given remains the same only for the moment of its happening; this moment is therefore not added to its definition—it enacts it" (BG, 139). In this sense, Marion is depicting the ever-changing encounter of human beings with phenomena of any kind. Note, though, that in the encounter that is each time different for each phenomenon, Marion seeks to uncover the unique figure of how this encounter gives itself each time: whether it be an object, a being, or the given phenomenon itself, they all arrive on the screen of consciousness in a contingent manner, deciding to appear from themselves and confronting us with the very fact of their appearance. It is in this sense that Marion will say that "no phenomenon can appear without coming upon me, arriving to me, affecting me as an event that modifies my field (of vision, of knowledge, of life [. . .]). It takes place, picks a date, takes its time to take form (anamorphosis); there is no neutral phenomenon, always already there, inoffensive and submissive. It makes a difference solely by its coming up" (BG, 125). Marion will thus seek to describe the subject in the very *alteration* that it undergoes through the appearance of this or that phenomenon.

An example will perhaps make this clear. In a persuasive fashion, Marion maintains that even ideals such as the sum of all corners of a triangle being the same 'always and everywhere' is determined by the contingent arrival of this particular phenomenon. Indeed, "[i]deality does not perhaps possess facticity, but its appearance does. For me, who learns them from a master or rediscovers them in pure reason, the ideals impose themselves in precise times and places as facts that are accomplished for, before, and without me. There was a place and a day when I thought I understood for the first time the cogito, integral calculus [. . .]" (BG, 149). In any case, the encounter with the happening of the phenomenon is unique, and therefore unrepeatable. The self of the phenomenon individualizes itself "by its very event" (BG, 171). Therefore, each event "arrives only once [. . .] and once for all" (BG, 171). Furthermore, each event is defined by its excess towards its possible causes and by the fact that something new appears in immanence: "each phenomenon [. . .] adds to the visibility and phenomenality of the world [. . .] What is valid for the painting—it increases the sum of available visibility through the unseen's anamorphosis in the painting—is valid all the more for worldly phenomena. From surplus to surplus, the finitude of the world shelters [a] nonconstitutable, saturating phenomenality. Phenomena [. . .] devise a limitless manifestation—undefine the world in the twofold sense of rendering it non-finite and forbidding it any definition" (BG, 172).

Each given phenomenon, then, introduces newness in what I, prior to it, held as visible and conceivable: the event, being irreducible to the preceding situation, "redefines a partially or entirely different situation. Essentially [. . .] the event begins a new series, in which it reorganizes the old phenomena [. . .] by the right that events have to open horizons" (BG, 172). With this eventlike character of the phenomenon, and its newness, one is close to the stakes of Marion's theory of saturated phenomena.

The Saturated Phenomenon

These stakes of the saturated phenomenon will be developed here by means of Marion's conception of 'possibility' in metaphysics, and later in technology, because it is the domination of technology that increasingly forbids us to encounter saturated phenomena. Through this Marion's "phenomenality of the unforeseeable" (BG, 111) takes on more relief.

Marion states:

> In technological terms, we declare possible the object that is thoroughly calculated and studied, for which [. . .] 'feasibility' studies guarantee that it can be produced. [. . .] The manifestation of the technological object radically precedes, that is, always gets the upper hand chronologically over whatever intuitive fulfillment might be, that is to say, over the product itself. *Possibility* here means a full, or at least imaginable, intelligibility, a sufficient foreseeability, and a calculation—to reach actuality, all that is lacking is the transition to production. In this way, we come upon

> the metaphysical definition of existence as a mere complement
> of essence. [. . .] The product confirms—at best—the 'concept,'
> and this without any surprise (BG, 172; 223–25).[7]

The technological mastery of the concept and of the intention over
manifestation is, according to Marion, obvious on the two registers of delay
and foresight: delay, in that "the concept (in the sense of the concept of
a product) renders this product visible before production actually gives it,
and sometimes even without production" (BG, 223); foresight, in that the
preeminence of the concept over intuition means that "production and
intuition [. . .] remain beneath the watchful gaze of the subject. From its
vantage point, it sees them coming from afar, without surprise and without
expecting anything new from them" (BG, 224–25).

    In this description of the technological object, which concept controls
the very production and actuality of the object, Marion seems to confirm
Heidegger's point on the intimate link between technology and metaphysics:
the concept's preeminence over the (actual) product conserves it "in
permanent presence through postulating its identical reproducibility" (BG,
214). Marion's important text "The Banality of Saturation," which is taken
up in *The Visible and the Revealed*, again is reminiscent of Heidegger when it
declares that the "frequency of technological objects and their phenomenality
[. . .] accumulates day by day. It could even be said that the world is covered
with a [. . .] layer of poor phenomena [. . .], which ends up eclipsing what
it covers over [namely] saturated phenomena" (VR, 125). Just as Heidegger
envisioned a retreat of being in and through our preoccupation with beings,
so Marion deplores the loss of the possibility of 'seeing otherwise' in and
through our everyday preoccupation with technological and present-at-hand
objects.

    According to Marion, it is in particular modern rationality that has
limited the appearance of any phenomenon to both the principle of sufficient
reason and to that of noncontradiction. It conferred conditions to every
possible experience. All that is real is real only if it is possible, that is, if
it does not contradict the conditions of possibility of experience. What is
possible *here* does not stem "from the phenomenon but, by contrast, from the
conditions posited for every phenomenon" (BG, 181). These conditions are,
according to Marion, first the transcendental subject purportedly possessive
of universal reason (Descartes/Kant), and second, the idea of a horizon
(Husserl) according to which every phenomenon has to and can only appear
in a certain light and interpretation. The transcendental subject corresponds

to the law of noncontradiction (I=I), and the idea of a horizon to that of sufficient reason, since in metaphysics, "nothing appears without attesting that it is possible. This possibility is equivalent [. . .] to the possibility of knowing the sufficient reason of such an apparition" (BG, 182). "Possibility [. . .] could be defined as an existence already absolutely conceived but simply awaiting actualisation" (BG, 172). An architect, for example, will consider it possible to build a house if and only if the representation of the house *in mentis* is not contradicted by or in any other way inhibited by the available material, financial resources, and so on.

Kant, on Marion's account, aligns the phenomenon to the categories of the subject's understanding and its transcendental makeup: what we can *know* is what can *appear*. Let us once again turn to the example of a table to make this clear. First, the table is nothing more than the sum of its parts; a table is nothing more than a plateau with four legs (quantity). Second, a table is nothing more than that which in reality *is* or *is not*, and this difference is dependent upon the foreseeable intensity with which it appears (quality). Third, a table appears in accordance with and analogous to other experiences; the table appears usually alongside the chair, and so on (relation). Fourth, the table can only appear if it aligns itself to the epistemological constitution of the subject, such that a table can and must appear only to a transcendental subject (modality). The first three points describe the idea of a horizon, and the last aims at erecting the transcendental subject as the starting point of all epistemology. In Husserl, Marion detects a similar restriction of the ability of the phenomenon to appear. Husserl investigated the intentional structure of consciousness through the pair intention/intuition according to what he called the "principle of principles": "[E]very originarily giving intuition is a source of right for knowledge, that everything that offers itself originarily to us in 'intuition' is to be taken simply as it gives itself but also only within the boundaries in which it gives itself there" (BG, 184). Marion's exegesis of this passage is in fact quite simple: the phenomenon's right to appear is limited both by the fact that it has to appear 'to us' and by the fact that the intuition that the phenomenon gives admits of 'boundaries.' The former limitation again intimates the transcendental subject, whereas the latter indicates the fact that the appearance of anything whatsoever always occurs from out of a certain horizon.

When I, for instance, aim intentionally at a table, intuition always falls short of that which is intended. For instance, when I aim at the table as a plateau with four legs, strictly speaking, this intention is not fulfilled, since intuition only offers me two or three legs of the table at a time. That

I still refer to the table as a table, that is, as a plateau with four legs, arises from the fact that I constitute its fourth leg. Constitution is that mental act with which I somehow add to the perception of three legs, the fourth leg. Though Husserl allows for a transcendence of the object toward the ego's constitution, a transcendence that forces one to walk around the dinner table and make 'adumbrations' of it to verify if what I constituted as a brown table really is a brown table (the fourth leg can be, for instance, colored green), the constitution of the table as a table still requires an invariant idea or essence of the table (an idea beyond which the table would not be a table anymore). This constitution, Marion will say, is a mental act in which the subject enacts its mastery over this particular table: the deficiency of intuition, that is, seeing only two or three legs of the table, is complemented with the signification of the table that the subject already adheres to in advance of seeing this particular table, namely, the table as a plateau with four legs. This particular table will therefore always already appear from out of the horizon of tables with which I was already familiar. In Marion's terms, the unseen of an object therefore immediately has "the rank of a pre-seen, a merely belated visible, without fundamentally irreducible novelty, in short a pre-visible" (BG, 186; also IE, 35–36).

The problem, according to Marion, is not so much that the phenomenon appears from out of a certain horizon, but rather that the horizon functions in such restrictive a manner that no room is left for that which is unforeseeable, for that which escapes every anticipation, leaving us enclosed in a "visual prison [. . .] a panorama without exterior, forbidding all genuinely new arising" (BG, 187). Another problem concerns the fact that intuitive givenness is yet again referred to the I, and so betraying "a classic ambiguity of transcendental phenomenology: the givenness of the phenomenon on its own basis to an I can always veer toward a constitution of the phenomenon by and on the basis of the I" (ibid.).

With the saturated phenomenon, then, Marion envisages an "absolutely unconditioned" (BG, 189) phenomenon that gives itself with no regard for the conditions set out for any 'ordinary' phenomenon in order to find out whether that which metaphysics regards as impossible is a possibility in and for phenomenality itself, that is, whether that which "contradicts [these limits] cannot still be deployed paradoxically as a phenomenon" (BG, 189). The method used here by Marion is once more indebted to Husserl, that of imaginary variations (ibid.).[8] For Husserl, in the period of the Ideen at least, the reduction is twofold in that it requires both the phenomenological 'epoche' and the eidetic reduction. The 'epoche' requires that one bracket any assumption about the existence or actuality of the thing in question in order to see how the thing appears to consciousness. The method of eidetic variation tries to elucidate the 'essence' ('Wesen') of the phenomenon by varying the appearances of the thing to such an extent that the essence of the thing in question lights up. For instance when one stretches the appearance of a table to consciousness to such an extent that one comes up, as if a contrario, with the invariant essence of the thing in question, it is from varying the appearance of a table to the point that that which appears cannot be considered to be a table anymore that one discovers the essence of a table as, say, a plateau with four legs. A similar mode of procedure is used by Marion, but in this case it concerns the invariant idea of a phenomenon: by imagining what possibly can appear to consciousness, even extending to the possibility of what, in metaphysical thought, is considered impossible, Marion tries to trace the unique, invariant 'essence' of the phenomenon and phenomenality, namely, as that which always and everywhere is able to give itself of itself to consciousness. Hence Marion's assertion that the "determinations of the given phenomenon [. . .] modulate with variable intensity" (BG, 178). And even when this intensity is raised to its maximum—in the case of revelation—this "ultimate variation" maintains all the determinations of the "unique figure of the given phenomenon" (BG, 243).

The saturated phenomenon defies the conditions of possibility traditionally conferred upon phenomena. It contests both the idea that, for a phenomenon to appear, it is restricted to and limited by a horizon, and the idea that its appearance depends upon the anteriority of the transcendental subject. Phenomenology is that enterprise that investigates that which appears as 'that which shows itself in itself.'[9] Perhaps indeed Marion's most important proposal is to extend Heidegger's definition of the phenomenon as follows: the phenomenon shows itself not only of itself but also as its self. When it gives itself of itself, it gives its self to consciousness (as the other of consciousness). The saturated phenomenon shows itself from itself and as its self, that is, the phenomenon appears in phenomenality and visibility (shows itself), autonomously (of itself) and individually (as its self).

Marion tries to think the human being's encounter with phenomena as a singular encounter. Consider this example: I inherit a table from my deceased grandmother. Marion's point is that whatever anticipations I make in receiving the table in my house—be it rearranging my space so that the table, as an object, can be placed, or rearranging my time so that the table can be used, as a being ready-to-hand, to eat or write on it—this still does not exhaust the significations that can be attributed to the table. What happens, indeed, when this table at the time of delivery overwhelms me by the stories that give themselves to be told on the occasion of its gift, when I am bedazzled by the memories attached to this singular table? The table gives itself as an event: it defies whatever kind of anticipations I undertook to receive it. First, the table alters the conception of a horizon: instead of provoking one single horizon according to which it can appear (being or object), it provokes an infinite amount of horizons that altogether forbid constituting it as one single object. It defies the anticipations of the transcendental subject, in that the table now appears as much more than the sum of its parts, as well beyond the subject's limits to determine if it is or is not,[10] as unique and unrelated to other phenomena, and, finally, as an event that provokes me to align myself to its appearance (BG, 119–31). Or, to return to Husserlian vocabulary, the table gives its self with an excess of intuition over against my (anticipating) intentions, which arise only on the basis of a certain horizon and the transcendental subject.

Thus, contrary to modern thought, which limited the phenomenon to what is possible, the saturated phenomenon extends the domain of the possible to that which, in the eyes of modern reason, is impossible, to *the possibility of the impossible* (BG, 218). What is (im)possible, then, is that phenomena appear in their own right, defying the principle of contradiction as much as the principle of sufficient reason (BG, 160, 172). Marion's saturated phenomenon is therefore not so much smuggling in a theology of the supernatural as raising the stakes of the natural, transcendental, conditions of possibility to the level of incorporating the possibility of the impossible. For indeed, Marion has asserted more than once that the saturated phenomenon has nothing exceptional about it; on the contrary, without saturation "none of the real phenomena with which we traffic daily and obligatorily can be analyzed adequately" (BG, 195).

The saturated phenomenon gives nothing exceptional to see, it only shows that, in fact, there is more to see than that which we, through our familiarity with technological foreseeability, are accustomed to: even "the objects that are supposedly the most simple [. . .] in fact always give more to see, and from afar, more than we can think [. . .] The concepts, by which we know what there is to see so well that we no longer take the time to go and truly see, serve only [. . .] to mask [the] exuberant splendor" (BG, 201) of what there is to see already. The saturated phenomenon is therefore an invitation to see and think otherwise.

And yet, it is not that the saturated phenomenon gives nothing to see; it is that that which gives itself to be seen goes well-beyond the capacities and intentions of the subject such that its mastery over the phenomenon is suspended, and the gaze "experiences only its powerlessness to see anything, except the bursting that [. . .] blinds it" (BG, 205). The intuition without a concept is, in case of the saturated phenomenon, not only blind but also blinding. Over and against the saturated phenomenon, the gaze is exposed to an "essential passivity" that entails "a real recognition of finitude" (BG, 206).

Saturation in terms of relation denotes the irreducibility of the saturated phenomena to any other experience: it is an "absolute phenomenon" (BG, 209). As for saturated phenomena, " 'their relation to thought in general'" (BG, 212), Marion asks: "[W]hat would happen if a phenomenon did *not* 'agree with' or 'correspond to' the power of knowing of the I?" (BG, 213). Marion agrees with Kant in that the subject would then undergo "a confused perceptive aberration without object" or the "disagreement between an at least potential phenomenon and the subjective condition for its experience" (ibid.). Marion differs from Kant in arguing that "this failure to objectify in no way implies that absolutely nothing appears there" (ibid.). What appears in the saturated phenomenon is precisely "a nonobjectifiable phenomenon" (ibid.). Such a counterexperience is not a nonexperience but "the experience of a phenomenon [that] offers the experience of what irreducibly contradicts the conditions for the experience of objects" (BG, 215). In such a case, Marion adds, the eye "sees nothing distinctly (in particular not an object), but clearly experiences its own powerlessness to master the measurelessness of the intuitive given—therefore, before all, the perturbations of the visible, the noise of a poorly received message, the obfuscation of finitude. It receives a pure givenness, precisely because it no longer discerns any objectifiable given therein" (BG, 216).

Saturation, then, reverses the relation between the I and that which it experiences. Instead of constituting the phenomenon as an object, the I finds itself constituted by the phenomenon and is turned into its witness. Marion defines this witness as "a subjectivity stripped of its characteristics that gave it the transcendental rank" (BG, 217). As with the work of art and the gift, here it is not a matter of *Sinngebung*, but of receiving the meaning of the saturated phenomenon. In and through the counterexperience the I loses its anteriority is turned into the interlocuted one, preceded by an "always already there interpellation" (BG, 217 mod.). The subject is turned into a witness "despite itself" through the surprise of "this more original event" (ibid.) of an "auto-manifestation" (BG, 219).

The Adonné

How does one receive such an automanifestation, if at all? Recall that Marion does not deny the subject the right to occupy the center of phenomenality but contests rather the way in which this occupation takes place. Unlike the Cartesian cogito, the *adonné* is given over to this center, and it has to receive this center in an appropriate manner. The *adonné* retains epistemological priority. Although the phenomenon giving its self turns the subject into its witness, the given and saturated phenomenon appeals to be shown in phenomenality, and it is this epistemological task that will fall to the *adonné*: "manifesting what presents (gives) itself, but which must still be introduced into the presence of the world (show itself)" (BG, 264–65), for if "all that shows itself must first give itself, it sometimes happens that what gives itself does not succeed in showing itself" (BG, 309), it falls to the *adonné* to "make possible [. . .] the opening for the givennesses of all other particular givens" (BG, 269).

This epistemological priority is, however, first attested to in affectivity, because "it is one thing to say that no phenomenon escapes its representation (understood in the broadest sense of a presentation to . . .) [. . .] But this is something completely different from interpreting the accompaniment of each thought (presenting to . . .)" (BG, 250), through an act of understanding. Indeed, "the representation which accompanies all representation is not said in an "I think" (therefore in the spontaneity of the understanding," but in an "I feel" (in terms of the affection of sensibility)" (ibid.).

Marion returns to Descartes' famous example of the piece of wax to explain this substitution of the 'I think' for the 'I feel.' Descartes' argument runs like this: the piece of wax certainly has a particular color, and certainly a particular form, and a particular odor too, but when we, for instance, heat the wax, the form and the color change. Though it remains the same piece of wax, it cannot be the senses that instruct us regarding what the wax really is. What is certain, in and through the changes that occur to the senses, is only that the substance of the wax appears this time in this particular form and another time in another form. Therefore, the piece of wax is, essentially, a *res extensa*. Marion comments that the extension of the piece of wax (its chemical formula, the quantity of molecules, its spatiotemporal coordinates) certainly defines the wax; it does not suffice to see it: "[T]he concept of the wax does not yet show it, its intelligibility does not always phenomenalize it" (BG, 263). On the contrary, the wax we can see, and that therefore shows itself, shows itself first and foremost to the senses. The conclusion to be drawn from this is evident: the wax does not show itself to the constituting ego but to "the receiver of the sensible manifold" (ibid.).[11] The thing shows itself in its "unsubstitutable selfhood" (BG, 264) to the senses only: "[C]ounter to metaphysics, it must be said that "feeling" does not result from the "thing" as its effect, [. . .] but that it shows it as its one and only possible apparition" (BG, 264). How the wax gives itself determines how it shows itself: the wax shows itself as a fluid only when it is warm; the wax shows itself as solid, only when the candle is not lit. The concept of the wax, constituted by a transcendental ego, does not allow the wax to appear; in fact it is the other way around, the concept 'hides' what there is to see of this particular piece of wax.

In the case of the saturated phenomenon, Marion argues, the impact of that which gives itself of itself is radicalized into a call, and the receiver turns into the *adonné* (BG, 266). It is here that the reversal of intentionality that we already noted in the case of the given phenomenon, plays in full (BG, 267). Marion mentions four characteristics of the subject that undergoes the appeal or the call (BG, 268–71).

First, the saturated phenomenon *summons* the subject to align him- or herself to its appearance in order to hear its appeal. This hearing puts the subject into the dative as a 'me, to whom' (givenness occurs). Givenness giving itself to the *adonné* is what accounts for the alteration of the *adonné* and that makes of human beings an "originally altered, called identity" (BG, 268), altered by it knows not what. Second, the subject is surprised by the appeal that seizes it. Surprise entails a "loss of knowledge" (BG, 269).[12] Surprise, then, is not knowledge but accounts for "a more originary affection" (ibid.) which tonality is best described as "admiration" (cf. ED, 371). Third, the *adonné* finds itself *interlocuted*, "as the 'unto whom' of an addressed word" (BG, 269). Thus the *adonné* is given to itself "from the call that gives me to myself before giving me anything whatsoever" (ibid.). Marion points to birth as an example of this opening to an alterity. This opening is also attested in the fourth characteristic of the *adonné*: its *facticity* derives from the always already given fact of the appeal. Paradigm for this facticity is one's birth.[13] Through birth also, the *adonné* receives the very fact of language in and through hearing the word from an Other. "Thus the gifted is delivered straightaway—with its birth—from solipsism" (BG, 269).

This has a consequence that the *adonné* is first and foremost defined from out of its response to what is given to it. This is what Marion calls "the responsal." Since the hearing of the appeal has always and already begun, even without me knowing or agreeing with it, every denial of the appeal is nonsensical: "[I]t is necessary to have already heard something to deny that a call was heard" (BG, 288). The response, therefore, "is nothing like an optional act, an arbitrary choice, or a chance," although "the meanings invested by the response can be chosen, decided, arrive by accident" (ibid.). I cannot not hear the appeal of givenness, but I can nevertheless choose to 'see' nothing other than objects and beings. However, to see only objects and beings therefore involves a certain 'irresponsibility' (as a *privatio*, a lack of responsibility) toward givenness. It is important to note that this 'response' seems to be a new version of the Heideggerian *Jemeinigkeit*: as much as *Dasein* always has to be its own being, my response toward givenness always and already depends upon me and upon me only. *Reduction and Givenness* still conceives of the situation of the *adonné* in Heideggerian terms. Recall that, for Heidegger, the term *Dasein* is best translated as 'being the there.'[14] Marion, who does not contest that the human being occupies the center of phenomenality, rather contests the way in which such an occupation takes place: "[T]he claim [. . .] poses *me* as the *there*" (RG, 201). One might say therefore that the *adonné*, resulting from givenness, is 'given to the there,' given to the center to give himself or herself over ('*s'adonner*') to "make possible [. . .] the opening for the givennesses of all other particular givens" (BG, 269).

Conclusion and Critical Remarks

What matters to us in this final section in Marion's account of the decentering of the modern subject is how this interplay between givenness and the *adonné* is interpreted phenomenologically. In other words, what happens to intentionality? Marion gives an answer that is strikingly similar to that of Lacoste: "[I]ntentionality is inverted: I become the objective of the object" (BG, 146).[15] It is important to note that in formulas such as these, *Being Given* attests to its continuity with Marion's earlier theological works: the exact same phrase occurs in his 1991 book *The Crossing of the Visible*. This book, considering the extent to which the visibility of a painting is permeated with invisibility, declares our passivity toward the work of art as follows: "[I]t is a matter of an inverted perspective, a counter-perspective, which is no longer organized in terms of the external gaze of the spectator, but [it is] as if the painting climbed back up from the unseen under the direction of its spectator, *object and objective of the perspective*, no longer its author" (*CV*, 39). This simple reversal of the subject-object distinction can be argued for in another way as well: whereas, according to Marion, the transcendental ego 'controls' that which shows up in phenomenality by the very fact of conferring conditions of possibility upon appearances in order to "keep the visible under the control of the seer" (*BG*, 214), the *adonné* finds him- or herself placed "under the guard of the paradox (saturated phenomenon) that controls it" (*BG*, 217). Whereas the transcendental I is the master and possessor (cf. *BG*, 214) of phenomenality, the *adonné* is radically dispossessed by the phenomenon giving itself of itself (cf. *BG*, 249); finally, whereas the phenomenon is always and already judged according to the measures of "the tribunal of the transcendental I" (*BG*, 188), the *adonné* now lets him- or herself "be judged [. . .] by what he himself cannot say or think adequately" (*BG*, 217, also 188).[16] However, most telling with respect to this reversal is the fact that when Marion writes that, for the giver and the receiver of a gift, their autonomy needs to be broken and that this means that both will have to abandon the autarchic position of not owing anything to anyone (e.g., *BG*, 101, 108, 111, 115)—Marion's colloquial rendering of the *ego*—it remains the case that it is nevertheless "the given" that will occupy this strange status of "owing nothing to anybody" (*BG*, 2).

What does this mean? It means that the subject is stripped of its subjectivity; that is, it is reduced to a mere receptiveness and passivity toward givenness. In the words of Marion, the subject becomes the "clerk"[17] and the recorder of that which gives itself, a mere screen on which givenness can testify to itself. Thus, we can recognize in Marion's discourse the very same movement that we perceived in Lacoste: a mere reversal of intentionality accounts for the decentering of modern subjectivity. However, one needs to be wary about such a reversal. Two main arguments help to explain this wariness. First, I will show in what manner the subject-object distinction recurs in Marion's thought and what the consequences of that recurrence might be. This argument will lead us to *God without Being*. Second, I will try to demonstrate that such a reversal cannot escape the structure and metaphors of transcendental subjectivity.

The subject-object distinction recurs in *Being Given* in quite an obvious manner. On the one hand, one notices a kind of 'subjectivization' or singularization on the part of the given. In the same way as Lacoste seemed to point to God as the sole subject, the phenomena or the given acquire an "individuation" (BG, 139, 159), even amounting to an "unsubstitutable selfhood" (BG, 264). On the other hand, the subject must refrain from all autonomy, and the human being is turned into a witness that "lights up as on a control panel at the very instant when and each time the information he should render phenomenal [. . .] arrives to him from a transistor by electric impulse, without initiative and delay" (BG, 217–18). The witness does not and cannot invest the phenomenon; rather the phenomenon invests and submerges the witness to such an extent that this witness cannot but, indeed as a simple 'clerk,' "register it immediately" (ibid). Is not this subjectivity, as the passivity of Lacoste's liturgical experience, only a sign of a more fundamental objectivity, as if the human being is a mere epiphenomenon of that which gives itself of itself?

To answer these questions, we will need to recall how phenomenology conceives of an 'object.' Let us return to the example of the table. When I look at it, I evidently see only one side of it. Constitution is that mental act with which I somehow add to the perception of three legs, the fourth leg. The constitution of the table as a table thus requires an invariant idea or essence of the table (an idea beyond which the table would not be a table anymore), which accounts for the fact, according to Marion, that the unseen part of an object immediately has the rank of a preseen. The point is: *objects do not have secrets*; they are entirely submitted to the power of the subject.

If this is the case, the question posed to Marion, and a fortiori to Lacoste, is whether we, in our relation to God, guard our singularity (which, obviously, involves some kind of secret) or whether we, on the other hand, are exposed to God to the point at which our visible and ontic being-in-the-world (for God, for others) and our finitude are only to be considered secondary. Since we already know that, in Lacoste's account, our thinglike existence before God is preferred over our embodiment, we now have to consider how Marion depicts (our) materiality in *God without Being*. In the iconic encounter with the divine, a specific relation between the visible and the invisible is at issue. Whereas in the case of the idol, the visible, that is, being(s), is the measure of all things invisible, in the iconic relation the interplay between the visible and the invisible is, precisely, reversed: I find myself envisaged by invisibility. In order to see what happens to worldy visibility in this encounter, several passages are noteworthy.

In the iconic relation, the intentional gaze of the other, aiming at us, *transpierces*[18] the (visible) wood of the icon in such a way that this visibility is downplayed to such an extent that the icon no longer consists in anything other than this encounter between two gazes (cf. CV, 20–22). For the icon to consist of two gazes crossing each other, the visible must be "dulled, dressed-down [. . .]—in short, transpierced" (CV, 61). It is important to note that this transpiercing pertains not only to the visible wood of the icon but to my own visibility as well. My visibility and my being undergo an "apocalyptic exposure" amounting to being "visibly laid out in the open" (GWB, 22). 'I' consists in nothing other than my referring myself to the intention of this invisible gaze (GWB, 23 *et passim*) as if the 'I' is as transparent as an object! Note, moreover, that even after *Being Given*, Marion adheres to this reversal of intentionality even in the case of God's revelation, for "[with the phenomena of revelation] it is not a question of [. . .] the constitution of objects starting from a transcendental subjectivity, which controls them by the initiative of intentionality [. . .], but of the reception of phenomena that show themselves, beginning with *the intentionality of God*, such as he reveals himself in and from himself, contrary to our expectations, predictions and intentions."[19]

In fact, these results might point to the fact that a simple reversal of intentionality does not suffice to decenter the subject: either one invokes another instance that displays a sort of autonomy, whether givenness in the case of Marion or God in the case of Lacoste, or this recurrence of an autonomous instance simply masks the fact that one still adheres to the transcendental version of subjectivity. Note that what is at stake here is not primarily a theological question. The question pertains in the first instance to a phenomenological issue: if the critique of the subject, as we have encountered it in Marion and Lacoste, is that the subject in and through its intentional aim enacts an unjustified power claim over objects and beings—the *pretention* to be autonomous—have we then really decentered this subject when asserting that its autonomy yields to passivity in and through the autonomous aim or appeal of either God or givenness? Are we not left with the very same problem with which we began, that is, intentionality as a question of power?

It is only when this reversal of intentionality is applied to God that, first, we seem to be left with a theological anthropology that is open to question because God's intentional aim would simply turn *us* into mere objects. Second, it is also when intentionality is attributed to God that the ontotheological turn of Marion and Lacoste plays itself out in full. For upon what grounds other than the ontotheological would one ascribe and attribute intentionality to God? Why would these thinkers, such as Marion, otherwise so committed to negative theology, ascribe intentionality to God? This second claim will be worked out in more detail in the two last chapters of this work. Now I will underline the recurrence of some form of the transcendental subject in *Being Given* by showing how the reversal of intentionality in this text still adheres to a transcendental logic. At the same time I will point to more striking similarities to Marion's earlier theological work.

First, the "phenomenal autonomy" (*BG*, 213) that the phenomenon acquires in *Being Given* resembles the autonomy Marion refuses to ascribe to the 'modern' subject. Whereas this subject is to be condemned for its power and its pretension to be autonomous and deciding on the phenomenon in an active manner, Marion's givenness simply repeats these two characteristics, but this time on the part of givenness. So one reads that "activity falls to the phenomenon and to it alone" (*BG*, 226)[20] and that "every phenomenon [. . .] exercises by itself the initiative of making itself visible" (*BG*, 133) and that it can do so on the basis of the power of givenness only. One should ponder also whether this claim of 'the power of givenness' is not retrieving precisely that which Marion objected to in Heidegger. Already in the opening pages of *Being Given*, Marion makes a sweeping claim toward Heidegger's naming of the 'Es gibt' as 'Ereignis.' Marion's argument is that Heidegger, by baptizing the 'Es' of 'Es gibt' as 'Ereignis,' fell in the metaphysical trap of evoking the instance that gives as an "indeterminate power," even "to the point where it would appear as an ontic agent" (*BG*, 36). Yet Marion's givenness is repeatedly attributed a similar indeterminate power. So for instance the gift that is irreducible to a being or object, as for instance the giving of time, is described as a gift "raised to a higher power" (*BG*, 80).[21] Therefore, givenness at least seems to point in the direction of the 'indeterminate power' that accounts for the reason of the gift. Over against the autonomous power of givenness, one therefore finds the powerlessness of the *adonné*, reduced to being a mere clerk of that which gives itself. It is here that one should dare to ask whether Marion succeeds in overcoming metaphysics, since it is not at all clear how a reversal of a metaphysical statement avoids the metaphysics it wants to overturn.

Moreover, while everything gives itself of itself with "neither limit nor remainder" (*BG*, 309), it does not follow that everything that gives itself in such a way will be shown in phenomenality. It is up to the *adonné* to make the given appear, and, in this sense, the *adonné* remains "the sole master and servant of the given" (*BG*, 319. This "responsal," however, does not differ much from modern subjectivity at all, since the manner in which that which gives itself of itself shows itself "in the world" (*BG*, 264–65) depends upon the resistance of the *adonné* toward givenness.[22] Marion's vocabulary may be abstract, but his point is quite simple: I can choose to see for instance the table simply as an object, and I can refuse to resist the shock of the event of the table since then the event as such will not 'appear' in the world (it will appear only as an object). Toward givenness, my response thus depends upon me and upon me only: one has "to decide on the gift" (BG, 111).[23] This, however, is a retrieval of precisely that which Marion condemns in modern subjectivity and in Heidegger's *Dasein*: "In fact, the reflective characteristics of *Dasein*—to decide itself, to put itself at stake [. . .]—are such good imitations of the transcendental subject's subjectivity that they should also suggest the character of subsisting ground for *Dasein*. The aporia of solipsism implies that of subsistence" (BG, 261, mod.). Thus, Marion seems to be stuck in a dilemma: either affirming some mythic power that accounts for the gift deciding itself—hence the importance of Horner's remark that Marion displays a tendency toward personifying the gift—or simply returning to an autonomous understanding of the gifted, deciding to render himself or herself to givenness.

We will see later in this work that even Marion's account of the *adonné* does not escape a similar solipsism. For now, it is to be noted that this decisional character (on the gift, the given) is close, indeed very close, to the Heideggerian account of *Jemeinigkeit*. Whereas for Heidegger being is in each case mine, in the sense that it is I, and I alone, who has to be 'my' being, for Marion the response to givenness in a similar way depends on me and on me only. Recall that in the counterexperience, the *adonné* is brought into a situation where nothing can be seen clearly and distinctly. The *adonné* is thus brought into "a pre-phenomenological and pre-rational obscurity," wherein "the choice or the refusal of the 'great reason'" has to be made (BG, 306). The *adonné* will choose either "a nonsaturated phenomenon [. . .] susceptible to a response that is adequate" or "a saturated phenomenon that shows what it gives only inadequately, in an endless series of always partial and provisional responses"; in short, the *adonné* must either choose "the enjoyment of a power adequate to constituting" or "expose [itself] to the humiliation of never constituting [. . .] in order to gain the enjoyment of a givenness of paradoxes" (ibid.). This situation, then, is described as one wherein "givenness enters into conflict with the gifted, the given with its reception, the call with the response. *No advice or counsel, no friend or enemy, can do anything for the gifted in the situation of giving itself over or not*" (BG, 307). This, of course, is nothing less than solipsism. Thus, not only does Marion rehearse the insubstitutability characteristic of Heidegger's account of *Jemeinigkeit*, in that no one can decide for me on the given, it also mimes the '*Vereinzelung*,' of Heidegger's existential solipsism, in that no one can offer any help to the gifted in this "space of indecision that cannot be imagined without fright" (BG, 306).[24] Marion's critique of the Heideggerian *Jemeinigkeit* as being yet another heir of transcendental subjectivity can therefore be turned against Marion himself.

To illustrate this hypothesis, I will now give a brief example of the similarities between Marion's notion of the painter in the theological work *The Crossing of the Visible* and the *adonné* of the later book *Being Given*. For, indeed, one more argument deserves our attention here: if that which is manifested of givenness depends entirely on the response of the gifted, and if that 'responsal' is dependent upon the extent to which the gifted is resistant toward givenness, and if finally there are degrees of resistance toward this givenness, then is this not precisely the same distinction that Marion condemns in Heidegger's analytic of *Dasein*? In other words, is this differentiation between different *adonné*'s on the basis of their amount or resistance toward givenness not re-invoking, albeit in a subtle way, a difference between an 'authentic' and 'inauthentic' *adonné*? Consider Marion's definition of genius: "Genius only consists in a great resistance to the impact of the given revealing itself" (IE, 52). Is the genius more apt or even more courageous to carry the burden of the given? One is reminded here of Marion's description of the painter in *The Crossing of the Visible*, as an example of true genius: "[T]he true painter does not know what he painted, and devoted his knowledge only to begging for the surprise of discovering what he had not dared to foresee. The whole mastery consists, precisely, in ultimately letting the unseen burst into the visible by surprise, unpredictably" (CV, 32). The mastery of the 'true' painter consists, therefore, in a nonmastery, in "no longer attempting [. . .] to be able to make (or to see) that which he is still able to desire or master." (CV, 32, mod.). Only the painter, then, is able to register the unseen's bursting into the scene of the visible, for the

> authentic painting fulfils the expectation of the painter and the visitor, strictly speaking, by surprising it, disorienting it, and flooding it. It fills not the expected expectation but rather another expectation—the unexpected. Its reality ['*effectivité*'] does not accomplish an already-defined possibility; it opens up a possibility to that point not anticipated, unthinkable, impossible. Not that such a picture robs itself of our desire to see: it robs us of our very meager desire—prudent and restricted—to see only what we had foreseen in all of its quoddity ['*quotidienneté*'], in order to open us up to a pure desire to see otherwise. (CV, 32; CeV, 61)

Let us interrupt this long citation and ponder what is being said here, for both what is stated here of the true painter and of the authentic painting and how it escapes the logic of 'prevision' in order to 'see otherwise' flow neatly into the terminology used for the description of the *adonné* and the saturated phenomenon of *Being Given*. Perhaps, therefore, Robyn Horner has a point when saying, surveying Marion's career, that "the accusations that Marion's phenomenology is a covert theology were possibly reinforced by the publication in [1991] of *La croisée du visible*."[25] In any case, just as the *adonné* is to be conceived of as a clerk that registers and records that which gives itself, so too the painter's task will consist in nothing more than "record[ing] the rising of the unseen to the point of appearance" (CV, 41).[26]

Over and against this mere recording, then, stands the autonomous appearance of the work of art: indeed, "the true painting [. . .] implores the visible already seen to allow itself to be increased and opened by a new glory. The unseen [. . .] climbs toward the visible [and] imposes upon it that of which the visible remained still unaware [:] the presentable par excellence, the brute unseen, the miracle" (CV, 29). The autonomous appearance of the artwork amounts to a miracle, since it renders possible that which otherwise would have remained impossible. We see here how, already in *The Crossing of the Visible*, Marion meditates upon that which will later in this work come to serve as a sort of definition of the saturated phenomenon. What, in effect, does the work of art teach us? We "learn from a painting to see a nonobject" (CV, 42), since it "purifies" the gaze in that "it offers to it, beyond every opposing object, what phenomenology holds for the phenomenon par excellence—that it shows itself on its own terms [. . .] And thus, in this self-showing on its own terms alone, it shows us above all what this is—to show itself, to appear in full authority, full glory" (CV, 43).

All this, however, raises the question as towhether Marion is not invoking a sort of elitist election in the case of the saturated phenomenon. Here we encounter the (in)famous objection of Jocelyn Benoist: "[D]ear Jean-Luc Marion, [. . .] what will you answer me when I say that there where you see God I see nothing or something else? [. . .] I am not sure that your thought has assured the necessary conditions [. . .] for responding in another manner than a ruse or the violence [. . .] of a reduction."[27] Indeed, the question is whether those who are not able to 'record' and 'register' that which gives itself will have to be considered as 'inauthentic' with regards to the power of givenness. In the next chapter I will indeed show that Marion does not avoid such ethical qualifications with regard to one's responsibility toward givenness altogether.

For now it is important to note that in Marion's phenomenology of givenness either givenness takes on the posture and the contours of an autonomous instance, in which case the decentering of the subject Marion evokes amounts to a similar 'objectification of the subject' as I perceived in Lacoste, or the *adonné* still resembles the modern subject, in that it takes over precisely those characteristics that Marion attributes to Heidegger's *Dasein* as one more heir of transcendental subjectivity (decide oneself, *Jemeinigkeit*, and solipsism). In the next chapter, I will examine the question of the miracle in Marion's work in order to retrieve Marion's possible answer, if any, to Benoist's remarkable objection.

Chapter 4

On Miracles and Metaphysics

From Marion to Levinas

Being given that, for Marion, the event as much as the autonomous appearance of the artwork can take the form of the miracle, one might, especially from the viewpoint of the Enlightenment, and with a bit of irony: a miraculous return of the miracle. For Marion indeed, miracles are no longer to be conceived of as exceptions to ordinary phenomena; it is rather the other way around: ordinary phenomena give themselves from themselves and as themselves; in short, they are *events* and, yes, the event can take the figure of the miracle.'

One might object that the miracle of the saturated phenomenon has nothing to do with the well-known definition of the miracle, according to which a miracle contradicts the laws of nature. However, our focus here is not on the 'laws of nature,' or on whatever contradicts them, but on the contradiction itself. Indeed, a great many definitions of the miracle insist, in one way or another, on the exception the miracle brings to the rules of 'ordinary' phenomena, be it one's expectations (Augustine), the laws of nature (Aquinas/Hume), or one's experience (Rahner).[1] In Marion's vocabulary: how is it that the same phenomenon can appear as both an object *and* a saturated phenomenon?

Miracles and Saturation: John Caputo versus Merold Westphal

First we have to make sure that we understand the miracle of the saturated phenomenon correctly. To do this, I will now stage a debate between Jack

Caputo and Merold Westphal. Caputo asks, "[F]rom Derrida's point of view, has Marion simply offered a more refined definition of hyperessentialism in terms of givenness?"[2] According to Caputo, Marion exposes himself to the danger of 'phenomenologizing theology' and so risks bringing to theology, through this danger of reading New Testament miracles phenomenologically, a "magical realism" and "a historical literalism of the events of the New Testament."[3] Westphal, however, suspects Caputo's contention to be a "modern, all too modern, product of the dogmatic naturalism of the Enlightenment" and even "a bondage to the principle of sufficient reason."[4] Caputo's reading is that Marion, while trying to describe the possibility of revelation, falls in the trap again of a metaphysics of presence (in which the intuition/presence fulfils the intention/absence) because Marion introduces a hermeneutics of faith at the heart of the given. Marion indeed resorts to faith and theology as the only instances that "can judge [the] actual manifestation or ontic status" (BG, 236)[5] of Revelation. It *is* striking that Marion has recourse to the language of being and actuality when referring to the possibility of Revelation: "[S] uddenly the language of *sans l'être* becomes quite ontic and existential. In the classical manner of negative theology, these phenomena beyond or without being thus acquire a kind of *hyperentitative* or *hyperousiological* status," giving them "onto-phenomenological status, as if they were literal, actual, and ontical occurrences that true believers would have witnessed."[6] But if only faith can bridge the gap between the possibility of revelation and its actuality, Caputo contends, the fact remains that this faith is, then, once again described as in search of actuality and the full presence of what offers itself only as a possibility to phenomenology. Any hermeneutic of faith, according to Caputo, will see Revelation *as if* it had actually occurred: faith will supply "an interpretative slant [. . .] that allows the believer to intend something that is precisely *not* given."[7] And here Marion's phenomenology of givenness, Caputo contends, thus "finds itself resubmitted to the most classical Husserlian constraints."[8] If this is the case, Caputo argues, Marion might not so much prove the possibility of a saturating intuition and givenness as testify to the fact that this longing for full presence is precisely what defines faith as an excess of intention over intuition.

Thus we are left, once again, with the prayers and tears of deconstruction. Or so it appears! For Marion has responded to this debate—say, *par avance*. The "blasphemy" of modern thought, according to Marion, is to think that "faith serves [. . .] to compensate faulty intuition," not seeing that we "should believe [. . .] rather to confront the excess of intuition."[9] In fact, "the most common and rude error with regard to the miracles of Christ consists in characterising them by a deficiency of intuition, givenness and manifestation that faith should compensate [for]."[10] Modern metaphysical thinking has limited the field of phenomenological manifestation in a very thorough way. While Marion contends that faith consists in believing what there is to see already, Caputo argues that faith consists in believing what is not available to sight. Faith, for Marion, would thus amount to a particular case of the saturated phenomenon, because the saturated phenomenon opens the possibility of seeing otherwise, or at least more than the gaze, which is acquainted only with objects, would take into account. Let us take Westphal's lead to escape the impasse: "the phenomenologist, who describes the possible event of revelation, does not qua phenomenologist affirm the actuality of the supernatural."[11] He or she should only take note that this revelation may have been *experienced* as miraculous. The phenomenologist focuses on the lived experience of that which is experienced as miraculous rather than on the actuality of any supernatural event. Westphal, indeed, seems to be more loyal to Marion's position when the latter states that "in this sense, the miracle [. . .] no longer bears on a physical event, but on consciousness itself."[12] Marion is therefore trying to bring into description the everyday concept of the miracle. Sentences such as "It's a miracle" attest simply to the fact that what I held as impossible shows itself to be possible after all: "[B]efore questioning the 'laws of nature,' [the miracle] puts into question what I can recognize as possible and the part I sacrifice to the impossible—in short, the miracle reveals the limits of that which I construct as my world."[13] This incites Emmanuel Falque to state that Marion comes close to Rudolf Bultmann here: "Marion [. . .] can no longer accord his faith to an objectivity of revelation." Indeed, "the objectivism of revelation is definitely abandoned" and substituted for "a transformation of the subject as such."[14]

The phenomenon of revelation is therefore, just as with the saturated phenomena, an encounter with that which we, prior to it, held as impossible (and thus shows itself to be possible after all). Indeed, *both* degrees of saturation are described by Marion as the possibility of the impossible (BG, 218; BG, 235–36). It is thus in this sense that even revelation "remains inscribed within the transcendental conditions of possibility" (BG, 235). Falque therefore contends that the miracle, contrary to what Caputo suggests, is not so much a literal event, but rather that revelation is attested to in its bearing on my consciousness. In this sense, lurking behind the phenomenology of givenness is not so much a transcendent giver as an immanent God creeping into consciousness even "if unbeknownst to it" (cf.

ID, 20). In *Being Given*, Marion indeed points in this direction when stating that the phenomenological reduction puts into parentheses the transcendent and metaphysical God as foundation of the factical world but as such leaves intact the fact that, concerning matters of revelation and *theology*, "God is likewise, indeed especially, characterized by radical immanence to consciousness" (BG, 242).[15] The question, then, is, of course, whether in the case of the experience of the miracle or of the saturated phenomenon what we experience in face of the miracle amounts to much more than a subjective narration of experiences. Indeed, Marion's stress on imaginative and imaginary variations on the level of consciousness could have as a consequence that one never leaves the level of consciousness altogether. This is a difficult question, and I will come back to it later in this work. For now it is important to see that everything perhaps hinges on the ability of the *adonné* to recognize that the impossible is possible indeed, that the miracle is possible without needing to be referred to a literal account of "what happened." It is here that we will locate Marion's response to Benoist's objection that the saturated phenomenon concerns a sort of elitist election.

To See or Not to See? Marion's Response to Jocelyn Benoist

Falque asks whether all this emphasis on the universal character of the saturated phenomenon does not leave us in the dark with regard to "the most ordinary limitation of our existence," finitude?[16] In other words, is evoking the infinity of intuition of the saturated phenomenon not, once again and *inevitably*, responsible for the metaphysical view that finitude and the finite response to the given fall short with regard to the excess of the given? Is there, behind this univocal sense of the miraculous given, not once again a recurring of binary oppositions, such that the excess of the given *is relative to* the inability of the gifted to make the given appear so that the excess of whatever phenomena can only be asserted *at the expense* of that instance which ought to receive it? Indeed, our finite being is once again described as a defect and as a shortage: not seeing the given corresponds to a "*vouloir défaillant*" (ED, 431), that is, a lack of willingness to make the given appear. This is Marion's explanation of why unconditional givenness does not appear as such and why we usually see only objects and beings: it is due to the perturbations and unwillingness on the part of the finite receiver. For indeed the decision that the *adonné* has to make regarding the reason of things is not one that can be made on the basis of rational arguments; on the contrary, it is regulated entirely by "the will to see," to have a proper look, a "*vouloir bien voir*" (BG, 307/ED, 422, 420).[17] Falque, therefore, is right when saying that *Being Given* comes at a great cost: "[C]onsecrating the excess as the rule, [the phenomenology of the gift] tends to place the 'fault' of its non-phenomenalisation on a powerless and faulty subject," thereby losing the "neutral and constitutive horizon of human beings, for whom it was, at first, conceived."[18] Although Marion time and again tries to avoid qualifying this 'ill will' ethically (e.g. BG, 314), he does not succeed in freeing this 'faulty will' from an ethical horizon altogether. For, if this space of indecision is the place where one has to decide on the reason of things, which, in the case of the phenomenology of givenness, is the decision to see the 'visible as a gift,' then we are returned to the decision of the receiver with regard to the gift. To see the gift as a gift, one will recall, the receiver must give up his or her autarchic position and recognize a debt of owing something to someone, which is described by Marion as "phenomenologically and *morally* [. . .] the hardest ordeal" (BG, 100).[19] Therefore, although one can perhaps avoid the conclusion that anyone who fails to phenomenalize what gives itself of itself shows his or her bad will or can be deemed 'inauthentic,' one cannot understand this 'faulty will' otherwise than from out of a privative understanding: the 'faulty will' is the absence of that which, properly speaking, ought to be there, the will to see the given. All nonphenomenalization of the given is understood as a lack, an unwillingness, or irresponsibility[20] to see the given as given. Here, then, is Marion's response to Benoist: if you do not see anything there where I see the excessiveness of saturation, then, this is due to your unwillingness to see what there is to see already. Thus Benoist's objection seems confirmed, in that Marion's response can only be violent or by ruse: when one or the other *adonné* does not see the excessive intuition of the given, this is and cannot be due not to a hole in the theory (for instance: something is simply not given) but to the absence of a certain will that, properly speaking, *ought* to be there.[21]

According to Falque, then, the phenomenology of givenness' inability to think finitude as such must be *complemented*[22] with a phenomenology of poverty (vis à vis Marion's emphasis on excess) and proximity between human beings and God (vis à vis Marion's emphasis on distance). It remains to be seen, however, whether this would solve the problem, for if it is possible that Marion did not succeed in overcoming metaphysics then the deficiency associated with finitude might not be accidental—something that can be compensated, complemented—but rather structural, simply repeating the age-old metaphysical disdain for finitude. Falque had asked "whether it suffices to reverse Kant to take leave of Kant, thus whether to reverse metaphysics is sufficient to overcome metaphysics?"[23] and suggests that, because Marion's statement that with the phenomenon of revelation "it is necessary that we no longer define the saturated phenomenon simply by the inversion of the determinations of the common-law phenomenon [. . .] but even [must free ourselves] from their destruction" (BG, 245), Marion perhaps means to say that only theology overcomes metaphysics. In my view, however, it is precisely this destruction by inversion that did not succeed, not only because an inversion simply repeats these determinations in another form but also because I have in effect already shown that there is no clear-cut distinction between the saturated phenomenon and the phenomenon of revelation: both are defined as the possibility of the impossible.[24] Thus even the phenomenon of revelation remains trapped in what it wanted to overcome: the simple inversion of the logic of common-law phenomena, of metaphysics.

To sum up: according to Marion, the possibility of the miracle has nothing to do with the actual occurrence of a violation of the laws of nature. On the contrary, the miracle is in the eyes of the beholder: something can be experienced as miraculous. There's nothing exceptional about that. However, since most often human beings do not see what there already is to see, since indeed most often we only see objects or beings, someone or something must cause or lie at the origin of this nonappearance. Here Marion points the finger to the human subject, for either there is a lack of will to see what there is to see—what is given—or one, structurally,[25] lacks the ability to do just that.

Longing for Ockham: Of Other Gifts and Other Lovers

But did not Marion say that the event, the miracle, or the gift gives itself autonomously and individually "independently of every position we would have taken in its regard"?[26] However, it might be that the crux of the problem arises here, since the question of overcoming metaphysics becomes all the more pertinent once one considers not only the part of finitude but also that of excess. And here one will have to side with Caputo again. For the intrusion of the language of being into the phenomenology of givenness is not accidental and perhaps more grave than Caputo seems to think. For Marion describes the reception of the given as given in a quite problematic way. Experiencing the given is, one will recall, to experience a *counterexperience*.

This counterexperience "contradicts the conditions for the experience of objects" (BG, 215). It is not that the superabundance of intuitive givenness gives nothing to see or hear, but rather that its witness is drawn into an obscure prephenomenological field wherein nothing is seen or heard clearly and distinctly and is summoned to a space wherein *the* decision concerning the reason of things has to be made. This space of (in)decision toward givenness is, however, the place where a doubtful *doubling of the logic of the gift* takes place. As we have seen, Marion insists that the gift decides (on) itself more than human beings decide on its appearance, or, more precisely, the gift decides and persuades human beings to give themselves over to the gift. But, on the other hand, *how* exactly does the gift decide itself? And how is it experienced? Note here that just as the miracle has nothing to do with an actual violation of the laws of nature, the gift does not consist in the actual (gift of a) being or object but rather in the way consciousness relates toward its being given.

What is as remarkable as it is doubtful, then, is that another gift comes in to explain the logic of the gift. According to Marion, the gift is exempt from presence and therefore distinct from the actual transfer of an object or a being from a giver to a receiver. The gift resides in the decision that persuades the *adonné* to see it as 'giveable' or 'receivable': suddenly an object appears as givable and appeals to the giver to be given (or to the receiver to be received). However, this givability of the object is, according to Marion, itself a gift, and, therefore, all gifts are dependent upon "another gift" (BG, 108). This *other gift*, then, is supposed to explain why this or that object appears to consciousness as givable or acceptable. The gift is explained through a gift: hence a longing for Ockham. Therefore, Marion's attempt to distinguish between the object and the pure gift can and needs to be questioned, for one understands that a saturated phenomenon can sometimes pass into the rank of an ordinary object; it is still unclear how an object passes into the status of a saturated phenomenon.

Note, in passing, that the very same objection might be raised against Marion's account of love in his recent *The Erotic Phenomenon*.[27] The 'bond' between my lover and me consists in the oath she and I take to gather our different intuitions in a single signification: 'here I am.' But this oath suffers from a lack of durability and visibility: it lasts as long as we, as lovers, perform this oath. This performance takes place in our erotic interchanges and in fecundity. Both performances, however, suffer from an essential finitude: eroticization ends with the orgasm, and our offspring takes on its own oath and therefore its proper (in)visibility. The 'eternal' bond between her and me seems unable to show itself in visibility. Our love, according to Marion, is therefore abandoned to the constant and endless repetition of the oath. To save our love from its temporal repetition, which is, literally, the contradiction in terms enacted by successive monogamy (*EP*, 166–71), *and* to save 'the unconditional love without being' from its entanglement with being and visibility, Marion has recourse again to "another lover" (*EP*, 215) who assures and secures the visibility and durability of our (all too finite?) oath. This lover turns out to be God. God is a 'better lover' than we are and is, therefore, able to assure our love of its visibility and durability even when we lovers do not (or no longer) confirm our oath to one another.

In order to question Marion's distinction between the object and the pure gift, I will now consider Caputo's comments: "In order to shield the gift from being and presence, Marion is forced to trade on a positivistic sense of the gift,"[28] that is, the visible object or being is bracketed in a phenomenological reduction only to give way to the 'hyperappearance' of the invisible givenness. Caputo is questioning here that which seems to run like an axiom through *Being Given*: "[A] fundamental rule [is] that the more considerable a gift appears, the less it is realized as an object and by means of a transfer of property" (*BG*, 106). For Marion, "the more the gift is radicalized, the more the object is reduced to the abstract role of support, occasion, symbol" (ibid.). With Caputo, one needs to ask, however, whether, even when the object is reduced to the role of a simple support, this suffices to speak of a gift 'without' being. Does not the simple fact that the gift *requires* the object as a support, an occasion, or a symbol, point to the fact that a gift, if there is such a thing, gives itself always and already in being? Caputo therefore notes an ambiguity between the reduction to the given, in which the gift gives itself to consciousness without the intermediary of an object or being (as we have seen earlier with the aid of the example of the work of art), and the reduction of the gift, which attempts to prove that a gift can be given without precisely an object or being. According to Caputo, "the reduction *to* the gift and the reduction *of* the gift trade on equivocal senses of the gift."[29] In other words, whereas the reduction to the pure given as an effect on consciousness excludes any positivistic, reified sense of the gift, the reduction of the gift presupposes and includes precisely the gift in the sense of a real object or physical counterpart "which [. . .] takes the hit for the genuine gift."[30] This leads Caputo to suspect that it is this "positivistic blocking of the gift as a visible thing, [that] allows the phenomenology of the unapparent to swing into action, allowing the invisible 'horizon of givenness' to appear or to 'hyper-appear.'"[31]

Just as the valorization of the excess entailed the downplaying of the finite receiver, so the invisibility of the 'pure' gift requires the outstripping of the object as a visible thing. Just as the excess of givenness commands a corresponding 'faulty will' on the part of the finite, the excess of the gift over objects and beings reduces the latter to "merely an extra, interchangeable, and optional support" of the gift (BG, 103–04). Thus, not only does the phenomenology of givenness function at the expense of finitude (Falque), but it also posits its hypervisibility at the expense of the ordinary visibility of objects and beings (Caputo). This might once again mean that both are relative to each other rather than explaining one another: the saturated phenomenon might be described only when *presupposing* the object as its counterpart. This means also that the saturated phenomenon, though evoked to explain the extension of givenness to the whole of phenomenality, is nevertheless dependent upon the object to make givenness appear. One should ponder therefore why Marion proposes the decision concerning the reason of things as a choice between either saturated phenomena or objects, since if givenness is universal it ought to incorporate objects as well, leaving no room for a dilemma of the either/or kind. The *contradiction*, time and again evoked by Marion, between the object and the saturated phenomenon is therefore problematic.[32] Note that at issue here are precisely those examples, for instance revelation (BG, 5 and 246), that Marion has depicted as given 'without being,' intuition, or horizon (BG, 17–18, 187). Here Marion's phenomenology seems to slip into the imaginary, for, in the first place, there seems to be no object from which to contradistinguish, and second, without any object to suspend, what is revealed to consciousness seems to be but an impulse that consciousness gives to itself. Therefore, the real dilemma appears to be that if one admits that something gives itself without intuition, that is, as a pure gift or a saturated phenomenon supposedly devoid of all 'object-ness,' one is stuck with subjective impressions of some kind. If one admits, however, that such a pure given, precisely because it remains dependent on the visibility of the ordinary object, is inevitably intertwined with this visibility to such an extent that evoking their contradiction (as if they were mere logical opposites) is perhaps a phenomenological error, then the relation between the visibility of the object and the invisibility of the gift must be depicted otherwise.

Indeed, while one can grant Marion that the gift never simply coincides with the object given, this does not, in turn, imply that the visible object is totally distinct from or indifferent to the gift *as gift*.[33] When I, for instance, give a ring to someone to show her my love, this ring surely does not coincide with my (gift of) love for her. But this does not mean that this visible ring takes up the role of a simple support for my love for her. One might imagine situations (death, quarrels, etc.) in which this ring *as an object* becomes more, and much more, than a simple index of my love: instead of being an occasion and (necessary?) support for the 'pure' gift, the ring would then be the *condition* for its appearing: if this ring would be the only thing that remains of my deceased lover, then this object might assume the role of a unique and irreplaceable object rather than an 'interchangeable support' of the love between her and me. The gift would then never be a 'pure' given (without being), but always and already entangled with the visibility of beings and objects—the object becomes saturated *through* being, if you like.[34]

The problem, once again, is that in Marion's account the object cannot be a saturated phenomenon (since the object, the physical counterpart, is simply the support of it, but, in fact, has nothing to do with its pure apparition as a lived experience), *while* he maintains that givenness is original and universal. The conclusion seems to be that Marion is betting on two horses: describing the saturated phenomenon in its contradistinction with the object as a contradiction to "the conditions for the experience of objects" (BG, 215), while not always granting the object as an object the rank of a given phenomenon. But does not the saturated phenomenon *rest* upon this distinction for the simple reason that the reversal the saturated phenomenon performs on the subject-object distinction stands in need of precisely the object as an instance that it has to denounce to arrive at the excessive intuition of the saturated phenomenon? In this way, the description of the saturated phenomenon would remain indebted to the description of the object, and the contradiction between them would never be as clear-cut as Marion wants us to believe. In other words, the relation between the visible object and the invisible saturation should perhaps take into account their entanglement rather than their distinction or contradiction.

Marion's description of the icon in his earlier works can make this clearer. The icon is proposed as that which surpasses the idolatrous function exercised by whatever subject. The idol mirrors, albeit invisibly, the gaze of the subject, in that the invisibility the idol encounters is merely a privative invisibility: its invisibility is determined by relation to me—what I cannot see, does not exist. The icon, however, tries to surpass this privative invisibility, by introducing an invisibility that no longer is generated by a subject that distinguishes between what is visible to it and what is not, but an invisibility *sui generis*—invisibility *as such*, 'not an invisible that should remain invisible or that should become visible,' as is the case with the idol (cf. GWB, 17–18).

The icon does so by effecting, again, a *reversal of intentionality*: "The icon lays out the material of the wood and paint in such a way that there appears in them the intention of a transpiercing gaze emanating from them [. . .] the gaze [. . .] here belongs to the icon itself, where the invisible only becomes visible intentionally, hence by its aim. [T]he gaze of the invisible, in person, aims at man" (GWB, 19). In *The Crossing of the Visible*, Marion contends that it is precisely this play of the gazes that gives to the icon "the phenomenological basis for its subversion of the visible by the invisible" (CV, 21). It is perhaps noteworthy that the idol, as it is portrayed in *God without Being*, resembles the transcendence of the object. It is indeed much overlooked in the secondary literature that the idol does allow for a certain kind of invisibility as well. Indeed, the idol does not rid itself of all things invisible but encounters invisibility *in a particular way*. It is the latter understanding, I suggest, that Marion wants to overcome.

A Phenomenology of the Icon?

The idol, for Marion, operates from out of a logic of need: it fashions a divine face in order to "attract the benevolence and the protection" (ibid.) of the God. The need at issue is a certain relief: in its attempt to appropriate the divine as a means to its own ends, the idol casts out a certain fear, the fear of atheism "in the original sense: being deserted by the gods" (ID, 7). Since the idol cannot escape this logic of need, it "reflects back to us, in the face of a god, our own experience of the divine" (ID, 6). The latter sentence allows us to move to the terminology of *God without Being* and more in particular to the theme of the 'invisible mirror' that the idol is. In *God without Being*, Marion wants to avoid the simple opposition of the icon and the idol, between "the 'true God' (icon) [and] the false Gods," by stating that "the same beings (statues, names, etc.) can pass from one rank to the other" (GWB, 8). The idol and the icon "determine two manners of being for beings, not two classes of beings" (ibid.).

What the idol sees, then, is nothing but that which is taken up "into the field of the gazeable" (GWB, 11). In this field, the human gaze, looking for God, will be stopped, only to "allow it to rest (itself) in/on an idol" (ibid.). Every (idolatric) experience of God is, as we have seen, like an invisible mirror: 'Show me your idol, and I will tell you who you are.'

As such, this mirror goes unnoticed. The gaze is held by its idol, whose supreme visibility stops the gaze and offers a "first visible" that will contain and dazzle the idolatrer. This freezing of the gaze upon the first visible is twofold: "The invisible mirror that the first visible offers does not only indicate to the gaze how far its most distant aim extends, but *even* what its aim could not have in view" (GWB, 13). The gaze encounters that which it can aim at and will determine that which escapes the aim accordingly: what is beyond the aim is "invisible, because it is omitted by the aim *(invisable)*" (GWB, 17). The idolatrous gaze, therefore, only knows a logical distinction between the visible and the invisible: invisibility is only, and can only be, 'that which is unavailable to sight.' As such, the idol is close to what one hears out of public opinion: 'I only believe what I can see with my own eyes.' What is not available to 'my eyes' is deemed to be something that does not exist or that only comes to be when I can see it. Idolatrous is that which knows nothing other than its own gaze, that of which the gaze determines both its visibility and its invisibility (the latter however only by reference to the former and always in relation to the gaze). The invisibility of the idol is thus thought of as a privation, as invisibility that properly speaking *is not* or that simply will become visible in a later point of time. Just as the transcendence of the object, for instance a table, necessarily entails the invisibility of two or three legs with regard to my intentional aim, so the idol distinguishes between what is visible to it and what is not. But, just as the 'invisible' legs of the table are not properly speaking 'invisible' (because they will be visible to my gaze when I walk around the table), so the invisibility of the idol as '*invisable*,' is not an invisibility *sui generis*, but determined by reference to the gaze's aim. It is in this sense that the icon of God *without Being* foreshadows Marion's distinction between the transcendence of the object and what one might call the transcendence of the given. For in the icon something appears which is in no way whatsoever dependent upon my gaze, "thus not the visible discerning between itself and the invisible, hemming in and reducing it, but the invisible bestowing the visible, in order thus to deduce the visible from itself and to allow itself to appear there" (GWB, 17). The icon thus tries to surpass the privative understanding of the invisibility of the idol. Insofar as invisibility is conceived of as the lack or absence of visibility, the invisible as such cannot appear. That which is not aimed-at no longer appears in the icon as '*invisable*,' as that which pertains to the invisible as the (logical) opposite of the visible, that is, lacking visibility, but as the "unenvisageable" (GWB, 17). The latter does not *oppose* visibility and invisibility, since invisibility *here* cannot be reduced to the limits of the visible. Invisibility is no longer the darkness of something 'invisable,' but envisages us from beyond the simple distinction between visibility and invisibility—independent of the gaze gazing at the icon.

But how can the invisible envisage the visible? Because "it saturates the visibility of the face with meaning" (GWB, 21). This "meaning" is not something that we give to ourselves, but rather something that we have to receive, that comes to us from elsewhere: "contemplating the icon amounts to seeing the visible in the very manner by which the invisible that imparts itself therein envisages the visible—strictly, to exchanging our gaze for the gaze that iconically envisages us" (GWB, 21). The icon inverts the moments of the icon, amounting to an apocalyptic and perhaps violent exposure: "our gaze becomes the optical mirror of that at which it looks only by finding itself more radically looked at: we become a visible mirror of an invisible gaze that subverts us" (GWB, 22).

Not only does one encounter here a God, as we will later see in Levinas, who sees "with an eye that sees all" (ID, 30), and that, therefore, transpierces human beings as if they were objects, but one must also ask to what extent such a description delivers the phenomenological motive Marion was looking for. Indeed, it may be the case that one finds oneself being looked at while gazing at an icon, the fact remains that one can still splinter one's fingers when touching the wood of the painting. The icon *also* remains an ordinary object. Should not a genuine phenomenological account first admit this, and refrain from the 'spiritualization' of the crossing of the gazes? This is not to question the possibility of the iconic gaze, but to question whether it occurs independently of the objects in which appears, and to suggest that there would not be an invisibility as such *without* the visibility of the painted icon. In fact, if the 'same beings can pass' from the idol to the icon, we are returned to the description of anamorphosis as "two phenomenalities in a single phenomenon" (BG, 350 n. 5), according to which the phenomenon can either appear as an object or as a saturated phenomenon. I do not contest the possibility of 'seeing otherwise,' since in our technological age such a possibility seems to be no less than an urgent matter, but I do contest the way in which Marion distinguishes between these two phenomenalities, for the statement that these phenomenalities succeed one another because they are "essentially different from one another" (BG, 124) seems to be an imposition rather than a phenomenological requirement. The problem is that, in the icon for instance, visibility and invisibility are no longer logical opposites precisely because such a logical and dialectical opposition is presupposed on another level: *first* one delineates a region of idols or objects, *only then* to propose another phenomenality that differs essentially from it. Such a decision, however, presupposes one or the other subject that oversees the available possibilities from a disengaged distance: it is only if one first defines our obsession with objects as a "visible prison" (BG, 187), closed in on itself, that one can delineate another region which can be set apart from it as 'essentially different.' It is only by stating first that the saturated phenomenon is *not* an object or contradicts it, that one, in a second move, can give an account of that which, supposedly, is devoid of any 'object-ness.'

However, following Levinas, the negation of something takes refuge in that which it negates (cf. *TI*, 41; *OB*, 18), which is to say that the negation or evoking of the contradiction with objective intentionality does not suffice to escape the logic of objectivity. Therefore, one can legitimately suspect the saturated phenomenon to still be indebted to that which it contradicts, namely, the object. Here is the reason why Caputo, as we had seen earlier, can say that Marion trades on a positivistic sense of the gift: not only must the presence of an ordinary object be invoked to describe what possibly 'escapes' it, but it is also because of this unavowed negation of immanence (in this case: the visible object) that Marion must return to a mysterious 'other gift' that is supposed to explain why anything appears as giveable. This 'other gift' without being can only be put to work if one first has negated being and its visibility. In other words, the negation of ordinary visibility opens the door for invoking invisible instances of whatever kind.

One can indeed ask whether Marion has not left here the terrain of phenomenology proper, and query whether, from a phenomenological perspective, one should not say that these two phenomenalities happen at the same time. After all, if the work of art gives itself in the effect it has on consciousness, it is nevertheless also the case that this effect 'without being' would not have occurred without the presence of the work of art as a simple object or being. Therefore, to escape the logical opposition of the saturated phenomenon and the object, it is perhaps necessary to argue for their occurring *simultaneously*. Only then does one avoid the dialectical opposition of the saturated phenomenon and the object, which implies a subject overseeing them at distinct moments in time: it is not that one *either* 'sees' a saturated phenomenon *or* one sees an object—the one always at the expense of the other—rather, from a phenomenological perspective, one should say that when confronted with a phenomenon of excess, one is also and still immersed with the ordinary visibility of objects. In this case, the relation between objects and saturated phenomena would not be mutually exclusive, but interdependent. In the latter case, one is confronted with a situation that demands to be interpreted phenomenologically and hermeneutically: the saturated phenomenon would then no longer be the simple negation of the visibility of the object, but would take into account its dependency and its incarnation in the visibility of the ordinary object. This entails a more sober phenomenology than the ones endlessly hailing the excess of certain phenomena, and amounts to the recognition that no matter how excessive the bedazzlement one undergoes, one is, from the perspective of phenomenology and finitude, still obliged to consider such an excess from out of our encounter with ordinary visibility.

How to Avoid a Subject and an Object: Levinas' 'Relation without Relation'

I hope to have shown that, both on the part of finitude and on the pole of the excess, a metaphysical mode of procedure recurs. First, the subject (*adonné*) is to be blamed for the nonappearance of the saturating givenness, and second, even if this givenness would consist in a hyperappearing—the visibility *of* the invisible beyond ordinary visibility—this hyperappearance would nevertheless presuppose the presence of the ordinary object. This hyperappearance, then, functions only if a contradiction or a negation with the visibility of the ordinary object is entertained. Prior to our case study on the miracle in Marion's work, I had already pointed to the recurrence of the subject-object distinction. This recurrence underlined our hypothesis that a reversal of intentionality does not amount to a decentering of the subject at all. On the contrary, such a recurrence merely transposes the problem of the subject to another instance that takes on the contours of the subject. In Lacoste's work, human beings become the object of God's intention, and in Marion's work the human being is the object and objective of the counterintentionality of givenness (and/or God). The problem then is that the decentering of the subject as it takes place in the authors under discussion remains trapped in the problem it wanted to resolve, that is, intentionality as a question of power. This question is not primarily a theological question. It *does* become theological and even a metaphysical question when this counter-intentionality is projected even upon God, as Marion does explicitly. For, again, it is not at all sure whether we must ascribe intentionality to God, and if we choose to do so, then we are again confronted with the question of intentionality as a question of power: for when a God 'that sees with an eye that sees all' rears its ugly head, how indeed can we avoid the conclusion that God's intentionality—whatever this may be—reduces everything that this intentionality encounters to the contours of an object? Does not this God render derisory the privacy, the identity, and the secret that the subject or the human being is? Could the relation between men and women to God be described otherwise? Is it possible to think the relation of women and men to God as an encounter between *singularities*, that is, as free and embodied agents? For this, it is necessary that transcendence is not indifferent to ontic and immanent differences and the spell and spiritualization of the 'without being' needs to be cast out.

The question concerning ontotheology is, obviously, left hanging when the decentering of the subject amounts to a mere reversal of the subject-object distinction. It is Levinas, then, who was well aware of this problem. Levinas' relation without relation seems, at first sight, to counter the problem with a mere reversal. According to Levinas, the signification that arises in the encounter with otherness is not a signification by relation to another term (*TI*, 261). The face of the other signifies of itself. This otherness, therefore, cannot and must not be described as, to use Lacoste's words, a sketch of signification relating to a full presence of that signification. If relationality is depicted in this way, 'relationship,' according to Levinas, is conceived of logically or dialectically,[35] and thought remains in the onto(theo)logical and metaphysical "objectivity characteristic of relations" (*OB*, 82). To Levinas' mind, such a relationality always strips at least one of the terms of the relationship of its singularity. Hence Levinas' attempt to think the other as other by means of a "defense of subjectivity" (*TI*, 26).

The 'defense of subjectivity' that is undertaken in *Totality and Infinity* is possible only if this subjectivity engages in a "relation without relation," a relation in which "the terms absolve themselves from relation" (e.g., *TI*, 50, 195). The 'relation without relation' is proposed to surpass intentionality and its simple inversion, with its recurrent terms *subject* and *object*. What is this 'relation without relation'? It is, as already indicated, a relation in which the terms withhold themselves from 'relation.' What, then, does this mean? Let us first say what it is *not*. It is not the knowledge of an object. Knowledge of an object, according to Levinas, is not unlike Greek anamnesis. Anamnesis indeed consists in an interplay between the 'same' and the 'other,' but in such a way that any teaching the same might receive from the other does not escape that which the 'same' *already* knows. That the table's fourth leg is green, for example, surprises me: I didn't know that it was green. Thus, the table is to a certain extent exterior and transcendent to my knowledge. Knowledge is, however, still a reduction to the same, i.e. an exteriority that must be understood in its relation to me, since perceiving that it has a green leg does not alter my prior knowledge of a table at all. The fact that the table's leg is green does not, in any way whatsoever, alter my view of a table in general. That is why, according to Levinas, the (Husserlian) transcendence of an object is merely a quasiexteriority: the surprise of its otherness will be undone by further investigation.

'Fusion,' the second type of relation that Levinas envisages, functions quite differently: this is a relationship in which the terms involved lose their independence altogether. Consider the following, admittedly rather awkward, example: I am so obsessed with dinner tables that I tend to avoid them completely. In that case, the table has me in its grip. I lose my independence to the point that I cannot even exist in a normal way. The alterity of the table prevents me from being myself. So, in this fusion, I cannot absolve myself from the relationship with the table, and the table, consequently, dissolves my singularity.

Thus, what Levinas seeks is a relation to transcendence that, on the one hand, *is* a relation to transcendence, that is, a relation to something other that cannot be reduced to the same, as was the case with anamnesis, and, on the other hand, a relation that prevents me from dissolving in the relation to transcendence altogether—as was the case with 'fusion.' The 'relation without relation' then prevents the terms involved from being simply antithetical (cf. *TI*, 148). This means that, in the relation to the transcendent, I (or the other) can no longer be interpreted as a term that makes up the relationship. The relationship is not between clearly definable terms, perceived (and defined, systematized) by someone or something that would be outside the relation as a spectator, but it is a relationship in which I (or the other) am no longer capable of perceiving myself as a term. 'Relation without relation' means that I am implicated in this relationship without there even being the possibility to remove myself from it, remove myself, that is, as a spectator would do. This means the bankruptcy of any theology that, through its thematization of transcendence, "assigns a term to the passing of transcendence" (*OB*, 5). Although I do not experience God in this world, I will, probably, if I am patient enough, in the next (Lacoste). The alterity of the phenomenon assigns me as the term and the objective of its givenness (Marion).

The 'relation without relation,' according to Levinas, only ever occurs in the encounter with the *face of the other*. The face is that which cannot be reduced to its form. If reduced to its form, this face, this ab-solute otherness of the other, is murdered. I consider the waiter solely as a waiter; I did not even hear his voice when he presented the menu. This other is reduced to a visible form and represented in and through his or her social role:[36] the representation of the other through an ego is a mastery from out of his or her context, that is, from out of that which the other has in common with me and makes him or her comparable to me. Representation, according to Levinas, presupposes the presence of a subject that, in its very epistemological operation, grasps that which is different from out of that which makes the other, in one way or another, the same as me. It is in this sense that the representation of the other disregards that which would make him or her, precisely as an individual, totally different from me. My intentional aim, that is, the other as my representation and the aim and terminus of intentionality, does not do justice to the other as other. The Other interrupts precisely this tendency, for in the relation to the other, however, I am involved in a relation in which the terms of that relationship are always *more* than just terms: it is "this surplus [. . . that] throws me outside of the objectivity characteristic of relations" (OB, 82). The face is a "signification without context" (TI, 23); it signifies *by itself*, that is, "not *by relation* to something" (TI, 261), to another term—as an object can only signify by relation to a subject or finitude only by relation to infinity.[37] The face's otherness, its transcendence, remains at a distance, and to be at a distance is the way of existing of the other (TI, 35). When the infinite comes to mind, it immediately starts to withhold itself; it refuses to be grasped as, for instance, an intentional aim. Indeed, such a terminus to transcendence's movement terminates this transcendence altogether. It is, with this movement, as if the logical paradox is brought to life: "The subject is the more responsible the more it answers for, as though the distance between it and the other increased in the measure that proximity was increased" (OB, 139–40)—Achilles can never catch up with the turtle!

Of course, the other 'term' of this relationship has to undertake a similar 'absolving oneself of relationship.' Levinas calls this somewhat peculiar relation toward the transcendent "Desire." At the opposite of this desire stands the *conatus essendi*, a being that only cares for its own being. It is as this sort of a *conatus* that I eat, drink, know, and live.[38] The face of the other interrupts these natural tendencies. Only now do I regard my comportment toward my being to be egoistic and unjust, since all I eat, drink, and know could have been given to the other. It is this shocking consciousness of my injustice toward the other that stirs up metaphysical desire in me. This desire is "beyond satisfaction" and "does not identify, as need does, a term or an end" (GP, 67). This concretely means that my duties toward the other are infinitely great. Since the other withholds himself or herself from relationship, there can be no privileged other toward whom my debt would be contracted once and for all. Even if I would suppose that I could help the other to the point that my help was no longer needed, I would still have to notice, in the face of this other, a reference to the other's other, to the whole of humanity (TI, 213). It is this that awakens this strange and shameful desire that "nourishes itself with its own hunger" (TI, 34; 179) and that approaches the other, as Achilles once did with the turtle, that is, while remaining separated from that which it approaches.

In Levinas' later works, one encounters a radicalized version of this 'relation without relation.' For instance, whereas in Totality and Infinity, the other still "resembles God" (TI, 293), in Otherwise than Being this linkage of the other and God is less evident. The terms absolving themselves from relationship absolve themselves so much so that God has to be understood as "other than the other" and even as "transcendent to the point of absence."[39] This is the reason why, in the concluding pages of Otherwise than Being, the human response to God is emphatically stressed: if God absolves from the relationship 'to the point of absence,' then there is no other possibility for me, if I want to testify to God's presence, than to testify. While I "can not count on any god" (OB, 154), God's transcendence "does not come to pass save through the subject that confesses or contests it" (OB, 156). The humble 'transcendence to the point of absence' disposes of no other means to 'present' itself in the world than the response to the other.

This testimony is the 'Here I am!' uttered toward the other to communicate to him or her my total passivity and exposition. And, not surprisingly, this 'I' is devoid of any assignable identity or content.[40] Recall that the representation through an ego started from that which the other and I have in common: the reduction of the other to the same is the epistemological relation of a subject to its object in which the latter is identified by the former, and the former somehow identifies itself through the latter: what allows a particular table to be seen, one will recall, is the essence of a table in general. This essence is extracted and abstracted from what different particular tables have in common. This abstracted essence, however, is decided in advance of seeing a particular empirical table. It becomes a universal a priori concept to which this or that empirical table has to correspond.[41] This is why Levinas portrays the subject as a movement of identification (TI, 36); in and through its encounter with objects, the subject remains chained to itself, to the eternal return of its own a priori representations. Therefore, in the relation toward the other, I cannot identify myself with or relate myself to the other, for he or she is absolutely different from me and in and through this difference resists all adequate representation on my part. I cannot identify myself with God, for, when confronted with the other, God seems to be absent. And I cannot identify myself with myself, for the appeal of the other has already summoned me outside of myself. And yet, it is I, and I alone, who am responsible for the other. It is this *election* that constitutes both the form and the content of my identity. In *Otherwise than Being*, the kenotic response to the other is extreme to the point of sheer horror; my kenotic identity is always pointing toward an other, as if my breath already is an usurpation of the other's place. *Who* I am is beyond any autoidentification (e.g. *OB*, 123). It is the other, who, prior to any choice of mine, has chosen me to respond.

Overcoming Ontotheology with Levinas

It is argued that in the case of Marion and Levinas, the relation to transcendence is conceived of within the metaphysical subject-object distinction. Therefore, one must wonder whether these thinkers really escape what Levinas called "the objectivity characteristic of relations." Indeed, a simple reversal of the terms *subject* and *object* would, in Levinas' view, amount to nothing other than yet another reduction of the other to the same. Indeed, one can easily show how the thought of Marion and Lacoste cannot avoid the pitfalls of what Levinas has called "abstract thinking" (*TI*, 103) and "formal logic" (*TI*, 180–81). That the relation to the transcendent, as Marion and Lacoste see it, is a relation between two 'simply antithetical' terms should be clear: 'subject' and 'object' are, for Levinas, the examples par excellence of an antithetical relation in which "the relation connects [. . .] terms that complete one another and consequently are reciprocally lacking to one another" (*TI*, 103). God, in this line of reasoning, is interpreted along the lines of modern subjectivity: a powerless object over against a powerful Subject (Lacoste), a clerk over against an almost autonomous givenness (Marion). It is clear too that both Marion and Lacoste 'assign a term to transcendence.' Such a termination of transcendence, according to Levinas, would amount to both a reduction of transcendence to the same, since this term is inevitably a *return* to the same and, in consequence thereof, to a form of complacency in relation to transcendence. Such a terminus to transcendence manifests itself when we interrogate Lacoste's and Marion's work with regard to the presence of complacency in the relation to the other and to the urgency required for the response to transcendence. While Levinas repeatedly says that in face of the other's destitution the words 'I believe in God' are to be conceived of as a waste of time (e.g. OB, 149), both Marion and Lacoste seem to drop these ethical urgencies altogether. Another example of complacency is present here. Whereas the liturgical experience suffers from its ethical under-determination to the point that one rightly accuses the believer that his or her desire for God makes him or her deaf to the misery of human beings, the responsibility toward the given in Marion's *Being Given* is not determined by any urgency whatsoever. And though one might agree with Marion when he rejects Levinas' exclusive emphasis on ethics, it is difficult to understand why such a rejection should downplay the character of urgency in the face of the neighbour's destitution.[42]

The "nonallergic" (*TI* 47, 197) relation without relation that Levinas proposes is a relation, not between terms that complement one another, but between instances that remain *kath'auto* or on their own, sufficient to themselves (*TI*, 103) without being reconciled in a dialectical or theoretical synthesis. The 'relation without relation' tries to think the finite as finite as much as it tries to think the other as other. And finitude, for Levinas, means, among other things, the fact that people eat and drink to maintain their being, or even that they are "capable of atheism" (*TI*, 58). In this relation, and contrary to the relations that are formal or dialectical, the finite is not an object for the infinite nor is the infinite an object—a theme or representation—for the finite. Finally, this relation without relation is perhaps the opportunity to think the finite and the infinite in a nonontotheological manner. Levinas notes that a theoretical attitude cannot conceive of the creature and creation otherwise than as a diminution of a transcendent Creator (cf. *TI*, 103). Indeed, why would an infinite and perfect being create an inferior being? It is surely of importance to note here that this diminution, in metaphysics, is almost automatically projected onto the materiality and finitude of embodied beings. Even in Greek philosophy, where there is no mention at all of creation in the Christian sense, this inferior being is marked by a longing to return to the full-presence of that from which it proceeds.[43]

The theoretical attitude thus immediately relates this inferior finitude to the superiority of the infinite: it complements the supposedly inferior finitude with the superiority of the infinite. By doing so, this attitude reveals that it is unable to think the finite on its own terms, as finite. The finite is understood in relation to the infinite and this relation is conceived of as a relation between an inferior and a superior instance. While metaphysics as ontotheology flees from contingency and finitude, Levinas has in mind a *positive* evaluation of both the finite—the finite, living, and embodied subject—and the infinite: the creature's finitude or its 'separation'—both capable of atheism and marked by the transcendent—belongs to the glory of the infinite. Levinas is quite clear on this: "Life is not comprehensible simply as a diminution, a fall [. . .]. The individual and the personal are necessary for Infinity to be able to be produced as infinite" (*TI*, 218). If this is the case, one cannot but be surprised by the recurrence of the thought of finitude and materiality as being, in one way or another, inferior to or a diminution of the transcendent. For Lacoste, we recall, the painful nonexperience of the believer is summoned to patience. Of course, in this way the nonexperience always points to an absolute future in which it will be liberated from its incompleteness. Levinas' view also helps to explain Marion's negative appraisal of (worldly) visibility, for it might be precisely this unavowed negation of immanence that might lie at the root of the problems of the concept of a reversal of intentionality.

In this respect, it is noteworthy that our analysis of Lacoste's work came up with a similar kind of dialectics, just as much as Marion sets off the saturated phenomenon over and against the ordinary object, so too we have yet to understand how Lacoste plays out the liturgical experience over and against (Heideggerian) being-in-the-world. Verhack, for instance, has argued that underlying Lacoste's distinction between the liturgy and the world is a misunderstanding of Heidegger's account of factical being-in-the-world: whereas for Heidegger our factical relation to the world is always and already an ecstatic opening of and towards the world, Lacoste tends, to interpret "human beings' confrontation [. . .] with the world [as] the consciousness of a limit which encloses one's own 'inherence.'"[44] Therefore, one must note that, just as Marion could place the saturated phenomenon *next to* the 'visual prison' of objectivity, so too must Lacoste distinguish in all too rigid a manner between the ecstatic relation *coram Deo* and the disenchanted, since closed, factical being-in-the-world, for it might be that the reversal of intentionality simply points to the fact that such a downplaying of immanence must be presupposed in order to delineate a region (of saturated phenomena, of the liturgical relation) which perpetually escapes the imprisonment and the closedness of worldly immanence.

On this account, it would thus seem that Levinas' account of transcendence is better armed towards the criticism of a reversal I am raising here against Lacoste and Marion. Nevertheless, one should not forget that it is Marion who, already in his earlier work, raised a similar question towards the thought of Levinas, towards the Levinas of *Totality and Infinity* that is.[45] It is, according to Marion, Levinas' conception of the Saying—at the time of *Otherwise than Being*— that "cannot be confused any longer with a reversal of the terms inside the ontological difference to the benefit of beings."[46] Such a confusion was indeed addressed by Marion's *The Idol and Distance* in which he argued, roughly, that the Other in Levinas came to occupy the position of a privileged being and that such a move would reinforce metaphysical reasoning rather than constituting a break-through as regards its overcoming.[47] Marion thus seems to point to the problem that I already perceived in Marion's own work and in that of Lacoste: just as givenness and God would come to occupy the position of an autonomous instance, so too the Other in Levinas would play the role of a privileged being, which accounts for all other beings and grounds their manner of being in advance. The fact *that* I 'am' in face of the other stems from the very existence of the highest being which is the Other. But this Other would also determine the 'what' of my being in its entirety, my 'way of being' as it were: my being is in its entirety directed toward the attending to the Other.

One should note, however, that Marion has largely abandoned this criticism of Levinas later in his work. For this, it is important to note just what is at issue here. In *The Idol and Distance*, Marion is seeking a way to surpass the ontological difference without abandoning it altogether and without, as Marion claims Levinas does, "following its example" (*ID*, 220). Marion thus queries for a "metaphysical extraterritoriality"[48] which would institute a proper distance to the question of being: an "exterior terrain exceeds the exteriority of E. Levinas, it seems, in that it would not mobilize [. . .] Being and beings, but would reinscribe them in a place of exteriority [that] would situate and relativize them" (*ID*, 220). Such a situating and relativization, however, Marion will later argue, can occur *while* maintaining the one or the other privileged being.[49]

Marion's objection to Levinas is important in several respects. First, it teaches us not to be too satisfied with Levinas' account of a 'relation without relation,' since it might be that this account of the Other, at least at the time of *Totality and Infinity*, might indeed be subject to a similar reversal as I am trying to detect in Marion's and Lacoste's work. It is, thus, more than obvious that a critical examination of Levinas' thought is at issue. For this, one needs to keep an eye on Levinas' debate with Derrida, not only because Derrida will indeed argue that such a reversal might be at stake in *Totality and Infinity* but also because Marion's concessions toward the Levinas of *Otherwise than Being* seems to be largely dependent on Levinas' debate with Derrida on precisely this issue of ontotheology. It is then obvious, as well, that we will have to delve more deeply into the question concerning ontotheology, since we will need to understand why it is not so much the fact that there still is a privileged being that ought to concern us, but rather the ways in which such a being, whatever it might be, is erected. This will become clear once Derrida's "Violence and Metaphysics" is examined in the next chapter: for as much as the I, in Lacoste and Marion, is turned into the intentional aim of either givenness or God, so too the Levinasian other might be construed as an autonomous intentionality aiming at the ego and turning it into, merely, "a theme," in short a *noema*, an idea, "attended to by the other" (*TI*, 86). For this, a slow and patient reading of Levinas' development is in order. This development, however, was fueled by a criticism of Derrida, and it is this criticism that informed Marion's understanding of Levinas at the time of *The Idol and Distance* and made him wonder, as it will make us, about the peculiar status of *Otherwise than Being*.

Chapter 5

Levinas

Substituting the Subject for Responsibility

I concluded the previous chapter by focusing on Levinas' 'relation without relation.' In this chapter, I will expand upon that notion by pointing to the role of language in this peculiar relation, especially given the fact that Marion grants Levinas' account of 'the Saying,' thus of language, an exceptional status when it comes to the question of ontotheology.

The central role of language with regard to the otherness of the other offers one of the peculiarities of Levinas' thought and deserves our attention here because it is one of the main lines of argument for thinking through that which Levinas wanted to think in his entire oeuvre: the concrete human being. For, as much as 'Le Je pense transcendental' does not speak, and is the word of no one, so Heidegger's *Dasein* "is never hungry" (resp. *TI*, 299, 134), and in order to "nourish the hunger of another" (*OB*, 56), one needs to think human subjectivity in its very flesh and blood, "having hands for giving" (*GDT*, 188). It is indeed in this movement of giving to the other that Levinas will recognize the legitimacy of representation.

After the presentation of the role of language in Levinas' philosophy, I will point to the limits of Levinas' account of the decentering of subjectivity. For this, I will probe into Derrida's critique of Levinas in his famous essay, "Violence and Metaphysics," for it is well known that it is through this essay that Derrida rejected the 'absoluteness' of the other's alterity. The Other, according to Derrida, can never be, as Levinas wants, an absolute other but is always other in and through his or her appearing *to me*. It is in this way that I take Derrida's essay as paradigmatic for this attempt here to put some question marks around these dichotomies that try to erect a universal

givenness 'without remainder' of being and immanence (Marion) or try to
envisage a liturgy that would like to abandon our finite world altogether
(Lacoste), or even around, who knows, that otherness in Levinas that wants
to be 'uncontaminated by being.'

Language and the 'Relation without Relation'

For Levinas, the relation without relation only occurs in language and
expression: "a relation between terms that resist totalization, that absolve
themselves from the relation [. . .] is possible only as language" (TI, 97).
Language, our speaking to one another, would be the ultimate fact for Levinas,
underlying both Heidegger's emphasis on the being of a being and Husserl's
stress on the constitution of objects. Against Heidegger, Levinas contends
that "to affirm the priority of Being over beings is [. . .] to subordinate the
relation with someone, who is a being, [. . .] to a relation with the Being
of beings, which, impersonal, permits the apprehension, the domination of
beings" (TI, 45).[1] Levinas raises the same objection, that of an improper
priority of epistemology over ethics, against Husserl. Levinas contends, as
did Marion, that "thought remains an adequation with the object" (TI, 27).
Though Levinas praises phenomenology, he makes a move similar to that of
Marion when saying that "in the Husserlian phenomenology [. . .] horizons
are interpreted as thought aiming at objects" (TI, 27).[2] Thus we find Levinas'
statement that "the difference between objectivity and transcendence will
serve as a general guideline for all the analysis of this work" (TI, 49). The
object, as an *adequate representation* by the subject, "is a determination of
the other by the same, without the same being determined by the other"
(TI, 170, also 124). Of course, "the I that thinks the sum of the angles
of a triangle is [. . .] also determined by its object; it is precisely the one
that thinks of this sum" (TI, 125) and not, for instance, something else.
But this way of determining the I is determining the I "without touching
[it], without weighing on [it]" (TI, 124); in short, the object "gives itself,
that is, delivers itself over to him who encounters it as though it had been
entirely determined by him" (TI, 123, mod.)—the object cannot keep a
secret. The subject, then, remains unaffected by that which it thinks: within
the light and the perspective of a horizon "intelligibility [. . .] is a total
adequation of the thinker with what is thought, in the precise sense of a
mastery exercised by the thinker" (TI, 123–24). Levinas adds finally: "[T]
his mastery is total and as though creative; it is accomplished as a giving of

meaning: the object of representation is reducible to noemata" (*TI*, 124), to a function of thought itself. In this reduction, (Husserlian) phenomenology again "leads to transcendental philosophy, to the affirmation [. . .] that the object of consciousness, while distinct from consciousness, is as it were a product of consciousness" (*TI*, 123).

Yet Levinas does not abandon intentionality altogether, although intentionality in Husserl's sense as the correlation of *noesis* and *noemata* "does not define consciousness at its fundamental level" (*TI*, 27) and is not its "primordial structure" (*TI*, 294). What, then, does define this primordial structure? "We have reserved the term intentionality, consciousness of . . ." Levinas admits, "to [. . .] the attention to speech or welcome of the face, hospitality and not thematization" (*TI*, 299), for "thematization and conceptualization [are] suppression or possession of the other" (*TI*, 46). And this attention to speech is "attention to something because it is always attention to someone" (*TI*, 99). Intentionality as consciousness of . . . , which in Husserl always takes the contours of an object, is thus for Levinas possible only on the basis of the more primordial "relationship with the Other as interlocutor, [a] relation with a *being*" (*TI*, 48) preceding ontology as well as epistemology. The theoretical relationship is according to Levinas derived from the relation with another human person. This is one of Levinas' most basic intuitions and insights: no matter how abstract and erudite philosophical or other discourses are, for such a discourse to have meaning at all, this discourse and its theories will always have to be communicated to another human being. Signification or meaning only arises in interhuman relationships. Take, for instance, a glass of water on my desk. I can consider this glass as an object and make an inventory of its material components. I can just as well use the glass to drink and thus state and enact the fact that the glass is ready-to-hand. As much as the hammer serves for hammering (Heidegger), so the glass before me is used to drink of it. But when an other enters the room, the situation changes: I will have to get up, offer him or her a drink, communicate what I was thinking about, and endure his or her replies: "[T]he explanation of a thought can only happen among two" (*TI*, 100 mod.).

Levinas likens this emphasis on the basic fact of language, this "saying to the Other" (*TI*, 48), to the way in which perception, "to believe the phenomenologists" (*TI*, 53), lays the basis for the scientific enterprise (also *TI*, 58). Given the references to Merleau-Ponty in Levinas' work, one is returned to the former's description of the derived nature of scientific theories vis à vis concrete perception: "classical science is a form of perception which loses sight of its origins and believes itself complete. The first philosophical act would appear to be to return to the world of actual experience which is prior to the objective world, since it is in it that we shall be able to grasp the theoretical basis no less than the limits of that objective world."[3] Language and expression thus play the role of the revelation and the manifestation of the other. Why? Because not only do I not know what the other is going to say but also because I am unable to reduce the other to just what he or she says:

> Manifestation *kat'auto* consists in a being telling itself to us [se dire à nous] independently of every position we would have taken in its regard, expressing itself. Here, contrary to all the conditions for the visibility of objects, a being is not placed in the light of another but [. . .] is present as directing this very manifestation [. . .]. The absolute experience is not disclosure but revelation: a coinciding of the expressed with him who expresses, which is the privileged manifestation of the Other, the manifestation of a face over and beyond its form. Form—[. . .] adequate to the same—alienates the exteriority of the other. [. . .] The life of expression consists in undoing the form in which a being, exposed as a theme, is thereby dissimulated. [. . .] This way of undoing the form adequate to the Same so as to present oneself as other is to signify or to have a meaning. To present oneself by signifying is to speak. (*TI*, 65–66; *TeI*, p. 37)

Here we encounter Levinas' strict distinction between the face and the form. Unlike the object, which always appears in the light of a certain horizon and thereby is forced to give itself according to the position that the subject takes in its regard, the other is the master of its own manifestation, always able to take his words back, to unsay what has been said. Contrary to the objects that give themselves to a certain interpretation and horizon, "the Other who expresses himself precisely does *not* give himself" (*TI*, 202). The other appears on his or her own terms, in his or her own light, and is, so to speak, his or her own horizon.

Language thus effectuates a relation without the mediation of a horizon or, in Levinas' terms, a "signification without a context" (*TI*, 23). Such a horizon and a context here would mean that one is confronted with the other from out of that which the other and I would have in common, and what I can know or take in in concepts of him or her. This means that the other would be determined from out of his or her relation to me and my position towards him or her. The representation or the image one can make of the other disobeys the distance which is the way of life of the other: "[T]he distance [. . .] enters into the way of existing of the exterior being. Its formal characteristic, to be other, makes up its content" (*TI*, 35).

Levinas expands this line of reasoning when speaking of language: as much as the other always differs from our representations of a certain horizon, so the expression of the other may not be reduced to just what the other says: "the first content of the expression is the expression itself" (*TI*, 51). This is why Levinas envisions this relation with the other as teaching: since the otherness of the other constitutes the content of the existence of the other to such an extent that the other never coincides with what he or she says or with what we picture of him or her, approaching "the Other in conversation is to welcome his expression, in which at each instant he overflows the idea a thought would carry away from it. It is therefore to receive from the Other beyond the capacity of the I, which means [. . .] to be taught" (*TI*, 51). The *representation* of the other is for Levinas an injustice toward the other's transcendence. It denies the uniqueness and the individuality of the other and cannot recognize the "flight out of concepts" (*OB*, 126 *et passim*) constitutive of the fact of being always and already implicated in the encounter with the neighbor. The transcendence of the other thus lies in the fact that he or she is in no way whatsoever comparable to me: "there is no ipseity common to me and the others" (*OB*, 127). The encounter with the other is an asymmetrical encounter and always surpasses what the subject may feel, know, or presuppose in any other way. This is why the other, in the language of *Totality and Infinity*, is able to teach me, not in the sense that Socrates' maieutics attributed to it as the awakening of that which was already dimly present in the subject, but in instructing that which the subject did not *already* know. Teaching in this sense is for Levinas the mark of transcendence, the mark of the other's height—an absolute difference different from all other, ontic, differences between the other and I. And yet, Levinas' account of 'representation' is more nuanced than is often acknowledged.

Levinas and the Critique of the Critique of Representation

This emphasis on language will position Levinas with regard to both Husserl and Heidegger. Against Heidegger, Levinas will argue that " 'pure objectivity'

[as] a residue of this practical finality [ready-to-hand, JS] from which it would derive its meaning" underestimates the objectivity of the object" (cf. *TI*, 94). Levinas thinks, for reasons that will become obvious below, that "the ancient thesis that puts representation at the basis of every practical behavior [. . .] is too hastily discredited" (ibid.). Against Husserl, Levinas will argue that the objectivity of the object is overestimated and even extended in an improper manner to the thinking of the divine. Considering signification solely as a theoretical act of a monadic subject, or seeing "in the cogito a subjectivity without any support outside of itself, this cogito constitutes the idea of infinity itself and gives it to itself as an object" (*TI*, 211). Levinas will therefore choose midway between Husserl and Heidegger and derive the relations with objects and objectivity from out of the relation with the other. This relation with the other cannot do without objects and objectivity, and it is here that we will need to recognize that Levinas is not simply reiterating the critique of representation and why "the overcoming of the subject-object structure" is considered to be by Levinas "an *idée fixe* of all contemporary thought" (*HAM*, 17, mod.).

Let us start with Levinas' argument against Heidegger. For Heidegger, one will recall, the ontic realm of everyday experiences needs to be utterly separated from the more fundamental ontological realm. The ontic region of *Dasein* testifies to a more basic ontological structure, which is present in our ontic everydayness only in a dim or 'implicit' manner. The task of fundamental ontology, therefore, is to bring to the fore these implicit dimensions and make them explicit. If you like, this is how a phenomenological reduction operates: one makes certain things disappear in order to let others appear; one unravels the, in a certain sense, superfluous clothing of a phenomenon to make the phenomenon appear in its naked that and how it is. In *Being and Time*, for instance, the preoccupations of everyday *Dasein* in the realm of '*Das Man*' ('the They') are considered to be a covering over of the brute and naked fact that *Dasein* is and has to be its being. In our everyday occupations, the world is like a mirror[4] that reflects and fills, but thereby also obfuscates, the 'empty' structures of the being of one's being human. This ontological structure is, more or less, the fact that I *am*, and cannot but be, the span between my birth and my death. This is why, in *Being and Time* at least, anxiety plays such a central role. When anxious, the ties that tie us to our worldly occupations are loosened to such an extent that the world no longer reflects or mirrors the meaning of our existence. On the contrary, in anxiety it is precisely these worldly occupations that lose their meaning. However, from a phenomenological perspective, this loss is at the same time a gain:

the disappearance of idle talk and the busyness of everydayness allow one of *Dasein*'s most central features to appear: the fact that I have to be my being, once thrown into a world.[5] This is what Heidegger calls *"Jemeinigkeit,"* mineness. Note here already that the tendency to fall (*Verfallen*) is *not* brought to a halt: whereas 'inauthentic' *Dasein* understands itself from out of the world and its preoccupations in it, 'authentic' *Dasein* does not leave behind this understanding of itself from out of the world. On the contrary, it understands itself *as* this mirroring: what appears is that *Dasein* is and has to be his or her world. In short, *Dasein is* his or her world *as* world.

As Lacoste, we find in Levinas therefore a similar wariness towards the 'ontologism' of Heidegger.[6] By 'ontologism,' Levinas understands the very fact of reducing all things ontic (for instance eating, drinking, etc.) to the ontological structure of care. Levinas' wariness concerns the fact that the very being of the being human cannot and must not be understood from out of such an ontological but empty and 'naked' structure. Such an ontologism risks interpret,ing according to Levinas, the human being as merely *a* being among others. Levinas asks: "How would a total reflection be allowed [to] a being that never becomes the bare fact of existing, and whose existence is life, that is, life from something" (*TI*, 154)?

Levinas' response to Heidegger, then, runs somewhat like this: "The method practiced here does indeed consist in seeking the condition of empirical situations, but it leaves to the developments called empirical, in which the conditioning possibility is accomplished—it leaves to the *concretization*—an ontological role that specifies the meaning of the fundamental possibility, a meaning invisible in that condition" (*TI*, 173; Levinas' italics). Three things must be noted. First, at the time of *Totality and Infinity*, Levinas still adheres to Heidegger's project of a 'fundamental ontology,' in the sense of seeking a condition that precedes and lays bare the sense and signification of that which we empirically do.[7] Second, Levinas disagrees from Heidegger with respect to the conception of the *relation* between the empirical or the 'ontic' and the condition of possibility of the empirical—the 'ontological.' Whereas for Heidegger our ontic preoccupations are indeed to be conceived of as the concrete accomplishment or attestation of the ontological condition of possibility, these attestations as such do not add or alter anything to the fundamental, ontological possibility. For instance, for Heidegger, the fact that we eat and drink is, if you like, merely an instantiation or actualization of the more basic structure of care. Third, Levinas reserves an 'ontological role' for diverse empirical situations; that is, these empirical conditions allow something of the being of the being human to *appear* as such but they remain invisible or do not appear from out of fundamental ontology itself. For Levinas it is precisely the resistance of the human subject to such a reduction to a complete and total ontological structure that makes up the being of the human being. Again Levinas points to the fundamental fact of speech and says that "otherwise than being catches sight, in the very hypostasis of the subject, an outside of the absolute which can no longer be stated in terms of being [or] beings [. . .] The subject already resists this ontologization when it is conceived as a saying" (OB, 17–18, mod.). It is not because there is ontology that we speak; it is rather because of our speaking to one another that there is ontology. For Levinas, however, this resistance to ontology and its tendency toward totalization attest to the positive aspect of the subject's separation—its being irreducible to the unity and monism of being: "[T]he impossibility of a total reflection must not be posited negatively—as the finitude of a knowing subject who, being mortal and already engaged in the world, does not reach truth—but rather as the surplus of the social relation" (TI, 221).

This social relation will then need objects and objectivity in order to be able to welcome the other not with empty hands. Against Husserl, Levinas will return the theoretical act of constitution to its proper region, pointing to the region from which the theoretical relation emerges in the first place, life. But life, for Levinas, lives from the enjoyment of the things surrounding this life. Consciousness as consciousness of . . . —intentionality—has as its roots the life we lead as life from . . . (something). But this 'something' must not be understood as an object, but rather as what Levinas calls 'the elemental' or the *milieu* in which one breathes and takes one's stand: "The relation with my site in this 'stance' precedes thought and labor. [It] nowise resembles idealist representation. I am myself, I am here, at home with myself, inhabitation, immanence in the world" (TI, 138). Husserl's turn to transcendental phenomenology and idealism is thus countered by retrieving the condition for the activity of representation and constitution. This condition, according to Levinas, is first and foremost the building of and the dwelling in a home. It is due to the fact that we live somewhere and from something that we will be able to think and not the other way around. The home, for Levinas, counts as the "first concretization" (TI, 153). One "can formulate it in this way: the consciousness of a world is already consciousness *through* that world" (ibid.). For Levinas as for Marion, it is not the I or the ego that constitutes the whole of reality, but on the contrary, it is the subject that finds itself constituted by the reality in which it finds itself constituting. This explains why Levinas calls the critique of the subject-object distinction an *"idée fixe"* of contemporary thought. Levinas does not deny the subject's right to representational thinking but will localize it, as we will see below, in the concrete relations with the other. Finding a condition of possibility for the idealist subject that considers itself as the condition of possibility for whatever appears, will come to mean for Levinas that "[i]ts transcendental pretension is constantly belied by the life that is already implanted in the being representation claims to constitute. But representation claims to substitute itself after the event for this life in reality, so as to constitute this very reality" (*TI*, 169). According to Levinas, the fact that representation has the pretence to proclaim itself to be the *condition* of this life itself accounts for the "eternal temptation" of idealism (ibid.).

What would, to Levinas' mind, this temptation be? The answer to his question lies in the fact that representation substitutes itself after the event of living from something for this very life itself. Nevertheless, Levinas will value this peculiar temporal character of thought positively, for it attests the subject's separation and independence. Levinas points to the way in which Descartes discovers the cogito: "[T]he discovery of this metaphysical relation [the idea of the infinite, JS] in the cogito constitutes chronologically only the second move of the philosopher. That there could be a chronological order distinct from the "logical" order, that there could be several moments in the progression [. . .]—here is separation" (*TI*, 54).

Indeed, in Cartesian philosophy, the cogito itself is the first on the scene, without any other evidence than its own presence to itself. That the cogito is subtended by God as its cause is only discovered afterward, after the *fundamentum inconcussum* of the cogito itself. Whereas in the logical order the cause—God—precedes its effect, the chronology is reversed with respect to the order of thinking: the effect, that is, the cogito, discovers its cause, God, from itself. "The present of the cogito, despite the support it discovers for itself after the fact in the absolute that transcends it, maintains itself all by itself—be it only for an instant, the space of a cogito" (ibid.). It is this reversed chronology that grants the subject the secret of its interiority, its interior life invisible to others—its possibility to have, as it were, second thoughts. This interiority is possible only because the subject has a temporality of its own, distinct from the time of historians, who precisely disregard the interiority of the subject by describing it from the outside. "For by virtue of time this being is not yet—which [. . .] maintains it at a distance from itself" (ibid.).

The temptation of idealism would thus, first, be that precisely this temporal character is effaced from the act of representing itself:

"Representation is a pure present. The positing of a pure present without even tangential ties with time is the marvel of representation. It is a void of time, interpreted as eternity" (*TI*, 125). Though this "illusion" (ibid.) is to be valued positively, since it attests the subject's separation, it stumbles upon the reality of the body and the corresponding position and place upon the earth. Though "at the very moment of representation the I is not marked by the past [. . .] the I who conducts his thoughts becomes (or more exactly ages) in time" (ibid.). It is this a-temporal character of representation, in which it becomes "essentially memory" (*TI*, 169), that *Otherwise than Being* will denounce. For consciousness, forever in search of time lost, operates precisely with the presupposition that the time lost can be recuperated and represented, and so forgets "the absolutely passive 'synthesis' of ageing" (*OB*, 38), in which "self-consciousness [. . .] is no longer a presence of self to self, but senescence. It is as senescence beyond the recuperation of memory that time, lost time that does not return, [. . .] concerns me" (*OB*, 52).[8]

Second, the temptation of idealism resides in the forgetting of even the conditions of constitution: though "by virtue of the [interiority of] the psychism the being that is in a site remains free with regard to that site" (*TI*, 54), "the idealistic subject [. . .] constitutes a priori its object and *even the site* at which it finds itself" (*TI*, 153, mod.). The idealistic subject thus posits itself as a worldless (better: site-less) ego and disregards, after the fact, the habitation and the body as the condition of possibility of thought itself. Nevertheless, for Levinas, the body counts as "the 'how' of separation" (*TI*, 163). It seems that Levinas' analysis of enjoyment and happiness from out of the habitation of the separated being is exposed to two risks. Enjoying the element, the separated being is determined as the realization of its *independence in and through the dependency* of that which the element has to offer (e.g., food, etc). But the separated being runs the risk both of substituting its independence for dependency upon the element, and, vice versa, the risk of substituting its dependency on the element for complete independence. While the latter seems to correspond to the 'temptation of idealism,' the former is the risk undertaken by a being who sacrifices "its [. . .] being to happiness" (*TI*, 63) and who thus betrays its independence by depending too much upon the pleasures of the element. In this "betrayal" the subject's mastery is inverted into enslavement and sickness (cf. *TI*, 164). An addiction can serve as an example of this, since, once addicted, the subject's separation tends to fusion with that to which the subject is addicted, and so to the loss of independence.

But if Levinas does not dismiss representations altogether, then in what does the role of representation reside? For, surprisingly, one finds Levinas saying that the very concrete analysis of enjoyment "does not render the concrete man. In reality man already has the idea of infinity, that is, lives in society and represents things to himself" (*TI*, 139). Living in society with the other, therefore, renders the weal and the woe of concrete women and men.

Representation and Kenosis: *Giving* to the Other

The subject is, however, not only capable of 'sacrificing its being to happiness,' the subject can also "sacrifice to its Desire its very happiness" (*TI*, 63). This desire, as we have seen, is distinct from the logic of need and is immersed in an endless movement of giving to the other. Levinas' insight is that the other introduces a new event in the subject's relation to oneself: "Desire [presupposes] a relationship in which the Desirable [. . .] puts an end to power and emprise. This is positively produced as the possession of a world I can bestow as gift on the Other—that is, as a presence before a face. For the presence before a face, my orientation toward the Other, can lose the avidity proper to the gaze only by turning into generosity, incapable of approaching the other with empty hands" (*TI*, 50). Just as for Lacoste liturgy is engaged in a logic of the surplus, a night of "inoperativity" (*EA*, 80) opposed to the useful logic of everyday ethics, so Levinasian ethics is constructed as a possibility for a being that lacks nothing. Indeed, the signification and the orientation the other imposes on the subject does "not arise because the same has needs, because he lacks something [. . .]. Signification is in the absolute surplus of the other with respect to the same who desires him, who desires what he does not lack" (*TI*, 97). The kenosis enacted in the giving to the other is therefore the kenosis of a being that lacks nothing but which has plenty to give: "[H]aving recognized its needs as material needs, as capable of being satisfied, the I can henceforth turn to what it does not lack. It distinguishes the material from the spiritual, opens to Desire" (*TI*, 117). It is in desire that representation and knowledge find the role suited for it, since it is only in the presence of the other to the same that the I finds itself in face of the world, better: through the face of the other in face of the world. The relation with the other "is not produced outside the world" (*TI*, 173) or "outside of economy" (*TI*, 172). It is only in this social relation that knowledge—ontology, epistemology—arises. It is, again, through language that we encounter objects: in and through language the subject can speak both *about* something and give *something* to the other. "Objectivity [. . .] is posited in a discourse, in a conversation which proposes the world" (*TI*, 96). In discourse, as distinct from sensibility and enjoyment, things acquire "fixity," a "name," and an "identity" (*TI*, 139). This "subsistance of th[e] world is [. . .] possible only through memory" (ibid.), or, in other words, consciousness. It is through consciousness and memory that we can speak of the same things in the same way: for instance, that "the same train is the train that leaves at the same hour" (ibid.). Levinas, therefore, does not simply join the contemporary critique of representations but allows for consciousness and representation[9] if and only if they are redirected toward the subject in ethical kenosis toward the other. Kenosis, for Levinas, only makes sense if there is something one *can* give to the other.

This reorientation of knowledge is, however, only possible on the basis of that which escapes all adequate representation, namely, the face of the other. "To represent to oneself that from which I live [. . .] implies a new event; I must have been in relation with something I do not live from. This event is the relation with the Other" (*TI*, 170). The face's appeal makes me face my world so to say. It operates a phenomenological reduction on the I: in expression, my quiet contentment of things disappears only to appear in a different light—under the accusation of the other. The other does not diminish my possibilities, but alters them and calls them to the Good.[10] "The presence of the Other [. . .] does not clash with freedom, but invests it" (*TI*, 88): either the subject will persevere in its being, or it will take this 'occasion' to turn to the Good by attending to the Other. From now on, the horizon of my being will be inscribed in the horizon of ethics. The latter option will be that of kenosis, for in function of the other's revelatory speech "the world is oriented, that is, takes on signification. In function of the word the world commences [. . .] the world is said and hence can be a theme, can be proposed" (*TI*, 98). Language, therefore, "designates [the thing] to the other, is a primordial dispossession, a first donation. The generality of the word institutes a common world [. . .] The relation with the Other does not only stimulate, provoke generalization [. . .] but is this generalization itself. Generalization [. . .] is not the entry of a sensible thing into a no man's land of the ideal [. . .] but is the offering of a world to the Other" (*TI*, 173–74).

It is this kenosis that is placed at the extreme in *Otherwise than Being*: it would be to fail to recognize the nonanonymousness of the for-another [. . .] to think that the giving can remain a simple expenditure of the acquisitions accumulated. [G]iving [. . .] takes on full meaning only in stripping me of what is *more* my own than *my possession*" (*OB*, 55–56). For the later Levinas, possession simply does not make me irreplaceable enough. On the contrary; possession counts merely as something that "can be common to me and another man, who thus would be capable of replacing me" (*OB*, 59). *Otherwise than Being* envisions a kenosis and openness "beyond that of the wallet—that of the doors of one's home" (*OB*, 74, mod.). This radicalization can also be illustrated by evoking another difference between *Totality and Infinity* and *Otherwise than Being*. Whereas in the first book, the appropriate response to the other's appeal is apology (*TI*, 219), the pleading of one's cause under the accusation of the other, in the latter book, all apologies the subject would come up with to justify itself in face of the other are disqualified. Whereas in *Totality and Infinity*, the subject can be said to *be* its apology in the sense that its duties toward the other are infinitely great, in *Otherwise than Being*, the self "cannot defend himself by language, for the persecution is a disqualification of the apology" (*OB*, 121).[11]

In the next section, I want to point, however, and with the help of Derrida, to what seems to be yet another parallel of the reversal of the subject-object distinction I perceived in the works of Lacoste and Marion.

Conclusion: Derrida and Levinas

Though we have seen that Levinas' relation without relation tries to avoid the simple dialectical relationship that attaches a subject to an object, it is important to note that although Levinas criticizes Heidegger's ontology and Husserl's intentionality for being philosophies of power, the question of power and violence can be raised to Levinas as well. In *Totality and Infinity*, one finds that while it is not so much the subject that exercises power over objects and/or the other, it is the Other whose claim is not as nonviolent as Levinas time and again has stated.[12]

Derrida was one of Levinas' first readers to attract attention to this. According to Derrida, "every philosophy of non-violence can only choose the lesser violence within an economy of violence."[13] Recall that, for Derrida, every critique of Western (and thus Greek) philosophy's emphasis on light and vision in the name of the prophetic voice stemming from Israel remains indebted to that very emphasis on the point that one can attack light only with light, its violence only by employing another violence, and so on. Hence Derrida questions why a transcendence that does not want to designate a spatial relationship still uses the word *exteriority*? Why would a philosophy that assaults the philosophies of light still speak of an 'epiphany'?[14]

Derrida's critique is perhaps most clear in his critique of the Levinasian critique of the Husserlian *alter ego*.[15] According to Husserl, it is on the basis of my own experiences that I determine the existence and the signification of the other's experiences. For example, if I see someone crying, I infer from seeing his or her tears that he or she must be sad, since I know that when I cry, I am sad. For Husserl, the other is an other ego, the other is *like* me. But, Levinas would add, such a conception presupposes that between the other and me there is room for comparison or at least a common horizon from which to judge our different experiences. And this horizon is, of course, my own. Derrida counters Levinas' quest for the other as an *absolute* other by stating that for Husserl the analogical appresentation of the other *is* already the development of respect for the other in his or her otherness: "It is the other as other which is the ego's phenomenon: the phenomenon of a certain non-phenomenality which is irreducible for the ego as ego in general [. . .]. For it is impossible to [. . .] respect [the other] in experience and in language, if this other, in its alterity, does not *appear* for an ego (in general). One could neither speak, nor have any sense of the totally other, if there was not a phenomenon of the totally other."[16] It is true, Derrida admits, that Husserl conceives of the other person as analogous to the transcendence of the object, with one crucial difference, however. Whereas in the case of the transcendence of the object, the 'adequate' knowledge of the object in question is possible by making further adumbrations of it, in the case of the transcendence of the other person, such adequation is out of the question, since "the alterity of the other, which is also irreducible [adds] to the dimension of incompleteness (the body of the other in space, the history of our relations, etc.) a more profound dimension of nonoriginality."[17] Although the other for Husserl is a phenomenon for the ego, this does not mean that the other is comparable to me or would in one way or another lose his or her alterity. On the contrary, it is just because of the fact that the other does not offer himself or herself to the completion of my perception (as an object does) that he or she remains inaccessible and irreducible to my ego: "the stranger is infinitely other because by essence no enrichment of profiles can give me the subjective face of his experience *from his perspective*, such as he lived it"—I can see that your body is similar to mine, but I cannot see what you think.[18] Thus, for Derrida as for Husserl, "the other as alter ego signifies the other as other, irreducible to my ego, precisely because it is an ego."[19] Derrida adds that "no dissymmetry would be possible without this symmetry,"[20] not even the one Levinas evokes. Hence Derrida's startling claim that "Levinas' metaphysics in a sense presupposes [. . .] the transcendental phenomenology that it seeks to put into question."[21] This transcendental symmetry, to be sure, is a return to the other as precisely an intentional phenomenon of the ego; this is "to give oneself over to violence, or to make oneself its accomplice at least, and to acquiesce [. . .] to the violence of fact; but in question, then, is an irreducible zone of facticity, an original, transcendental violence."[22] But, thinking the other from out of his or her appearance to (my) ego, Derrida wants to suggest, is to opt for the least violence possible or at least "the most peaceful gesture possible."[23] If it is a simple reversal of the subject-object scheme that is at issue, then it should be possible to localize this violent reduction of the same by the other, to show, in other words, that even in *Totality and Infinity* the relation with the other is *not* so incommensurate with a power exercized.

In her *L'envers de sujet*, Christine de Bauw has pointed to a similar problem. Commenting upon statements made by Levinas that the face of the other provokes ipso facto "the consciousness of guilt," "unworthiness" and "injustice" (*TI*, 83, 86), de Bauw asks whether "the term consciousness is not a return [. . .] to theoretical determinations"?[24] Furthermore, de Bauw asks how it is possible for the very idea of a reversed intentionality to make sense at all, if not for a subject to whom it appears: "in other words, there where Levinas introduces the idea of an inversion of intentionality to advance a radical passivity of the subject, must one not see, in that very inversion, the intervention of a certain subjectivizing activity"?[25] Indeed, the idea of an inverted intentionality *presupposes* the idea of a subject that represents to itself the experience, if any, of the other. De Bauw concludes that "a certain imprecision accompanies the notion of a 'consciousness of unworthiness.' Levinas underlines its non-theoretical character, but the notion [. . .] guards a reluctant status, still reminiscent of theoria: unworthiness presupposes an object (unworthy *of what?*) and a measure (unworthy *by relation to what or to whom?*)."[26] The latter sentence indeed suggests that Levinas' 'relation without relation' did not succeed in developing its nontheoretical character to the very end, in which case, it should be possible to locate the violence Levins attributes to theory in the very discourse of *Totality and Infinity*. In other words, is it possible to show that the role of the powerful, 'traditional' subject is never left altogether but simply repeated by another instance?

Note that this is the very same objection that I raised earlier against Marion and Lacoste. Robyn Horner, relying on John Milbank, mentions this argument:

a potential criticism of Marion's work is that it places the gaze of the infinite within the same frame as the observer. John Milbank undertakes an extensive analysis of the crossing of regards, which, he maintains, can only be supported by *a prior projection of the I.* The evidence is readily available in Marion's work. For example, he maintains that the other is like me in that each of us is characterized by an intentional 'aim.' Further, he speaks of my experience of the regard of the other as a 'weight,' but as a weight that is only recognized after I become aware of my obligation to the other [. . .] Marion's 'reverse intentionality' may be part of iconic theology, but it cannot be sustained phenomenologically without the (metaphysical) presumption that the Other is in some way like the Same, and, therefore, without the loss of the otherness of the Other.[27]

Though Horner's conclusion is somewhat at odds with Derrida's line of reasoning, the conclusion we need to draw is that one cannot maintain the idea of an inverted intentionality without presupposing the transcendental violence of a necessary appearance of the other to the ego. This will lead us to reconsider the decentering of the subject at issue in Marion and Levinas, since, to my knowledge, Marion has never subscribed to the critique of the alter ego as it occurs in Levinas,[28] and Levinas seems to have left this critique (in his later work, *Otherwise than Being*) altogether.

It remains to be shown just how the subject-object distinction occurs in Levinas' *Totality and Infinity.* That the relation without relation is not the relation 'incommensurate with a power exercised,' seems to be obvious, first, from the fact that it is time and again stated that the other "dominates" over the same: "The Other imposes himself as an exigency that *dominates* [my] freedom" (*TI*, 87).[29] Might it be that the presence of such a domination in the relation between the Same and the other simply points to the fact that Levinas is substituting one center, namely that of the egoistic I, for the other, the ethical other? The text seems to confirm this thesis: "The I, which we have seen arise in enjoyment as a separated being having apart, in itself, the center around which its existence gravitates, is confirmed in its singularity by purging itself of this gravitation, purges itself interminably, and is confirmed precisely in this incessant effort to purge itself" (*TI*, 244–45), which "tears consciousness away from its center by submitting it to the Other (*TI*, 207, mod.), so as to arrive at the I as a being whose responsibility "places the center of gravitation of a being outside of that being" (*TI*, 183).

Again, just as Marion maintains that the phenomenon giving itself of itself, *kath' auto*, "possesses phenomenality's center of gravity" (*BG*, 131), so too the other will, at least in *Totality and Infinity*, be erected as *another center* around which subjective existence gravitates.

It is here that one can notice the consequences of the linkage between the other and God: "the Other [. . .] resembles God" (*TI*, 293). Considered from this perspective, it is indeed striking how Levinas handles his metaphorical play with the mythological figure Gyges. Gyges, the one who sees without being seen, stands for the pretension of modern subjectivity to be autonomous, since the possibility of the separated being to maintain the secret of its interiority will occur at the cost of "unpunished crimes" (*TI*, 61), "of injustice and radical egoism" (*TI*, 173). Would it be a coincidence that at least *Totality and Infinity* orients the subject towards the other in such a way that it finds itself responsible before a God "who sees the invisible and sees without being seen" (*TI*, 244)? Is God Gyges? Or is God another other, perhaps even the *first* Other?

It seems, therefore, that Marion is right, then, when he, in *The Idol and Distance*, criticizes *Totality and Infinity* for being merely an inversion and therefore a continuation of the ontotheological tradition of a privileged being. Nevertheless, it is all the more strange that we could raise a similar criticism toward Marion and could point to the fact that givenness at times plays the role of another center turning the subject into its object and objective. The fact, however, that Marion abandoned this criticism in his "Note concerning Ontological Indifference," where he seems to allow that one privileged being—*me*, or the Levinasian 'Here I am'—escapes the absoluteness of the ontological difference, should makes us wonder whether the problem of the inversion of intentionality I am addressing here does not point to yet another problem, as if it were the side-effect of a yet more grave ill-ness. This is why I will, after Derrida's take on what this problem might be, turn to the Levinas of *Otherwise than Being* and, later, to Levinas' account of the ontological difference.

For it seems indeed the case that it is again Derrida who was the first to point to this problem in Levinas. It will be no surprise that Derrida formulates the same criticism of Levinas' treatment of Heidegger over against Levinas' critique of Husserl: "Just as [Levinas] had to appeal to phenomenological self-evidences against phenomenology, Levinas must ceaselessly suppose and practice the thought of precomprehension of Being in his discourse, even when he directs it against 'ontology.'"[30] Derrida goes on to list some citations in which Levinas shows his complicity to ontology in order to hint at Levinas' commitment to metaphysics as ontotheology: "By refusing in *Totality and Infinity*, to accord any dignity to the ontico-ontological difference, by seeing in it only a ruse or war, and by calling the intra-ontic movement of ethical transcendence (the movement respectful of one existent toward another) metaphysics, *Levinas confirms Heidegger in his discourse*: for does not the latter see in metaphysics (in metaphysical ontology) the forgetting of Being and the dissimulation of the ontico-ontological difference?"[31]

Levinas would thus do no more than persevere in the oblivion of being that, according to Heidegger, dominated Western philosophy. But Derrida's reasoning is more complex than that, for Derrida already announced the real stakes in a preceding note. Commenting upon a book of Birault, Derrida launches the following remark: "This [. . .] does not signify that the beyond of metaphysics is impracticable; on the contrary, it confirms the necessity for this incommensurable overflow to take support from metaphysics. A necessity clearly recognized by Heidegger. Indeed, it marks that only difference is fundamental, and that Being is nothing outside beings."[32] Therefore, if one wants to surpass metaphysics, one can only surmise what this might mean from *within* metaphysics, from *within*, to use Levinas' words, the logic of the same. The question of Being needs to be taken up from out of Being's appearance in and to beings. Levinas' ontotheology, according to Derrida, misses precisely this point: just as the other must appear in and to the same (contra Levinas' Husserl), so too the question of being can only be addressed from out of its historical 'epochal' determinations of beings (contra Levinas' Heidegger). This means that, from out of the ontological difference, the 'beyond' of metaphysics can never lead "beyond Being itself," but always only "beyond the totality of the existent or the existent-hood of the existent,"[33] that is, beyond the totality of beings or the being of a being. For metaphysics, according to Heidegger, is precisely that "which remains a closure of the totality, and transcends a being only toward the (superior) being, or toward the [. . .] totality of beings."[34] Approaching metaphysics from within means precisely that one cannot view that which one transcends, namely, the totality of beings, as it were from the outside or from a point beyond being that would not be *implicated* in (the) being (of beings) itself. In this sense, such a "beyond being" would only be able to be posited as another being *over against* the totality of beings. It would, first, delineate the totality *as* a totality—implying one or the other subject that is capable of overseeing such a totality—only then to mark an instance that is supposed to escape this totality permanently. This being, then, would ground the totality of beings in an a-historical fashion, that is, without taking sufficiently into account being's appearance in the historical unfolding of beings, and by simply presupposing a dualism and a dichotomy between the same (or being) and the other. It is to such a dichotomy that Derrida points Levinas when criticizing the 'intra-ontic movement of ethical transcendence' for propping "up thought by means of a transhistoricity."[35] And Derrida proceeds: "this anhistoricity of meaning at its origin is what profoundly separates Levinas from Heidegger, therefore. Since Being is history for the latter, it is *not* outside difference."[36] Just as Levinas interprets Heidegger's thinking of Being as an *arche* which is outside of beings as a sort of foreign power,[37] so too, it seems, does Levinas explore, at the time of *Totality and Infinity*, the link between the human other and God: God as a supreme being bestows the face of the human other with the power to appeal to the subject and put it into question. Hence Derrida's critique, for, in his words, "the question of Being is nothing less than a disputation of the metaphysical truth of this schema."[38] What Levinas proposes, therefore, is a very classical schema: "it is a question of attaining, via the royal road of ethics, the supreme being [. . .] ('substance' and 'in itself' are Levinas' expressions). And this being is man, determined as face in his essence as man on the basis of his resemblance to God. Is this not what Heidegger has in mind when he speaks of the unity of metaphysics, humanism and onto-theology? [. . .] 'The Other resembles God.' Man's substantiality, which permits him to be face, is thus founded in his resemblance to God, who is therefore both the Face and absolute substantiality."[39] And Derrida closes his critique of Levinas by pointing to his resemblance to the work of Nicholas of Cusa: "in the many different images of that face one face would appear in many different ways."[40]

    This reasoning of Derrida seems to offer some clarification on the problem of the inversion of intentionality I noted in the works of Marion, Lacoste, and, now, in the thought of Levinas, for the intraontic movement of ethics does indeed explain just why time and again another subject, that is, another being, appears in the discourses of the authors under discussion. The inversion of intentionality seems to be dependent upon another problem, since it time and again sets off one region of phenomenality against another region: just as Lacoste tries to utterly separate the atheistic realm of immanence from all things liturgical, and just as Marion's givenness seems to stand in need of a region of objectness, which it contradicts, so too then Levinas' account of the other posits a point 'beyond' being—the other—to delineate and 'dominate' the totality of beings—the same. Our problem, then, seems to reside more in the dichotomies that are instituted in this way, that is, between liturgy and world, between the object and the saturated phenomenon and finally between the same and the other, than in the fact that one can time and again perceive a subject, transcendental or not, appearing on the scene. Whether it be God, givenness, or the Other that surrounds, circumscribes, and 'sees with an eye that sees all,' common to these thoughts is what I call a "metaphysical mode" of procedure: at issue in each case is a certain disavowal and perhaps even a very classical negation of the immanence, visibility, and finitude of the world that is ours and that first allows these thinkers to delineate this immanence, closed in on itself, as standing apart from or next to the transcendence they are invoking. To illustrate this problem, we will later show to which point such a negation leads, that is, why the inversion of intentionality in each case results in what I call here "the objectification of the subject," in which the singularity of the human being is downplayed to such an extent that it *can* appear to be merely an object without secrets.

For now, it seems suited to ponder to what extent Derrida is perhaps a bit too hopeful when saying that the beyond of metaphysics is not impracticable, for as much as it is not possible to criticize phenomenology without presupposing phenomenology, and as much as it is impossible to criticize the primacy of being without presupposing in one way or another the comprehension of being, another thesis also comes into view: it may not be possible to criticize metaphysics without presupposing it.[41]

Otherwise *than Being*: Condemned to Be Good

Totality and Infinity in Light of Otherwise than Being

We have seen Milbank's and Horner's formulation of the problem of the recurrence of the subject, a suspicion that also seemed to play a role in Derrida's extensive analysis of *Totality and Infinity*: it is only because of a 'prior projection of the I' that Marion's reversal of intentionality in the crossing of the gazes is put to work. Similarly, de Bauw mentioned that the occurrence of statements as 'consciousness of unworthiness' pointed to a residue of theoretical violence in the relationship with the other in Levinas' work.

What I want to suggest, then, is that it is this prior projection of an I that lies at the root of the recurrence of the subject-object distinction that I am discussing, for it seems that it is precisely because of such a projection that, as Derrida noted, a scission and a dichotomy between the same and the other occurs. Indeed, it is precisely because of such an I supposedly capable of overseeing the order of the Same (or the order of objects)—in short, the realm of immanence—that it can *oppose* dialectically a transcendent realm to it. It is, I suggest, in this logic that a metaphysical procedure recurs, for such an opposition presupposes precisely one or the other cogito that can oversee the logic of immanence in a clear and distinct way only then to value or will (Nietzsche) another realm, transcendent or not. It is such a subjectival operation that occurs in the works of the authors under discussion here. Nevertheless, it is precisely such a movement of projection and willing (of a prior I) that Levinas will attack.

I have already noted that Levinas in his later works abandoned the critique of the alter ego altogether and that Marion, at least to my knowledge, never subscribed to this critique (see above). In this sense, it is important to note that in *Otherwise than Being* Levinas modified his critique of Husserl and intentionality. To be sure, one still finds in *Otherwise than Being* Levinas' critique of the primacy of the theoretical (OB, 32–33, 65–66), but this critique is now no longer extended toward the other as an alter ego.[42] A new element comes to the fore in Levinas' critique of Husserl when Levinas argues that "intentionality bears the trace of the voluntary and the teleological" (OB, 96). Levinas demonstrates how, through this voluntary aspect of intentionality, consciousness retains the measure of every appearance: "[The intentionality of consciousness] retains the initiating and inchoative pattern of voluntary intention. The given enters into a thought which recognizes in it or invests it with its own project, and thus exercises mastery over it. What affects a consciousness [. . .] does not knock without announcing itself, leaves [. . .] the leisure necessary for a welcome" (OB, 101–02). The ego's intentionality thus is able to represent things at will and at command. There is no obstacle it cannot take; it encounters nothing that cannot be reduced, no lack of intuition that signification cannot fill: "signification is signifying out of a lack [. . .] like a hunger [. . .] at the presence which is to satisfy it" (OB, 96).[43] In this sense, intentionality always gets what it wants. It is this voluntary aspect of the ego that Levinas in his later writings will seek to undermine, for the goodness and the ethics Levinas envisages are precisely what precede any choice: "[G]oodness [is not] an altruistic inclination to be satisfied. For signification, the one-for-the-other, is never enough, and the movement of signification does not return. This is also *not* to conceive of it as *a decision of the will*, an act of consciousness beginning in the present of a choice, having an origin in consciousness, or in the present of a choice conditioned by inhabitation [. . .]. Goodness [. . .] as a responsibility for the freedom of the other, it is *prior to any freedom in me*" (OB, 138). This *involuntary* aspect is what delineates the figure of subjectivity as *the other in the same* (OB, 25): people are not condemned to be free (Sartre); they are condemned to be good. This pattern of the 'other in the same,' the fact of being always and already the other's hostage, is what is proposed by Levinas (and later Marion) to counter Derrida's deafness to the dichotomy between the other and the same. Whereas *Totality and Infinity* hesitated, so to say, between an I that, at first, was allowed its interiority and its 'as for me,' only then to be opened up unto the Other, in *Otherwise than Being*, the I is, from the outset, caught in the mazes of the other's web. The I is no longer the first on the scene. On the contrary, when it enters the theater of the world, it discovers itself to be already elected to respond to the presence of others. In this way *Otherwise than Being* proceeds to a complete abandonment "of the sovereign and active subjectivity" (OB, 47). What Levinas points to, therefore, is precisely that the phenomenological reduction is not between *one* ego and an *alter* ego (as opposed dialectically) but that the very performance of the reduction is somehow 'à l'insu' (i.e., without me knowing that it is *already* affected by other human beings). The ego, then, is originally dependent upon its alter; it is altered from the outset by the other, and this alteration is its summation to be good.

It is this figure of the subject as the 'other in the same' that Levinas tries to convey when insisting on an originary accusative, *without nominative* (e.g., OB, 112, 124; GP, 68), for "subjectivity is not called, in its primary vocation, to take the role and the place of the indeclinable transcendental consciousness [. . .]. It is an irreplaceable oneself. Not strictly speaking an ego set up in the nominative in its identity, but first constrained to . . . It is set up as it were in the accusative form, from the first responsible and not being able to slip away" (OB, 85).[44] Marion comments: with this idea of a hostage, "the term 'decentered' is not even suitable, for no center could ever have been decentered since originally no I assured even the least bit of center."[45] In this way, Levinas seems to have resolved Derrida's objection that privileging an encounter with rather than a constitution of the Other seems to presuppose "that there is a time and an experience without 'other' before the encounter."[46] Since the Other is the first on the scene, such an experience without the other is now indeed omitted. This is perhaps best explained by the paragraph despite oneself, 'malgré soi' (OB, 51–53), since

> the despite here is not opposed to a wish, a will, a nature, a subsistence in a subject, which a foreign power would contrary. The passivity of the 'for-another' expresses a sense in it in which

no reference, positive or negative, to a prior will enters. It is
the living human corporeality, as a possibility of pain [. . .].
Pain is not simply a symptom of a frustrated will, its meaning
is not adventitious. The painfulness of pain [. . .] the pain of
labor and ageing are adversity itself, the against oneself that is
in the self. (OB, 51)

Again we find Levinas stressing the phenomenon of ageing, as that which
is outside of the simple 'consciousness of . . .':

[I]t is not possible that responsibility for another devolve from a
free commitment, that is, a present; it exceeds every actual present
or represented present. It is thus in a time without beginning. Its
anarchy cannot be understood as a simple return from present
to prior present, an extrapolation of presents according to a
memorable time, that is, a time assemblable in a recollection
of a representable representation. [Such a] passive synthesis, is
ageing. [. . .] In self-consciousness there is no longer a presence
of self to self, but senescence. It is as senescence [. . .] that time
[. . .] is a diachrony, and concerns me. This diachrony of time
is not due to the length of the interval, which representation
would not be able to take in. (OB, 51–52)

The responsibility for the other, therefore, escapes all retention and protention,
in short: representation. Its intrigue, and its 'already' being present in the
self that the self can only discover afterward, does not come from a past that
is too far away to be able to be represented in and through retention. Nor
is it unrepresentability due to a lack of clarity from out of which the self
would be able to anticipate its signification as if it was something 'to come.'
And, finally, that the excess of the diachrony over representation escapes all
presentation to the present of consciousness is not due to the length of the
interval means that it is not simply because the interval takes, for instance,
too long that it escapes being held present in consciousness. It is important
to note that with this account of diachrony, Levinas tries to differentiate the
infinite that traces itself in this intrigue from the unrepresentability of the
mathematical and the numerical infinite. The latter infinite indeed proceeds
from present to prior (or future) present in a numerical series that is infinite
only because it regresses (or progresses) *ad infinitum*. This 'bad' infinite,
however, knows only the infinite as a negation of the finite, as the infinite

of n+1 possibilities. In Levinas' wording, "A linear regressive movement, a retrospective back along the temporal series toward a very remote past, would never be able to reach the absolutely diachronous pre-original" (OB, 10).[47] For the question of metaphysics, which will concern us in the next chapters, it is important to note that *Totality and Infinity* relates this problem of an infinite regress to the question of a foundation for knowledge. Levinas reasons that if we were "to identify the problem of the foundation with an objective knowledge of knowledge," the "sterile course" of infinite regress would be inevitable (*TI*, 85, 43). For, as such, the problem of foundation indeed leads unto an infinite regress: it is always possible to ask how the ground of reality is itself grounded.

Levinas' rephrasing of the asymmetry of the other's approach as 'the other-in-the-same' in another way as via a critique of the Husserlian conception of the alter ego is, perhaps, what allows us to conceive of a decentering of the subject *without* the prior projection of an I: if there is no prior I that needs to be decentered, as Marion argues, then there is also no such I that can project the reversal of intentionality! It is to this that Levinas' repeated criticism of the concept of "finite freedom" points (OB, 121–29, TI, 223ff). Just as the concept of 'finite freedom' presupposes an initial unlimited freedom, so indeed would the very idea of a reversal of intentionality presuppose a prior and immanent ego that is conscious of its intentionality being reversed. With the idea of the 'other in the same,' it seems that it is precisely this critique that Milbank and Horner raise against Marion and that I, with Derrida, raise against Levinas that is put out of play. For indeed, Levinas distinguishes his account of the other-in-the-same from "the Fichtean conception, where all suffering due to the action of the non-ego is *first a positing* of this action of the non-ego *by the ego*" (OB, 124). This is why one does not find, at least in *Otherwise than Being*, statements such as 'consciousness of proximity,' of obsession and so on. On the contrary, it is this fact of being thrown outside of the objectivity characteristic of relations that "cannot consist in a becoming conscious of this situation" (OB, 82). But over and against the cognitive capacity of consciousness that reduces everything that appears to its being present to and contemporaneous with consciousness, the subject now has to reckon with the traumatic forging of an entrance without knocking, with a "penetration" (OB, 49)—if not rape— through the other, with his or her advent as a thief in the night, incognito. No longer, as in *Totality and Infinity*, the "non-violence par excellence" (TI, 293), but the "violence par excellence" (OB, 197n. 27).[48] And yet—in what again seems to hint at Derrida's writing—it is "a good violence" (*OB*, 43) because this violence of the other orients the subject toward the other.

Another argument that explains the idea of subjectivity originally in the accusative is yet another remarkable difference between *Totality and Infinity* and *Otherwise than Being*: whereas the first book describes fecundity and sexuality as an exemplary instance of the 'relation without relation' (cf. *TI*, 121) because it allows for a "transubstantiation" of the egoistic I, the latter denounces the very notion of "transubstantiation," since the term itself again seems to presuppose one substance deciding (or projecting such a choice) to become another substance. In this sense, it would remain too indebted to the substantiality of the subject which, precisely, Levinas wanted to overcome: "[S]ubstitution of one for another, as me, a man, I am not a transubstantiation, a changing from one substance into another, I do not shut myself up in another identity, I do not rest in a new avatar" (*OB*, 14).[49] It seems that all possibility of a choice between the for-the-other or for my own has been abandoned, for "*already* the position of the subject is a deposition, *not a conatus essendi*. It is from the first a substitution by a hostage [. . .] We have to conceive in such terms the *de-substantiation of the subject* [. . .] its subjection, its subjectivity" (*OB*, 127).

However, the abandonment of a prior I—the abandonment of the a priori—and this desubstantiation of the subject is not without its price. For, as we have seen, *Totality and Infinity* still undertook a defense of subjectivity; *Otherwise than Being* will be immersed in a movement that cannot be depicted otherwise than as a complete hollowing out of the interiority of the subject. It is this abandonment of the interiority, the privacy, and the secret of the subject that is, again, accompanied by that which I have called an "objectification of the subject" itself, for one should ponder what the difference would be between this interiority 'without secrets' that we will see Levinas describing enacted by the subject in face of the other and the Sartrean account of the other, where the other who *cannot* do anything other than objectivize me? Indeed, what, if anything, would be the difference, to turn to Levinas' words, between "the extraversion of the interiority of the subject" (*GP*, 75) through the other that leaves this subject "without secret" and the object of which "all [. . .] is exposed, even their unknown" (*HAM*, 43)? The latter tendency, I will suggest, is not only the recurrence of an old metaphysical figure in Marion, Lacoste, and Levinas; this tendency also points to the persistence of metaphysics in contemporary philosophical discourse and culture.

The Subject's Self Otherwise than Being

What should we make of this "extraordinary everydayness of my responsibility for other men" (OB, 141), this responsibility in which the Other "concerns me for the first time (even if he is an old acquaintance, an old friend, an old lover" (OB, 86), extending to "responsibility with regard to men we do not even know" (OB, 100), and so obfuscating "the distinction between those close and those far off" (OB, 159)?

Levinas admits that such a responsibility and its asymmetrical structure "[impose themselves] upon meditation in the name of a concrete moral experience: what I permit myself to demand of myself is not comparable with what I have the right to demand of the Other" (TI, 53). It is this direction that *Otherwise than Being* will pursue when describing the subjectivity of the subject in "a quasi-hagiographic style" (OB, 47).[50] The sovereign subject is substituted for the duty to be a saint as if, for the Jew Levinas, the absence of the Messiah means that I myself will need to be the Messiah, who, in this world, has no place to lay his/her head.[51]

It is this responsibility that singularizes or individuates me: no one can be responsible for the other in my place: "The subject [. . .] is someone who, in the absence of anyone is called upon to be *someone*, and cannot slip away from this call. The subject is inseparable from this appeal or this election, which cannot be declined. It is in the form of *the being of this entity*, the diachronic temporality of ageing, that there is produced despite myself the response to an appeal, direct and like a traumatizing blow" (OB, 53). This passage calls for several comments. First, if *Otherwise than Being* drops the distinction between the I in the nominative and the I in the accusative, then, as Rodolphe Calin argues, "the other does not address himself or herself to a particularity that would precede it, he or she provokes [. . .] my uniqueness, he or she effectuates that I am me through his or her calling."[52] Second, from whence comes this strange claim that it is in the form of *being* that 'the despite oneself' is produced?[53] Here we should note that Levinas seeks to think the 'otherwise than being' not at the expense of being but, as it were, at the crossroads of being and otherwise than being. Again, the relation between being and 'otherwise than being' is not a dialectical relation in which the one would take precedence over the other. On the contrary, Levinas does not dismiss 'being' (or epistemology) in favor of what would be its contrary or antithesis, namely 'otherwise than being.' 'Otherwise than being' is not floating in the air, above or alongside being. "[I]t cannot be situated in any eternal order extracted from time that would somehow command the temporal series [. . .]. It is then the temporalization of time [. . .] that must also signify the beyond being" (*OB*, 9). It is therefore *in* being and *in* time that something otherwise than being signals itself while not being reducible to either of them. It is here that Levinas finds the answer to and the name of that which was his main goal all along: the uniqueness of the human being, not reducible to being one more being among all others, for "the exception of the 'other than being,' beyond not-being, *signifies subjectivity or humanity*, the *oneself* that repels the annexations of essence" (*OB*, 8).[54] It is, therefore, the human being that is otherwise than being. This 'oneself' will designate the uniqueness of the human being, and it is precisely this that, according to Levinas, is forgotten by the larger part of Western philosophy, since, "to reduce men to self-consciousness and self-consciousness to the concept, to deduce from the concept [. . .] the subjectivity and the 'I' in order to find meaning for the very singularity of 'that one' in function of the concept, by neglecting, as contingent, what may be left irreducible after this reduction, what residue there may be after this deduction, is [. . .] to forget what is *better than being*, that is, the Good" (*OB*, 18–19). The subject, then, is a break and rupture with being and being's pretension to the absolute by, as the bad infinite, "cover[ing] over all ex-ception" (*OB*, 8) and "filling every interval" (*OB*, 125). But this break at the same time binds the subject to the other: the subject is at the same time a "breaking-point and binding place" (*OB*, 12), "of essence *and* essence's other" (*OB*, 10). This "knot in subjectivity [. . .] signifies an allegiance of the same to the other" (*OB*, 25).

It is therefore a question of the relation between being and otherwise than being. This relation is not a dialectical relationship in which the one provokes, as if automatically, the other. It is not a symbolic relation, in which the presence of the same reflects and narrates the absence of the other. According to Levinas, it is nothing less than an enigma,[55] for the signification of the one-for-the-other touches at and is befriended with being as if its was its neighbor "to the point that the one-for-the-other can be expressed as though it were a moment of being" (*OB*, 80). The otherwise than being is exempt from proof and speculative audacity, and there is therefore no clear and distinct way to testify to its transcendence, to the point "that the diachronic ambiguity of transcendence lends itself [. . .] to this option for the ultimacy of being (*OB*, 95). The otherwise than being shows itself to the finite, by leaving the trace of its 'otherwise': not the presence of an absence, as in symbolic relations, but rather as the presence of an absence *as* absent.

In the concluding pages of *Otherwise than Being*, Levinas explains why the intrigue of the otherwise than being must appear to and show itself in being: "thematization is then inevitable, so that signification show[s] itself [. . .] in the betrayal which philosophy is called upon to reduce" (*OB*, 151–52). The otherwise than being therefore shows itself necessarily in the logos of being and in the said.[56] However, in this appearance the trace of the infinite shows itself *in a particular way*: the enigma of an alternating and simultaneity of meaning, which, "is the very pivot of revelation, of its blinking light" (*OB*, 154) is, when appearing to thought and consciousness, brought back to a dilemma, as if it shows itself to be up for choice after all.[57] But this choice or dilemma shows itself only to "reflection on the condition of the statement that states this signification" (*OB*, 156) beyond being. And Levinas adds that it is only "in this reflection, that is, only after the event, *contradiction* appears: it does not break out between two simultaneous statements, but between a statement and its conditions, as though they were at the same time" (ibid.). Thus, it is between the statement of the beyond of being and its condition, that is, being and language that a contradiction appears: it is impossible that the beyond of being be said from out of being. Levinas' point is that this contradiction only appears when thinking starts to reflect upon the (finite) conditions from out of which the infinite gives itself to thought. Note that Levinas mentions the same line of reasoning while trying to understand how the other can animate and dwell *in* the same: "this signification in its very signifyingness is an accord or peace between planes which, *as soon as they are thematized*, make an irreparable cleavage. They then mark two Cartesian orders [. . .] which have no common space where they can touch [. . .] Yet they are in accord prior to thematization, in an accord, a chord, which is possible only as an arpeggio. [T]his kind of accord is the very rationality of signification in which the tautological identity, the ego, receives the other" (*OB*, 70).[58] Thematization and reflection *oppose* being and otherwise than being and become "a contestation of the infinite" (*OB*, 154): "A God was revealed on a mountain or in a burning bush, or was attested to in Scriptures. And what if it were a storm! And what if the Scriptures came to us from dreamers! Dismiss the illusory call from our minds! The insinuation itself invites us to do so."[59] It is in and through thinking, that is, in representation and in reflection, that the infinite is "belied without any ambiguity," is taken as "an extrapolation of the finite," as "the invisible behind the visible" (*OB*, 154), and appears, perhaps, as "a great Other," a being par excellence.[60] According to Levinas, such a (Feuerbachian) contestation already presupposes the very signifyingness of signification, for "how would the contestation of the pretension beyond being have meaning if this pretension were not heard" (OB, 156)? This pretension and insinuation of the beyond of being "does not allow itself to be walled up in the conditions of its enunciation. It benefits from an ambiguity or an enigma, which is [. . .] the effect [. . .] of an extreme proximity of the neighbor, where the Infinite comes to pass" and leaves but the trace "of its impossible incarnation" (OB, 161).

As a consequence of this contestation, "everything is incumbent on me" (OB, 154), and responsibility stretches to a responsibility "for everything and for everyone" (OB, 114), even God: "It is up to us, or, more exactly, it is up to *me* to retain or to repel this God without boldness."[61] It is here that the figure of 'the other in the same' takes an unexpected turn, for with this emphasis on *my* responsibility, the subject is granted a uniqueness as indeclinable as Kant's '*Ich denke*' (OB, 56), but here it is not Kant's '*Ich denke*' that accompanies every experience; every experience is on the contrary accompanied by an attachment to the other for whom I am responsible. This subject, then, is "a *sub-jectum*, under the weight of the universe" (OB, 116). It is this "incessant event of subjection to everything" that marks the "exceptional uniqueness" of the ego (cf. OB, 117), "always [emptying] oneself of oneself, [absolving] oneself [. . .] to the point of the quasi-formal identity of being someone. But is always to be *coram*" (OB, 92). It is this reduction of the I of transcendental consciousness to a self, to the "pure someone" (OB, 50) that Levinas designates as a subjectivity older than consciousness. It is however not to the abstraction of the '*Ich denke*'—form without content—that Levinas leads us, but rather to an embodied 'me,' for "the oneself is provoked as irreplaceable, as devoted to the others, without being able to resign, and thus as incarnated in order to offer itself, to suffer and to give" (OB, 105). It is thus that Levinas queries "to restore to the soul its egoity which supports no generalization" (OB, 127).

With this last citation, we are again brought back to Derrida's critique of Levinas' Totality and Infinity, for the critique of the alter ego that Derrida attacked in Levinas' book was, as we have seen, an attack precisely on the fact that Levinas had to presuppose the other as an alter ego to make the appeal of the 'absolute' other heard. Hence Derrida's remark that surely "the other is not myself [. . .] but it is *an* Ego, as Levinas must suppose in order to maintain his own discourse. The passage from Ego to other as an Ego is the passage to the essential, non-empirical *egoity* of subjective existence in general."[62] The least that one can say of the other is, therefore, that he or she, in the very same way as me, must be able to say 'I' or me. An important result of this chapter is that via Derrida's critique, Levinas seems to have left the critique of the alter ego by a re-appraisal of the phenomenological Reduction.[63] After all, if the abandonment of the critique of the alter ego is accompanied by an abandonment of the nominative I, than the very act of performing the reduction must point to this originary accusative that Levinas seeks to describe. In "Philosophy and Awakening" (1976), then, Levinas "returns to the Husserlian description of the constitution of the stranger in the sphere of 'ownness' by re-interpreting it deliberately in favour of ethics"[64] and investigates whether the transcendental reduction itself is perhaps not simply "just another fold in the certainty of the cogito [. . .] but the teaching of a meaning, despite the incompleteness of knowledge and of identification."[65] Already in the transcendence of the object and of the body, which testifies to the separation of "the knowing being [. . .] from the known being" (TI, 48), Levinas now distinguishes a "self-presence" that already attests to a certain rupture with the cogito to the extent that "the lived experience is a lived experience for a self that within immanence distinguishes itself from it, that, beginning with *Ideas I*, is recognized as 'transcendence in immanence.' "[66] Levinas thus envisages an ego that cannot be reduced to the simple "movement of identifications" (cf. *TI*, 36) that *Totality and Infinity* proclaimed, and wherein Derrida saw a false "adequation of Ego to the Same."[67] Levinas now sees "in the identity of self-presence [. . .] an avowal of difference between the same and the same, out of phase, a difference at the heart of intimacy."[68]

Nevertheless, it is only in the "intersubjective reduction" that "the Reduction shows it true meaning,"[69] and it is here that Levinas comes back to Husserl's reduction of the other as an alter ego. We recall from Derrida's analysis that the other ego appears to an ego precisely by not appearing, that is, by not submitting himself or herself to what Levinas considers to be a constitution of the I, and thus by maintaining the secret of its interiority. It seems that Levinas, at the time of *Otherwise than Being* comes to realize precisely this, for we find him stating in the article "Notes on Meaning" (1979) that "what we take as the secret of the other man in appresentation is precisely the flip side of a significance other than knowledge."[70] Therefore, not only does Levinas now recognize the Husserlian version of intersubjectivity he decried in the early stages of his career, but Levinas also admits that the very performance of the (ego-logical) reduction presupposes "this relation with the other self where the self is torn from its primordiality."[71] This means, therefore, that the 'other' of *Otherwise than Being* is no longer opposed to the alter ego of the phenomenological reduction (of Husserl), but on the contrary that the phenomenological reduction to the other as an alter ego already testifies to the structure of the subject as 'the other in the same.'[72] And with this concession to Derrida's essay, another remarkable shift in Levinas' understanding of the subject seems inevitable: a subscription to the most basic phenomenological law possible according to which all that appears must, first, appear to me. As for Marion, it seems that for Levinas, too, the decentering of the subject is not so much a matter of contesting that the subject occupies the center but rather the way in which it does so.[73] Indeed, it is only toward the end of *Otherwise than Being* that Levinas concedes to Derrida that, in phenomenology at least, nothing, not even transcendence, "comes to pass save through the subject that contests or confesses it" (OB, 156). It is in this statement that a return to a particular understanding of the Heideggerian *Jemeinigkeit* is insinuated. Not only does *Otherwise than Being* indicate that "it is as *my own* that substitution for the neighbor is produced" (OB, 126).[74] This "ethical reprise of the Heideggerian notion of *Jemeinigkeit*"[75] is also obvious in Levinas' later writings on the reduction, for if the intersubjective reduction depicts the way in which the other tears the I out of its (egoistic) hypostasis, it is precisely "in this tearing [that] the meaning of my mineness is revealed."[76] Levinas then concludes that the reduction "re-does the disturbance of the Same by the Other."[77]

Levinas acknowledges, too, that this redescription of the reduction is, in fact, indebted to Heidegger, for it is the latter that has shown Levinas how such a bringing back takes place, for "[Heidegger] does not at all say that the *Dasein* is *Jemeinigkeit*, because it is an *Ich*; on the contrary, he goes toward the *Ich* from the *Jemeinigkeit*, toward I from the 'superlative' or the emphasis of this subjection, from this being-delivered-over-to-being."[78] To conclude the queries of the previous chapters, I will therefore note a parallel between the Heideggerian notion of *Geworfenheit* (thrownness) and Levinas' idea of responsibility.

Chapter 6

Intermediary Conclusions and the Question concerning Ontotheology

The Turn to *'Jemeinigkeit'* in Levinas and Marion

In the preceding chapters, I have tried to critique the notion of a 'reverse intentionality' at issue in the works of Lacoste, Marion, and Levinas. I have tried to show that the very idea of a reversal of intentionality remains stuck in the problem it wanted to resolve, for time and again the subject under critique is replaced by another instance, whether God, the other, or givenness, that takes on the contours of modern subjectivity. In the remaining chapters of this work, this problem will be examined from the perspective of ontotheology. Indeed, if another subject is needed to decenter the subject, are we not left with the metaphysics that these authors tried to criticize?

And yet, through a reading of Derrida's "Violence and Metaphysics," we have seen that Levinas adjusts his understanding of the subject in his later works, especially in *Otherwise than Being*. In this book, Levinas tries to think subjectivity without presupposing that it is first in the nominative in order to, in a second move, decenter it by turning to the other. It is thus not that the human being *first* constitutes and posits itself and *then* needs to be decentered—roughly the movement we recognized in *Totality and Infinity*—it is that we in each case already *have* a self that is, from the outset, summoned to ethics. It would be too simple to say that for Heidegger this comportment would be an ontological one (being-toward death), whereas for Levinas it would be a matter of taking up one's responsibility for-the-other, since this distinction relies on the fact that both *Dasein* and Levinas' 'self' are depicted from out of the idea of *Jemeinigkeit*. For Heidegger, 'mineness' means saying that being is in each case mine: I cannot talk about being otherwise than from out of *my* being. And for Heidegger too this 'existential' of *Dasein* serves to *distinguish Dasein* from entities that are simply present-at-hand or objects.

Dasein cannot be taken as, and we know Levinas would readily agree, "an instance or special case of some genus of entities."[1] Such an understanding of the human being from out of the substantiality of present-at-hand objects is precisely what Heidegger wants to avoid, as Raffoul notes: "*Dasein* is thus mine, not in the sense of a substantial property, but in the sense of a finite and temporal event to assume."[2] Note too that I deliberately used the active "taking one's responsibility," despite Levinas' insistence on the radical passivity of the self. For the *Jemeinigkeit* Levinas envisions is precisely a "reverting of heteronomy into autonomy" (OB, 148).[3] To be sure, this reverting is, for Levinas, "the very way the infinite passes" (ibid.), but it passes in a particular way and with an ambivalence "that *is* the exception and subjectivity of the subject" (OB, 148) "to the point that it is I that only says [. . .] this unheard-of obligation" (ibid.). *Solus ipse?*

Earlier in this text we saw Marion reverting to a similar version of *Jemeinigkeit* while accusing *Dasein* of being yet another avatar of the transcendental subject. In this conclusion, I point to further resemblances between and the limits of Marion and Levinas' accounts and develop one of the criticisms Marion has raised against Levinas.

Let us first ponder an almost literal parallel between these two philosophers with regard to their thought of the transcendent appeal. It is striking that, for instance, Marion's definition of the response to this appeal corresponds almost exactly with how Levinas understands the impossibility of escaping one's responsibility for-the-other. Whereas for Levinas, "the will is free to assume this responsibility in whatever sense it likes; it is not free to refuse this responsibility itself" (TI, 218–19), Marion's notion of the responsal "is nothing like an optional act, an arbitrary choice, or a chance," although "the meanings invested by the response can be chosen, decided, arrive by accident" (BG, 288). Therefore, we must reconsider our account of the decentered subject in Marion's work and ask to what extent Marion would follow Levinas' later account of the subject that is decentered through an encounter with alterity against its will. In "The Banality of Saturation," Marion underlines the affinities between the *adonné* and the Levinasian hostage. Considering the question whether his account of the subject retains some form of the active and autonomous subjectivity that we know from modernity, Marion declares that, "[the witness'] activity always remains that of a response [. . .]. This responsive posture imposes on the witness [. . .] that she remain always in radical dependence on the event that gave her to herself. *The figure of the hostage [. . .] here finds its legitimacy*: de facto and de jure, the witness is herself only through an other, more interior to herself than the most intimate within her (VR, 144). In "Notes on the Ontological Indifference," Marion explains his adherence to the Levinasian version of subjectivity. Here Marion surprisingly acknowledges that "*Dasein* is itself also defined by a decenteredness which right away deports it outside the I before its even having been experienceable as a center."[4] Marion then moves on to distinguish *Dasein* from the Levinasian 'Here I am' precisely on the basis of its countered will: "Hostage: he who in advance and without having chosen it, depends on an other. *Dasein* can be put into play; it must, nonetheless, always decide to do so itself. Better, its being put into play is but one with 'anticipatory resoluteness' [. . .]: whatever happens to *Dasein*, in principle it always wanted it."[5]

At times, Marion affirms this figure of the hostage even in *Being Given*. The witness to the saturated phenomenon, for instance, is a "witness constituted *despite itself* by what it receives" (BG, 217).[6] This similarity between Levinas and Marion poses serious questions. For instance, if the *adonné* is himself or herself constituted as a hostage, and for this reason would share in Levinas' later movement for which the term *decentered* is not even suitable, then this might mean that our earlier analysis of a contradiction appearing in Marion's work between the subject constituting objects and the witness constituted by saturated phenomena does not hold because in Marion as well the prior I would be abandoned altogether. Or, is it on the contrary that this analysis revealed the limits of this enterprise evoking an other in me which is more intimate to me than I am to myself?

The Limits of the Other and/in the Same: Levinas

Levinas' notion of the 'other in the same' indeed seems to avoid the problem of a reversed intentionality in that the 'other in the same' abandoned the prior ego, which it only in a second step sought to decenter. In so doing, the criticism that the decentering at issue is possible only on the basis of a projection of an anterior I is deflected. With the figure of 'the other in the same,' such a distance from the self seems to be disqualified, for now the other is "in the midst of my very identification. The ipseity has become at odds with itself in its return to itself" (OB, 125). This is the reason why the later Levinas evaluates the phenomenological reduction positively: the reduction is no longer the work of a transcendental subject quietly contemplating and constituting objects in the world; the reduction now *rehearses* and attests to the split always already there in the identity of the subject. It is perhaps this that Marion adheres to when comparing the *adonné* to the hostage of Levinas. For indeed, this movement of another instance creeping into myself in the midst of my identification is precisely what Marion wants to underline when writing that "the I loses its anteriority [. . .] and cannot yet identify, except by admitting the precedence of such an unconstitutable [saturated] phenomenon" (BG, 217). It is for this reason that one needs to contest "the originary character of authenticity as self-appropriation": such self-appropriation "simply cannot be established or justified *phenomenologically*" (BG, 290), to the point that with "the ambition of accomplishing self-appropriation [. . .], what it's really all about is at best an *illusion* and at worst, if it's stubborn, a *lie*" (BG, 291).

If this is the case, then one would have expected that the nominative I, symbolized by Levinas as we have seen through the *conatus essendi* or the egoistic persevering in one's being, would have disappeared from *Otherwise than Being* or that it, because of the anteriority of the 'other in the same,' would be reduced to playing the role of a Kantian postulate or simply an illusion.[7] In short, the question as to what extent the nominative I is absent from *Otherwise than Being* is still hanging. If present, the difference between *Totality and Infinity* and *Otherwise than Being* would surely be diminished, for what I have denoted as distinctive of *Otherwise than Being*—the fact that it no longer needed a prior I in which it only in a second step seeks to decenter—would then nevertheless be present in the structure of the book. In other words, there might be, even in *Otherwise than Being*, a conflict between the two "concurring appreciations"[8] of *Jemeinigkeit* that Calin distinguishes in Levinas' oeuvre: on the one hand, *Jemeinigkeit* denotes the selfish and possessive persevering in one's being (the nominative I); on the other hand, *Jemeinigkeit* is caught up in the ethical intrigue as I depicted it above (the originary accusative). In fact, in *Otherwise than Being*, the nominative I is as in *Totality and Infinity* introduced in a chapter on sensibility and enjoyment. Enjoyment is again interpreted from out of the phenomenon of eating: "[T]he taste is the way a sensible subject becomes a volume, or the irreducible event in which the spatial phenomenon of biting becomes the identification called me, in which it becomes me through the life that lives from its very life in a *frueri vivendi*" (OB, 73). And Levinas concludes: "[E]njoyment is the singularization of an ego in its coiling back upon itself [. . .]. It is the very movement of egoism" (ibid.). This "enjoyment in its ability to be complacent in itself" is at the very same place even described as "the *condition* of the for-the-other" (OB, 74). Here, oddly enough, the alternation of meaning is not between that of a 'sick subjectivity' that does not know whether it fools itself when bearing witness to the Infinite and the Infinite itself, but rather between the (nominative) I and "the incarnate ego" itself which would "[lose] its signification" and affirm itself "in its *conatus* and joy" (*OB*, 79). It seems that the ego can remain calmly in its egoistic *conatus* after all! Just as we saw Marion preserving the possibility for the (nominative?) ego of constituting objects whilst declaring the universality of saturated phenomena, so Levinas' 'accusative' retains the possibility of the nominative I. How to understand this contradiction? How can there be any possibility for the ego to affirm itself when the subject is described as *without* a nominative? Or are we back to square one, that is, to the scheme of *Totality and Infinity*, distinguishing the same from the other, and preserving the latter at the expense of the other? Is it that Levinas, despite himself, has let a moment of *reflection* slip into his discourse, which, as we have seen, separates two orders that originally belong together? Could there be, in this unexpected return of the nominative I, a *return of the (modern) subject* thematizing and representing adequately what can happen to it as in the "total transparence" of the encounter with the other of which *Totality and Infinity* spoke (*TI*, 182)?

For the answer to these questions, we will have to examine what happens to the interiority of the subject and the nominative I in *Otherwise than Being*. In order to do this, I rejoin Rudi Visker's analysis of the impossibility of escaping the appeal of the other and of its consequences, and expand it to my analysis of Marion. Visker asks whether Levinas might "be yet another phenomenologist who by taking the intersubjective turn is purging the subject of everything in it that resists intersubjectivity."[9] Visker proceeds by questioning Levinas' identification between the I and morality[10] through an investigation whether "interiority [is] fully signifiable through ethics"?[11] What is at stake here, in *Otherwise than Being*, and perhaps more than in *Totality and Infinity*, is whether the ego can ever be assured of "the convergence of morality and reality" (*TI*, 306). Note, though, that Lacoste would pose a similar question to Levinas: by equating facticity with ethics, "the I can establish no distance, no caesura, between its worldliness and the order of duty," and so Levinas is "condemned to passing over in silence everything that does not constitute our being-in-the-world as moral obligation" (*EA*, 71). This ethical usurpation of facticity finally deserves our attention here not only because of its philosophical presuppositions but also because of its theological implications, for the God that intimates Godself in Levinas' thought (and a fortiori Marion's) is perhaps not all that discrete and reluctant to reign as Levinas wants us to believe.

Visker's major concern is indeed that the thinker who started out with a book 'on escape' tries to think the appeal of the other nevertheless as something from which there is no escape possible, such that my being is *only* perceived from out of the horizon of ethics. Visker distinguishes between two versions of the appeal, which roughly coincide with the movement from *Totality and Infinity* to *Otherwise than Being*.[12] Whereas in *Totality and Infinity* the appeal of the other is construed as an appeal that one cannot not hear, in *Otherwise than Being* Levinas allows the Transcendent a discretion that causes the appeal to be heard only by the one listening to it. Nevertheless, Visker argues, the two versions coincide in the priority given to responsibility and to the Good. Every nonresponse is immediately conceived of in the most classical manner of a *privatio boni*: as the lack of something that ought to be there. *Every* 'irresponsibility' is a lack of responsibility. Levinas indeed time and again resorts to the portrayal of an appeal accompanied by the impossibility evading this appeal "without fault" (OB, 135).[13] Just as Marion blamed the finite subject for not phenomenalizing givenness, so we find Levinas condemning as irresponsible all those persons not living up to the measures of the sacrifice imposed on me by the other. To be sure, such an ethical impossibility needs to be distinguished from a "real impossibility" (OB, 198n. 2), since, more often than not, "individuals may not rise to its height" (HAM, 28). Levinas explains that "if there were real impossibility, responsibility would be only an ontological necessity" (OB, 198n. 2) and would therefore be inscribed in the subject's ontological makeup without any fault on its part. The fact remains, however, that whenever individuals fall short of their responsibility for-the-other, Levinas will have, according to Visker, only one word at his disposal: evil.

Our aim here, however, is only to understand why and how Levinas maintains a différend between the nominative and the accusative aspects of the ego to the point of declaring that "we must give the lie to everything that is constructed as an internal world, as interiority" (GDT, 191). Levinas indeed fears such an interiority for the simple reason that "the I has the possibility of being a presented personage, and of representing himself in the form of the saint" (GDT, 190–91). Such a representation is the return of complacency in the relation toward the other, for in this way, the I takes pride in its suffering for-the-other and, of course, "the just person who knows himself to be just is no longer just."[14] It is here that *Otherwise than Being* turns to the extreme, for the denunciation and the effort to eradicate subjectivity of everything that even remotely resembles the nominative I *rests upon* the continuous return of the nominative I and the staging of a *perpetual conflict* between the nominative and the accusative ego. But this return of the nominative I is somewhat like a useless passion, for its return is only a necessary stage in a battle always and already won by the accusative ego. Thus, the kenosis and the sacrifice of the nominative I are *endless*, and "[have] to continue" (OB, 49), in order for the nominative I never to be able to take hold of its suffering for-the-other. Thus, to avoid the nominative I making sense of its suffering, the one-for-the-other "presupposes the possibility of pure non-sense invading and threatening signification. Without this folly at the confines of reason, the one would take hold of itself and [. . .] recommence essence" (OB, 50). Here is the reason why the I is not only responsible for persons it 'does not even know' but even for "the fault of another" (OB, 112). The I is for-the-other (*pour autrui*) by the other (*par autrui*). The suffering imposed on me by the other, my persecutor, without reason, is something for which I, in a paradoxical manner, am responsible. "Suffering [. . .] would lose [its] passivity, if it were not at every moment an overflowing of sense by non-sense" (OB, 73–74). Thus, to avoid the nominative I installing itself, its return must be forever postponed.

It is here that the *il y a* or the 'there is' plays an important role, for what hinders such a return of the nominative I is precisely the non-sense and the rumbling of the *there is*. Though the *il y a* still, as in the early works, "strikes with absurdity the active transcendental ego" (OB, 164), it is now at the same time "a modality of the one-for-the-other [. . .] through which expiation is possible" (ibid.). The passivity of the self is safeguarded by the everpresent nonsense of the there is. Visker comments:

> the il y a is made to work for ethics—its non-sense must prevent the subject under appeal from making sense of that appeal and thus from returning to itself [. . .]. Without 'the restlessness' and the 'insomnia' of the il y a, there would not be the 'non-coinciding of the ego with itself' [OB, 64] which Levinas needs in order for ethics to attain the dis-inter-estedness of a subject completely for-the-other. As a result the subject's being-for-itself can become *a necessary stage* for it to undergo that fundamental conversion which ethics, with the help of the il y a, will arrange for it.[15]

With this "ethicization of the il y a,"[16] Visker contends, "ethics becomes a sort of purgatory in which the subject is purged of whatever in it that might have attached it to itself."[17] Disagreeing with commentators who seek to establish a caesura between *Totality and Infinity* and *Otherwise than Being,*

Visker argues that in this "distance between *le Moi* et *le soi*," Levinas finally envisioned an 'interiority without interiority' or a self without an I. For indeed this 'ethicization of the *il y a*' has as a remarkable consequence that the terror with which the *il y a* was accompanied in the early works is now transferred to the ethical and religious condition of the subject: "[T]he 'no privacy' which was characteristic of the subject's predicament when the il y a has sneaked through its walls [. . .] this *'pas de privé'* becomes [. . .] the main characteristic of the ethical 'relation' with the Other, which Levinas [. . .] calls 'the religious condition of man.'"[18] This religious situation, however, is at the same time reminiscent of a *certain* theological situation, for Levinas not only points to Jonah's impossible venture to escape God (OB, 128) but also to "the glory of the infinite [which] leaves to the subject no refuge in its secrecy [and which] is glorified by the subject's coming out of the dark corners of the 'as-for-me,' which, like the thickets of Paradise in which Adam hid himself [. . .] offered a hiding-place from the assignation" (OB, 144). Here is the interiority without secrets of which *Otherwise than Being* testifies (OB, 138), in which the subject is made transparent without any opaqueness whatsoever (OB, 146). In this way, the intersubjectivization of the subject again amounts to an objectification of the subject. The subject's facticity is *adequately* determined from out of the appeal of the other. Levinas can then be exposed to the same objections I made against Marion and Lacoste. Indeed, if my being receives an adequate and transparent signification from out of the other's appeal to the point that every attachment to my own being or being in general needs to be eradicated, then how can we not conceive of this move as if it concerned one or the other subject that portrays that which happens to it as if it were merely an object that *can* in principle be adequately understood and interpreted? It is here that we must note another parallel with the work of Marion. We have seen that Marion considers the appeal of givenness as more basic than that of the Other. *Being Given* indeed continues the work of *Reduction and Givenness* and displays how the "pure form of the call, as such" (RG, 202; 248n. 82) is present in all diverse instances that supposedly utter an appeal. But what matters to us here is that the appeal that Marion describes rehearses the end of all privacy that I just detected, with Visker, in Levinas' work.

The Limits of the Other and/in the Same: Marion

At the end of *Being Given*, Marion describes Descartes' *Meditations* as one of those "privileged moments" (BG, 271) in which metaphysics, despite its aim to erect subjectivity as the first and last principle of everything that appears, does not fulfill its declared intention. It is here that we will again see the intersubjectivization of the subject. Note that this intersubjectivization in the works of both Levinas and Marion turns to an 'objectification of the subject,' insofar as this intersubjectivization is interpreted as an *adequate* and *transparent* determination or description of the subjectivity of the subject. According to Marion, then, what is at stake in Descartes' groundbreaking work is not so much the tautological affirmation of the ego that always (only) thinks itself, but rather, through the intervention of the evil genius, an ego that *is* thought by another instance. Marion then underlines the personal nature of this genius, "since this [genius] cannot be one of the bodies cast into doubt, it could be an other, even an Other" (BG, 273).[19] The evil genius therefore plays the role of an "originary alterity" from which my existence is "necessarily derivative" (ibid.), granting the radical dependent nature of the ego (BG, 274). The ego indeed exists, but in a secondary way, since "originarily thought by an other thought, one that always already thinks me, even if I cannot yet identify its essence or demonstrate its existence" (ibid.). Jocelyn Benoist has raised an important objection toward Marion's interpretation of the cogito, "this ego originally altered and interlocuted."[20] Benoist's question is whether Descartes' evil genius really can be taken as a (personal) other and therefore whether this originary alterity *within* the cogito indeed dismisses all bonds with the solipsism traditionally attributed to the Cartesian cogito.[21] Benoist argues, contra Marion, that it seems "that this alterity might very well be the mark of solipsism's true sense, not primarily theoretically, but existentially. Solipsism might indeed not first be the identification of the whole with me [. . .] but rather *an alteration of me to myself [altération de moi à moi-même]* a loss of the signs of recognition that usually permit the I to identify itself."[22] The interlocution of the evil genius, then, is not the intervention of a personal alterity, but rather attests to the ego's original duplicity. This duplicity testifies to, as it were, an anonymous and ambiguous double of the self *within* the self. "Expressing the formulation of the soliloquy, the cogito is then linked to a fundamental experience, namely that of error, or at least to the possibility of error. Insofar as this possibility of error exists, I exist as well: *si fallor, sum*."[23] Though Benoist agrees with the locutionary and performative nature of the cogito, he insists "that there is no dialogue here. The mystery of a word one hears must not be confused with the word of a response."[24] Benoist's objection thus indicates that one cannot conclude from this intimacy at the heart of the subject to an address by a personal other. Indeed, this appeal to the subject that, in the words of Marion, is more intimate to me than I am to myself, cannot be resolved by intersubjectivizing it, and this may be the true sense of solipsism. Such solipsism, Benoist writes, pun no doubt intended, "is what Jean-Luc Marion cannot receive."[25] Here finally is the reason why Marion argues that the *adonné* knows no solitude, that none of us mortals can ask, Why have you abandoned me? (BG, 313).

One must note here the continuity with Marion's early theological works, for not only is the one instance with which Marion envisages such a solipsism, namely, vanity and boredom as the "refusal of the other" but "a [pretension] to solitude" (GWB, 130), but Marion also has but one name to resolve this possibility of solipsism: God. This is reflected very well in the theme of God's indifference toward being in *God without Being*. This indifference of God is however but an indifference toward being, and in nowise an indifference toward beings.[26] Marion's point is that the being suffering abandonment is always and already taken up in a difference and distance more essential than the ontological difference itself. God's indifference to being dislodges being and beings only to appeal and to "approach being [*l'étant*] as such" (GWB, 91/DsE, 135). This is why, in boredom, the being experiences the bankruptcy of every attempt to "no longer have to receive any gift" (GWB, 97).

In *The Idol and Distance*, the theological stakes of this figure of the other-in-the-same are even clearer, especially when it states that the distance without being "demands to be received because it more fundamentally gives us [the chance] to receive ourselves in it. [W]e discover ourselves, in distance, delivered to ourselves, or rather delivered for ourselves, *given, not abandoned*, to ourselves" (ID, 153). In this way, "distance does not separate us from the Ab-solute so much as it prepares for us, with all its anteriority, our identity" (ibid.), our identity, therefore, as receivers, as the ones to whom it is given to receive themselves from what they receive: *adonné*. God gives Godself to a being, when and if this being, does not possess its being as a good to be possessed, but acknowledges that the horizon of being itself is to be received and is, therefore, subjected to the logic of the gift. At this instant, the being surrenders and gives itself over to distance by acknowledging that "distance [. . .] plays upon a withdrawal in which requestants not only experience the absence of the *Requisite* but above all discover, in the absence that abandons them, the Requisite that gives and gives itself" (ID, 246). Note that the very same dialectics surfaces in *God without Being* when being is portrayed as 'vain' and 'boring,' since the bored gaze has a "privileged relation" (GWB, 134) with its "contrary, God as *agape*" (GWB, 135). And where in *God without*

Being the bored gaze provokes the appeal of God, in the phenomenological repetition of *Reduction and Givenness* boredom liberates from being in order to open onto "the wind of every other possible call" (*RG*, 196) or operates a reduction of the appeal of being so as to make appear "the pure form of the call" (*RG*, 197). Therefore, although the bored gaze abandons beings as much as the call of being and so regresses to "a spectator disengaged from a rejected world" (*RG*, 192), this gaze endlessly encounters the appeal without being. Thus, just as in *Being Given*, where the *adonné* cannot experience its own abandonment, so in *Reduction and Givenness* abandonment opens onto an appeal that is always already there. Thus again one encounters an 'intersubjectivization' of the subject.

Theological Turns: Admiration against Abandonment

We cannot but conclude, therefore, that Marion's refusal to think a solipsistic abandonment rests upon a theological decision even in *Being Given*: just as the faithful would have to acknowledge the presence of God even when abandoned or experiencing vanity, so too the *adonné* knows no solitude, for even in utmost abandonment it is accompanied with the presence of another instance that alters and converts it—'God or whatever we may call it' *pace* Descartes.[27]

From a philosophical point of view, however, this decision is perhaps somewhat illegitimate, for not only, as Benoist indicates, does it take for granted that this nameless voice of the soliloquy can be identified with the appeal of a personal 'other,' but it also indicates that the 'pure appeal' underlying all of the other differences[28] nevertheless points to God. It is important to understand that the reduction to one single appeal such as occurs in Levinas and Marion almost necessarily leads to a theological usurpation of facticity; indeed, for those *looking* for a theological turn of French phenomenology, this equation of the other-in-the-same with the presence of God and that submits the I to the admiration of its opening toward a (personal) other, this would be the place to start. Not only does Levinas mention the possibility that the internal voice of the subject, that which accounts for the alteration of the subject, might be the voice of God,[29] but Levinas' and Marion's work also coincides in privileging the same (theological?) *Grundbefindlichkeit* as it were, namely, admiration. Indeed, why *admire* this other within the same if it is not the trace of God? In both

Levinas and Marion, then, one finds the abandonment of the philosophical 'thaumazein' in favor of admiration. For Levinas, as is well-known, this turn to admiration follows evidently from the end of the Third Meditation, where Descartes ponders the idea of the infinite "to admire and to adore, the incomparable beauty of this inexhaustible light" (TI, 212). And it is here that the relation with the infinite "becomes a personal relation" (TI, 211).[30] A similar substitution of amazement and astonishment (thaumazein) for admiration and adoration is present in Marion's works: whereas boredom and vanity suspend the claim of being and the corresponding astonishment (cf. GWB, 117), "the appeal that convokes [erects] the interloqué, who in this way originates in the first passion, admiration" (RG, 202 mod./RD, 302). This privilege of admiration is present in Marion's phenomenological works as well when, for instance, the appropriate response to the event of the saturated phenomenon is once again admiration.[31] In Marion's In Excess, finally, admiration attains the rank of the "most powerful exercise possible of the look" (IE, 59). But from the perspective of an originary finitude what or who is there to admire in an indeed finite world? I suggest that in this privilege of admiration that has slipped into Levinas' and Marion's works, a certain theological turn might indeed be at work, for the hint indeed seems to be that the one to admire is almost certainly a personal other, God for instance pace Derrida.

Reprise: Theology 'after' Ontotheology

Perhaps therefore we should try to rephrase the figure of the other-in-the-same, for this theme of an alterity within the ego itself, this 'alteration of the subject' with which Levinas and Marion at least hint at a certain theology, does not discriminate enough between the many possible names of that which transcends immanence. In this conclusion, I would like to point to both the similarity of the Heideggerian understanding of Geworfenheit, thrownness, with the Levinasian responsibility happening despite oneself, and to Jean Luc Nancy's portrayal of an 'other' other-in-the-same than the version Levinas' ethics has given us. For that which can be 'other' than the same can perhaps take on many names and allows for more expressions than Levinas and Marion have argued.

The equation of otherness with a personal other, which aims to reconfigure the subject's adherence to being—its egoistic conatus (Levinas), its clinging on to the safety net of the transcendental subject (Marion)—

as a decentering that is 'uncontaminated' or 'unperturbated' by being or immanence, and that makes appear the being of the human being from out of one, single appeal is, I suggest, where Levinas and Marion therefore are unfaithful to the sting and the ambiguities of finitude and facticity. In the Levinasian one-for-the-other, for instance, every attachment of the subject to itself, to its own being must be declined and directed toward the other in an ethical way. A complete eradication of everything in the subject that is attached to its context or to its form is at issue and is drawn into this signification of a single humanity united "before culture" (*HAM*, 6). Here is the reason why this defense of subjectivity amounts to a subjectivity "without secrets" (*OB*, 138). Such a subjectivity is *completely* turned to the other, for the simple reason that it is hassled by this 'enigma' despite itself and unbeknownst to it and receives its being entirely from the other.

The point, however, is that this redescription not only seems to resort to the vocabulary of the object but also uses the mode of procedure of the subject it wants to decenter to describe the subject in this way, in that it *presupposes* that the human subject can be determined in an adequate and transparent manner. First, the vocabulary of the object: Levinas in effect maintains that this ethical appeal is the rupture of the secret of Gyges, such that the subject "make[s] himself visible before making himself a seer!" (*GP*, 75). Visible to whom? From whence comes this appeal one cannot refuse? It seems that we are again bedazzled by the ontotheological God's permanent presence, for God is the name of the one who 'sees with an eye that sees all' (Marion) and who 'sees the invisible and sees without being seen' (Levinas). And so we will find in Marion's early works a rather unsettling echo of a statement of Levinas', for that "'force' that convinces 'even the people who do not want to listen,'" and that "no 'interiority' permits avoiding" (*TI*, 201), receives in *The Idol and Distance* an explicitly theological expression. The 'God' evoked in this book not only will convince the one who does not want to listen but also "will love those who do not love him, manifests himself to those who turn away, and all the more the more they turn away" (*ID*, 215). Once again, it seems, we are back to Sartre's account of the relation between God and human beings: "if I posit ['the they'] as the absolute unity of the subject which can in no way become an object, I thereby posit the eternity of my being-as-object and so perpetuate my shame. This is shame before God; that is, the recognition of my being-an-object before a subject which can never become an object [. . .]. The position of God is accompanied by a reification of my object-ness."[32] Second, one should ask whether such a procedure or redescription of the subjectivity of the subject is not itself indebted to the modes of procedure of the modern subject it wants to decenter, for eradicating the subject of everything in it that refuses to hand itself over to the other, in its turn *presupposes* that the fate of the nominative I *can* be adequately and transparently determined. The subject without being indeed rests upon the hypothesis that the being or immanence *can* be adequately depicted, only then to turn this being *in its entirety* to the other.

With this orientation and connection, the endeavor to think an instance 'without' or 'otherwise' than being connects too hastily and too easily, forgetting finitude's separation. Facticity signifies, yet again, from out of the 'total transparence' of the encounter with otherness. Death, which for Levinas as much as for Heidegger is essentially part of facticity, is nevertheless made to signify for the other: my death ceases to be meaningless, since I can now die for the other, and, in fact, I must.[33]

The immanence of the subject is completely at the service of—it befits—the other's transcendence. And yet such a perfect fit seems to adhere to the most classical mode of procedure of the modern subject, for as much as this subject was traditionally adequately determined by its capacity to think (itself), so too the intersubjective description of the subject, ethical or not, conceives of the subject as being able to be determined transparently from out of its capacity to respond. In fact, just as the cogito opposes itself to the world (by the act of negation), so too the ethical subject is to be distinguished from the immanent totality of being or immanence, which seems to imply that a clear and distinct account of immanence is possible after all. In this way, the account of transcendence I discovered in *Otherwise than Being* seems to suffer from the same problem that I noted in *Totality and Infinity* and Marion's opposition between objects and saturated phenomena. The suggestion is that despite a common insistence on an antidialectical thinking of transcendence beyond the ontological difference and the differences between beings, such a dialectics is precisely what recurs time and again. In Levinas, for instance, the transcendence 'uncontaminated by being' seems to rest upon the thesis that immanence can be portrayed "like an egg in its shell"[34] or a 'visual prison' (Marion). The mode of procedure is simple: if one first delineates immanence as closed in on itself, then it is possible to portray a transcendence that always escapes this prison of immanence. Only then, indeed, can one think transcendence as interrupting the supposedly self-concernedness of immanent beings. In short, it is not sure at all whether Levinas and Marion have surpassed the simple opposition between immanence and transcendence, between finitude and infinity. In this sense, what Derrida called a "silent axiom" of *Totality and Infinity*, "the amalgation of Same and ego," found its way to the discourse of *Otherwise than Being* and a fortiori to Marion's phenomenology of givenness.[35] According to Derrida, it is this equation that fulfills the "necessary condition of [Levinas'] anti-Hegelianism,"[36] for it entails that every negation enacted by the ego remains a moment of the same. Since every act of consciousness (representation, work, etc.) presupposes such a negation,[37] consciousness itself cannot attain the other by means of "a simple negation of the same" or the infinite by a negation of the finite (as did metaphysics).[38] On the contrary, every negation and negativity only confirms the ego as closed in on itself. Yet one should ponder whether the complete redescription of the same or the ego 'for-the-other' is not in turn dependent on some version of dialectics, whether, therefore, the thesis that is the same is not, because of the simple fact that it can be turned to the other 'without residue' and 'without secret,' reinscribed into a synthesis that functions as an adequate representation of the fate of the same. In short, the thesis that the ego equals immanence is what allows Levinas, in both *Otherwise than Being* and in *Totality and Infinity*, to determine and destruct *all* immanence in favor of the transcendent other. This is why, as we have seen, Levinas cannot abandon the nominative I altogether, for this ego will function not only somewhat as a thesis to the antithesis of an incessant and interminable kenosis. This ego in the nominative, that is, the modern subject therefore haunts the entire discourse of *Otherwise than Being* itself in order to describe the fate of the nominative I in such a transparent manner. Therefore, one should ask with regard to these phenomenologies of Marion and Levinas whether the subjectivity of the subject they describe is indeed "haunted by the divine" (cf. *ID*, 36) or rather whether it is the modern subject itself that haunts these phenomenologies.

Derrida was the first to point to the limits of this complete eradication of negativity and dialectics in Levinas' work by questioning whether the 'good infinite' of the Other can be distinguished in a clear and distinct manner from the 'bad infinite' that proceeds dialectically: "if I cannot designate the (infinite) irreducible alterity of the Other except through the negation of (finite) spatial exteriority, perhaps the meaning of this alterity is finite, is not positively infinite. The infinitely other, the infinity of the other, is not the other *as* a positive infinity, as God [. . .]. The infinitely Other would not be what it is, other, if it was a positive infinity, and if it did not maintain within itself the negativity of the indefinite, of the *apeiron*. Does not 'infinitely other' primarily signify that which does not come to an end, despite my interminable labor and experience?"[39] Questions such as these make one wonder whether the movement without terminus that we saw Levinas expounding from *Totality and Infinity* to *Otherwise than Being* is totally exempt from dialectics or from the 'bad infinite' after all. Is, for instance, the kenotic responsibility 'without any term' to transcend to or the 'endless repetition of responses' that Marion evokes that different from the infinite entailed in numerical series of the kind n+1?[40] Here Visker's 'the ethicization of the *il y a*' is important, for with this ethicizization it is precisely that instance that resisted the subtle dialectics between being and nothingness that Levinas opposed to Heidegger that is *incorporated* in the relation to the other: the *il y a* is *mis à l'oeuvre* as the French would say. But the *il y a* was precisely that which in Levinas' early works could not be domesticated in a "dialectic of being and of nothingness."[41] The *il y a* was described as "the impossibility of nothingness" through "promoting a notion of being without nothingness which leaves no holes and permits no escape."[42] In this way, the *il y a* intends to leave no room for a peaceful synthesis and to escape dialectics as a pure "interval and interruption."[43]

In this sense, it is all the more surprising that the 'there is' makes its way into ethics. It is as if that which could not be resolved—in the Hegelian sense—is nevertheless resolved: "[I]ts non-sense has become the carrier of a Sense."[44] One may therefore surmise a sort of reversed dialectics in Levinas' mature work: it is not a dialectics in the classical sense of the word, in which every non-sense will be redeemed and resolved by a (superior) sense, such as all absurdities already signify from out of a horizon of sense, but rather the other way around: the preserving of the non-sensical character of being for-the-other over the constant effort of the nominative I to make sense of the appeal. Or even the other way around, for this constant overflowing of non-sense to the point of suffering for-the-other without reason is the point where the "absurdity of the there is [. . .] *signifies*" (OB, 164). In this way, since the fate of the nominative I is completely at the service of the Other—this "sense of the senses, the Rome to which all roads lead" (HAM, 24)—one will need to ask whether the incorporation of the absurdity of the 'there is' into the framework of this superior sense is not yet again but "the entry of the subject into the play or designs of the Infinite" (OB, 153), as some sort of participation in the being of God. One should indeed reflect upon the reason why Levinas and Marion, otherwise so reluctant toward the dialectical use of negation and negativity,[45] return to this structural element of negation in their respective discourses: just as for Levinas it is precisely the infinite which cannot be denied or negated, for "the very contestation" of the infinite entails that the pretention of the infinite was already heard because of the fact that there is no negation "in which the sense of which the negation is a negation is not conserved" (cf. OB, 156), so too the negation of the appeal is in Marion's phenomenology of givenness the flip side of that which it negates, for "it is necessary to have already heard something to deny that a call was heard" (BG, 288).

What is of concern in statements such as these is again that Levinas' thinking of transcendence (and a fortiori that of Marion) intimates a *perfect fit* and *overlap* between the immanence of the subject and the transcendence of the other. This might mean that Levinas did not overcome that which he nevertheless rejected from the start, that is, representation as an adequation between what is represented and the representation itself.

If, however, the immanence of the subject cannot be fully signified by transcendence, this would mean that one would have to reckon with a modern subject that, although not fully signifiable, does not understand the art of disappearing completely. It is perhaps this that the unexpected return of the subject in the works of Lacoste, Marion, and Levinas has taught us. In this sense, the recurrence of some sort of adequation in all of these thinkers perhaps points to an unavoidable residue of the cogito and of the modern subject in the philosophical endeavor. These two points—the unavoidable solipsistic I taken together with its *Jemeinigkeit*—might point to a way to describe the contemporary subject in line with a tradition stemming from social anthropology: *participant observation*. Insofar as the subject enacts the cogito, the subject would remain a distant observer of the world into which it is thrown (for the I or ego is distinct from the world), but the subject would also simultaneously have to *be* this observer and therefore participate (for the I or ego *is* in each case his or her world).

What indeed if such an otherwise than being is not given? This would mean that it *is* awkward to affirm that, in our encounter with transcendence, our embodiment is secondary to our thinglike existence (Lacoste) or that visibility can be completely transpierced, dulled, or dressed-down by invisibility (Marion), and also that the face-to-face with the other is *never* transparent (Levinas). In short, if transcendence is *not indifferent* to ontic differences, so also immanence can never totally receive its signification from transcendence.[46] Transcendence would be meaningful only *through* and *in* immanence. Instead of a negative appraisal of particularity, we perhaps need to learn to value this immanent opening to otherness otherwise and overcome any axioms that equate immanence immediately with an egg in its shell (Levinas) or a visual prison (Marion) or a being-without-God (Lacoste).

Nevertheless, the idea of 'the other-in-the-same' does offer some opportunities for further investigation. Philosophically, it seems, it would provide a *rapprochement* between Levinas and Heidegger. If the subject's complete attachment to the other shows itself to be yet another illusion, then the attachment of a human person to his or her form needs to be taken seriously. The attachment to one's form, the fact of belonging to a certain culture that differs from other cultures, complicates the encounter with the other in a significant way, for if the immanence of the subject cannot receive a full and adequate signification from the relation to the other, then, of course, the encounter with the other cannot occur independently of culture, as Levinas maintains. Another response to metaphysics than the one Levinas has given us would then consist in thinking of the other person not as Other, but as a singular individual. This would return phenomenology to its original stance not only because it would find its starting point in an appraisal of the visible encounter with concrete, particular others but also because it would refuse to compare facticity to whatever instance in which its signification would be given in a complete manner.

The rapprochement between Levinas and Heidegger resides in the fact that Levinas' notion of the for-the-other as preceding any of the subject's choices might be extended to other peculiarities to the being of the human being as well. In fact, with this notion Levinas himself seems to have returned to one of the major characteristics of the Heideggerian *Geworfenheit* or 'thrownness.' *Otherwise than Being* insists, as is well-known, on the 'de-situating' of the subject, since the Other appeals, is a face, regardless of his or her form, regardless of his or her *Geworfenheit* in a particular world (e.g. OB, 48, 146). In *Totality and Infinity*, however, Levinas seems to have interpreted the Heideggerian *Geworfenheit* more in line with the in vogue existentialist interpretation of those days, as the absurd fact of being thrown into a world.[47] This fact of being thrown into the world, however, is also something that one has not and could not have chosen— it "is not a commitment" (OB, 136) and "non-chosen and impossible to choose" (TI, 223)[48]—andcan in this way be linked to Levinas' account of the encounter with others. Levinas' ethical intersubjectivity escaping all prior choice could then be integrated into an enquiry of what it means to belong to a determinate community (Christian or otherwise). For Heidegger indeed, *Dasein* has never freely decided whether it wanted to come into *Dasein* or not, and it will never be able to make such a decision.[49] The notions of *Geworfenheit* and authenticity are moreover explicitly related to the question of birth. According to Heidegger, I cannot *not* be the span between my birth and my death, and it is this span that *Dasein* will have to assume if it is to have the courage to exist authentically: "[B]irth is not and never is something past of something no longer present-at-hand [. . .]. *Factical Dasein exists as born* [. . .]. Thrownness and [. . .] Being towards death [. . .] form a unity; and in this unity birth and death are 'connected' in a manner characteristic of *Dasein*."[50] It is in this way that one may interpret the later Levinas' positive evaluation of the phenomenological reduction as a reflection on being-already-in-the-world-with-others. Such a Heideggerian understanding of Levinas is not arbitrary. In fact, in *Einleitung in die Philosophie*, a course taught by Heidegger and attended by Levinas, Heidegger clarifies his notion of *Geworfenheit* and again mentions the involuntary character of existence, "for no *Dasein* comes to existence on the basis of its own decree and decision."[51] One should note also that Heidegger here, as in *Being and Time*, warns about the interpretation of *Dasein* as an egoistic being or a *conatus essendi*, which, as we have seen, runs like an axiom through Levinas' entire work. Heidegger does not only mention explicitly that if *Dasein* in each case has to be its self, and is thrown into a self, this does not mean that it is "individualistic-egoistic returned to itself,"[52] but he also reiterates that this essential characteristic of *Dasein* is the condition of possibility for a proper commitment toward others.[53] Thus, not only can one agree with Françoise Dastur, who, after a reading of the *Zollikon Seminars*, concludes that "one could only reproach Heidegger for being deaf towards the voice of the other and for listening to the voice of being if being and the other would constitute a real alternative"[54] but also concludes that one should also wonder whether the Levinasian theme that knowledge and the representation of things present-at-hand can only function among beings that are able to speak to one another is not a theme Levinas picked up from Heidegger as well, when hearing the latter proclaiming that the "very discoveredness of things present-at-hand is therefore [. . .] necessarily also given away and shared, because of the openness of the there, i.e. Da-sein is necessarily being-with."[55]

An advantage of this interpretation of Levinas from out of Heidegger's notion of thrownness is certainly that Heidegger, unlike Levinas, refused to compare facticity to whatever instance in which its signification would be given in an adequate manner. On the contrary, the reflection on the facticity of *Dasein* rests upon a certain muteness of that which *Dasein* transcends, which follows from the fact that *Dasein* is thrown into a world, while "the 'whence' and the 'whither' remain in darkness."[56] The involuntary character of being-thrown-into-a-world thus seems to exclude the idea of an ontotheological God whose permanent presence ends all privacy of the ones who pray to and praise God: *Dasein* has neither *arche* nor *telos*. This is not to say that there is no transcendence, but rather, following Derrida, it envisions the possibility that "there is more than one appeal,"[57] because the involuntary aspect of the other-in-the-same allows for other others than the ones mentioned by Levinas and Marion. In a remarkable essay, Jean-Luc Nancy indeed seems to develop the idea of the other-in-the-same in a more Heideggerian fashion.[58] Nancy is pondering the heart transplant he had to undergo. The other-in-the-same, therefore, is no longer a personal other, but rather the intrusion of a stranger's heart by means of all sorts of technological devices. Nancy points to a strange shift in the history of these transplantations' representations: whereas at first one pointed to the symbolism of the "gift of another, and of a secret, shadowy complicity and intimacy between the other and I," Nancy points to the limits of such an intimacy, for "very soon the other-as-stranger makes its presence felt: no longer as a woman [. . .] man [. . .] but as another immune system, that replaced nevertheless the irreplaceable other. Such a manifestation is called 'repulsion': my immune system repelled that of the other."[59] One should note the strange complicity between technology and the identity of the subject here, for it seems to entail that the notion of an other-in-the-same extends way beyond the *interior intimo meo* that Levinas and Marion advocate. In this sense, one perhaps should not applaud Levinas' and Marion's accounts of being held hostage by another instance too much. For the intrusion of technology at the heart of the subject's identity and the *different* account of the other-in-the same that seems to emerge from Nancy's "self-portrait" might simply point to an infrequently reflected consequence of Levinas' and Marion's philosophies. Indeed, is the lack of privacy before the permanent presence of God not simply mirroring the invasion of all privacy that, in our societies, is assumed by the internet, by cellular phones, by surveillance cameras? Is their respective 'objectification of the subject' not simply a confirmation of Heidegger's view on technology, as the ever persistent ontotheology of our time? It is this similarity that ought to initiate a defense of the subject's privacy, a privacy, to be sure, that is a burden but that also maintains the uniqueness and individuality of the individual precisely because its facticity cannot and may not receive a complete signification by whatever instance one wishes here to invoke.

The fact of being thrown into a culture would therefore initiate a careful consideration of Heidegger's account of facticity. Indeed, for Heidegger, thrownness reveals, as we already noted, that being-with others is always limited to being-with a determinate circle of others.[60] It is in this sense, I want to suggest that Nancy develops Heidegger's understanding of being-with-others. Nancy, calling the prophet Levinas back to the community, as it were, insists that one needs to understand being-with-others as the proper problem of being.[61] Such a return to Heidegger's account would also throw a new light upon Christian particularity or upon belonging to a Christian community. If there is any sense to the saying that one can be thrown into a Christian culture, then a certain understanding of ontotheology could affect the Christian self-understanding just as well. One will recall that for Heidegger it is a matter of taking up one's *Dasein* in an authentic manner. '*Eigentlichkeit*,' however, is not opposed to the inauthentic manner of being one's *Dasein* in the everydayness of '*Das Man*' ('the They'). Rather, it is "in it, out of it, and against it [that] all genuine understanding [. . .] and appropriating anew, is performed," without the possibility of a complete "extrication."[62] It is further of importance to note that the everyday understanding of 'the They' is not without philosophical presuppositions. Rather, Heidegger is concerned with retrieving those residues of metaphysical conceptions from this everyday understanding in order to bring them back to a genuine ontological understanding. But the everyday understanding precisely speaks the language of the subject-object distinction![63] In Heidegger's words, it encounters beings, not from out of the thing itself, but out of its being 'present-at-hand' in public opinion. For Heidegger, this obsession with present-at-hand objects is a direct consequence of the idealistic representation of the subject as a 'worldless' ego that necessarily reduces *all* that it encounters to the contours of an adequate representation of an object. One could therefore argue that even for the Heidegger of *Being and Time*, 'overcoming' metaphysics is not a matter of leaving metaphysics behind us, but of understanding it from its origins in the everyday understanding of the They. It is this 'existential modification' of our everyday understanding that occurs in angst and death, and that for Heidegger will count as a "liberation"[64] for *Dasein*, albeit in no way whatsoever a *permanent* liberation. Nor is the 'step back' out of metaphysics, for the later Heidegger, the simple claim that one should stop thinking metaphysically, but rather that one can only surmise what this 'overcoming' might be if one understands metaphysics *from within*.[65]

For Christian particularity this means two things. First, it means that the temptation to think ontotheologically cannot be extricated totally and permanently. There is no point of view that avoids the ontotheological functionalization of God to the very end. This is why theology benefits from an interruption by its other (individuals, other religions, and so on) and why it cannot forget Levinas' point that the other interrupts the complacency of the same. Ontotheology in this sense is first and foremost the instruction that the charge of idolatry is above all a charge against one's own conception of the transcendent. The ontotheological constitution of metaphysics is therefore an invitation to persist in a permanent 'unsaying' of ontotheologically conceived residues in one's own theology *without the false hope of extricating it completely*. Second, an enquiry into ontotheology operates a decentering of subjectivity that therefore no longer succumbs to the temptation of a 'pure' encounter with transcendence and no longer even feels the need to demarcate the rigid boundaries of the community. In the end, this decenters the subject in such a way that this subject is aware both of its inevitable subjectivity and of the fact that its encounter with *particular* others (e.g., with individuals, religions, or objects) instigates a humble, somewhat nontotalizing, stance toward transcendence. 'Theology' would consist in the humble recognition of the fact that transcendence, and the word 'God,' is always and already incarnated in being and that, therefore, the encounter with transcendence is an uncertain, contingent, and ambiguous affair.

Did Levinas envisage such a blurring of the boundaries between immanence and transcendence? Is this transcendence of Levinas really a transcendence that refuses to reign? Perhaps Levinas' 'identity without secrets' can be avoided with what one might call an "incarnational" approach to the question of human beings' relation to God by the simple fact that facticity is not fully signified by an otherwise than being. I want to suggest, therefore, that the attempt to think of the encounter between human beings and God as "the relation of two freedoms" (*TI*, 211) or "the communion of two loves" (*ID*, 162) has not yet succeeded,and that in order to do this it is less a question of 'overcoming' metaphysics than a question of comporting oneself toward it in an appropriate way. Incarnation entails both God's freedom to appear and the freedom of human beings with regard to God: God's freedom, in that the encounter with transcendence is demarcated neither solely by ethics nor by liturgy. God is able to appear anew wherever God wills: in objects, sacraments, persons, or nature; the freedom of human beings to relate to God, since the secret and the sting of finitude is not made transparent either to the other or to God.

Chapter 7

"And There Shall Be No More Boredom"

Problems with Overcoming Metaphysics

This chapter portrays the way in which singularity and particularity make their appearance in Heidegger, Levinas, and Marion. It is true that Heidegger, Marion, and Levinas all frame their thought around that which might counter the reckoning with beings and objects. Philosophy, they argue, has preferred controllable, foreseeable, and 'present-at-hand' objects. Heidegger's *Being and Time* was concerned precisely with showing how our particular being-in-the-world hardly encounters objects at all. In our dealings with things ready-to-hand that Heidegger sought to describe, one notices that the critique of metaphysics is a critique of the tendency to regard 'objects' and 'objectivity' as the sole way to truth. Marion, as we have seen, tries to differentiate between the 'safety' of constituting and constituted objects and the surprising novelty of the saturated phenomenon. Levinas, as is well-known, attacked the wide-spread Western adage that 'knowledge is power' by pointing to the Other as that instance that both resists and makes possible the adequation on which knowledge thrives. It is in this sense that all these thinkers are querying for another account of our particular and historical encounter with world than the one that, in philosophy, came to be known as the "correspondence theory of truth": truth is '*adaequatio rei et intellectus*,' the correspondence between the thing in itself and the thing as it is thought or represented.

My aim in this chapter is twofold: on the one hand, I will depict the manner in which Heidegger, Levinas, and Marion try to surpass this narrow view of attaining truth, but, on the other hand, I hope to provide some evidence as to why these attempts seem not to succeed. Indeed, I will show how in all three of these thinkers the thought of an adequate and transparent view on particularity can, after all, be obtained. It, therefore, appears that *we can surpass metaphysics only by presupposing it*, that is, by never being able to surpass it. It is this paradox, I will contend, that needs to be thought through and that forces one to handle the phrase 'overcoming metaphysics' not only with the greatest care but also with suspicion. Hence the title of this chapter: it is somewhat stretching Levinas' contention in *Otherwise than Being* that the encounter with the other liberates one from boredom[1] in order to gain an understanding for the view that 'overcoming metaphysics' might itself be yet another metaphysical convulsion.

This chapter closes with the consequences this 'overcoming' of metaphysics might have for theology. It is indeed barely noticed that Heidegger and Levinas *share* a similar disdain for the theological enterprise. Therefore, my question is: does the turn to the particularity of being in a world necessarily entail a reluctance toward theology?

Dasein, Metaphysics, and Dasein's Metaphysics (Heidegger)

Already in *Being and Time*, Heidegger launched an attack on the idea of *truth as adaequatio* or truth as representation. This correspondence between the thing in itself and the thing-as-it-is-thought is said to have as its presupposition being-in-the-world.[2] Truth as correspondence, according to Heidegger, rests upon something like a condition of possibility that Heidegger calls "'true' in a still more primordial sense."[3]

Truth as correspondence tends to forget that, for something to be true in this way, this something must first *appear* or *show itself*—phenomenologically— to be true. Phenomenology investigates not so much the judgment as the appearing of a particular appearance of which we, in and from out of this appearance precisely, predicate something of something. For instance, for a judgment—say, 'the table is brown'—to be able to correspond to a certain state of affairs, it is first necessary that this table shows and reveals itself as brown. For something to reveal itself, however, it has to occur within *Dasein*'s comprehension of being-in-the-world. Truth, thus, presupposes *Dasein*: it is only as and to *Dasein* that something can show itself as true or that something (i.e., the table) is uncovered as brown. This 'discovery' is only possible since to be *Dasein* is essentially 'uncovering' (*Entdecken*), since to be *Dasein* is already to dwell among beings (*Entdecktheit*, uncoveredness).

However, this 'uncovering' is not at *Dasein's* disposal, since it is possible only on the basis of a more primordial disclosedness of the world that gives a particular existence (*Dasein*) to itself in the mode of uncovering being. *Dasein*, thus, presupposes truth. *Dasein* is already "in the truth," it is thrown—*Geworfen*—into truth, that is, I, and every individual existence, is thrown into the disclosure of being and world.

Heidegger is quick to point out that the 'truth' of this being-thrown into a world does not mean that *Dasein* is, or has, from time immemorial, been "introduced to all the truth."[4] Rather, Heidegger tries to convey that this being-thrown into the disclosedness of world is always and already twofold: not only do I understand my own being-uncovering in terms of the world, and from out of (an imitation of) the behavior of others but also from out of my ownmost disclosing of world. Heidegger, then, does not *oppose*—in a dialectical fashion—authenticity and inauthenticity as unconcealment over against concealment. The first is not, and can never be, a permanent state of *Dasein*, since being proper with respect to, for instance, this table necessarily entails that one is improper toward other beings in the room. The second, inauthenticity, is not the total absence of unconcealment. To be sure, the inauthenticity of 'the They' is a concealment, but it is a concealment that does not notice its own concealment. On the contrary, it considers this comportment toward beings as the only way to relate to being-in-the-world: "[I]dle talk [. . .] develops an undifferentiated kind of intelligibility, for which nothing is closed off any longer."[5] The fallenness of 'the They,' therefore, seems to consist in a certain temptation to conceive of its comportment toward beings as a total and transparent unconcealment.[6] The conclusion seems to be that 'authenticity' or a proper comportment toward the being of beings cannot be conceived of as the total absence or the privation of everything improper, whereas fallenness, out of which the proper comportment emerges, *does* not notice its own concealment and regards therefore its comportment to beings, as for instance, the table, as the total absence of anything that would be a concealment.

An example: suppose I look at this table and then say to you, "This table is brown." What is happening? I convey something about something to you. You look at the table, shrug your shoulders, and agree. But the very fact that you agree, Heidegger is implying, depends upon two things: first, upon the fact that in and through the assertion 'the table is brown,' I communicate myself as being a *Dasein* that always and already dwells among beings that are ready-to-hand, and second, that in and through my communication of this assertion you as well bring yourself into your awareness of a being as being-uncovering of entities within-the-world. The conclusion seems to be that, for Heidegger, truth does not so much reside in the judgment or in the assertion, taken by itself, but in speech, in our speaking together of being(s) always and already thrown into a world, that is, both in that its being-with is "limited to a determinate circle of others" and "alongside a definite range of entities within-the-world."[7] This is so because, at the moment of the assertion and our agreement, the uncoveredness of the table is still preserved. It is this preservation of the uncoveredness of this individual table as a brown table that accounts for the fact that the judgment or the assertion relates and corresponds to the entity about which it is an assertion.

Yet Heidegger stresses that for the judgment 'the table is brown' to be true, it is not necessary that one brings oneself face to face with the table, that one, as Husserl would say, has to experience the table "in person." After all, it is possible to speak about this table (or, of course, anything else) in a proper manner while not being near to the table. What matters to Heidegger seems to be a certain modification in the understanding of the relation between the assertion and the entity being spoken of. That there is this relation, one will recall, stems from the uncoveredness of the table, which is preserved in the assertion. However, once asserted, the judgement becomes "as it were ready-to-hand which can be taken up and spoken [of] again."[8] It is here that the tendency to fall as a peculiar relation to the uncoveredness of a being comes into play. As one will recall, 'the They' is portrayed by Heidegger as doing what everyone does, speaking about that which everyone speaks about, reading what others have read, and so on.[9] Heidegger understands the being-uncovering of the They as "the absorption in something that has been said"; that is, "that which has been expressed as such takes over Being-towards those entities which have been uncovered in the assertion."[10] Thus, in the idle talk of the They, the relation between the assertion and that which is spoken of changes: no longer is the assertion 'the table is brown' something that occurs within in a world and in our speaking of entities within-the-world; in its stead 'the table is brown,' and the relation between the assertion and that which it speaks of, becomes present-at-hand. The uncoveredness that was preserved in the utterance is taken to be *Dasein's* sole discovery: "Uncoveredness of something becomes the present-at-hand conformity of *one* thing which is present-at-hand—the assertion expressed—*to* something else which is present-at-hand—the entity under discussion."[11] In this way, "the uncoveredness (truth) becomes, for its part, a relationship between things that are present-at-hand (*intellectus et res*)—a relationship that is present-at-hand itself,"[12] or as it is stated in *Introduction* to *Metaphysics,* "truth loosens itself, as it were, from beings, this can go so far that saying again becomes mere hearsay."[13] What worries Heidegger here is that philosophy, instead of reflecting upon being thrown in a particular world, returns to the Cartesian and thus mathematical understanding of world as, say, a collection of things present-at-hand, a collection of objects that can be adequately defined and represented correctly by a subject. Philosophy, turning to Heidegger's critique of Descartes, "prescribes for the world its 'real' Being."[14]

In his later works, as is well known, Heidegger pondered the experience of being that the Greeks entertained. For this, he returned to the understanding of *physis,* as "a kind and mode of presencing."[15] How indeed do beings become present, and how are they uncovered? Beings present—show—themselves. If they appear, this simultaneously entails that they have a certain look (*idea*), which is both how a being "presents itself to us, re-presents itself and as such stands before us" and *that* something that comes to presence indeed is coming to presence or presences.[16] The table, for instance, presents itself, but both in the sense *that* there 'is' this table and in the sense of *what* the table essentially is—that is, a brown plateau having four legs. The look—*idea*—or what a being shows itself to be is equated with its being: *that* there is (this) being in this or that way is substituted for "that which comes to presence in the whatness of the look."[17] A being is determined thereby from out of its lying present as *a* being for a subject: a table is what it is because it shows itself most often as a brown plateau with four legs. The being of the being table is that it 'is' as being a plateau with four legs; the 'real' being of a being is held in thought, rather than encountered from out of a particular event. The consequence is that the very fact *that* a being is able to lie present for a subject is considered to be secondary. Herein lies the birth of the so-called modern subject: a being is if and only if it (a) shows itself *to* a subject, and (b) if this subject can determine both that a being shows itself at all and what this being shows itself to be like.

Thus, metaphysics loosens this second sense of becoming-present from the first sense and detaches the 'look' that a being gives 'to us' from the becoming-present of a being itself. In metaphysics, this what-ness—*essentia, hupokeimenon, subiectum*—becomes the norm and the criterion for anything to show up. That the table is brown, for instance, is no longer inferred from the fact that the table presents itself from out of a world, but it is because the table has this or that essence—chemical elements that produce a certain pigment—that this table *must* be brown. Metaphysics retains of the becoming-present of being(s) merely the 'whatness' of a being and understands the very appearing of a particular being, its 'thatness,' always and already from out of its 'whatness.' Therefore, this whatness or essence comes to determine also how beings in particular appear; that is, they will always and already appear as a privation, a fall, and a defect over against the whatness that "is most in being about beings."[18] It is, according to Heidegger, Plato who develops this metaphysical pattern for the first time: now "beings themselves, which previously hold sway sink to the level of that what Plato calls *mē on*—that which really should not be and really *is* not either—because beings always deform the idea, the pure look, by actualizing it, insofar as they incorporate in matter."[19] For Plato the pure abstract(ed) look matters, and the material being is only a deformed, inferior copy of the being as it is held in thought. Thus, now that which appears, that which makes an appearance, is but a seeming and a defect, in short, a fall over against the "whatness" of the particular being which "is now what *really* is."[20] Metaphysics, for Heidegger, is essentially the appearance of a range of distinctions or dichotomies in that which, for the Greeks prior to Plato, originally *belonged together*, namely, and among others, being and becoming or being and thinking. Whereas for the Greeks the being of beings is to be traced from out of the manifold appearances of beings, metaphysics distinguishes between the inferior appearance of a being in time and in materiality and the 'permanent presence' of the essence of a being that does not appear, but can be held in thinking. Heidegger does not dismiss all presence of beings but is rather looking for a more original (phenomenological?) account of the presence of beings in their very presencing or coming into presence in being and in time. Whereas for the Greeks being and thinking belong together in the sense that being *needs* the *noein* or apprehension of human beings so that "apprehension also necessarily occurs along with appearance," in metaphysics "thinking sets itself against Being in such a way that Being is re-presented to thinking, and constantly stands against thinking like an ob-ject."[21] Being and thinking no longer call for one another, but thinking assumes dominance over being in that the representation of the essence of a being decides over the appearance of beings. The appearance of a being no longer gives rise to thought; rather a being *is* only insofar as it can be represented in thinking. To conclude, it is important to note that, in this sense, the metaphysical appearance of such a cleft is always worked out from out of a privative term: for instance, 'becoming' appears over against being as something that really should not be and is therefore, from the perspective of being, proclaimed as something that in reality *is* not either.

How does all this relate to Christianity? Not only do we have here the means to grapple with that which Heidegger understood as ontotheology—'God' as the uncaused cause and unmoved mover who founds or holds together the (immaterial) essences of the diverse material (but imperfect) beings—but also one can understand Heidegger here as a thinker who is careful not to think of our particular being-in-the-world as a defect, or, to use theology's terminology, as a fallen or sinful creature that has to deplore its own status. Rather Heidegger is concerned to retrieve from this conception of a being's appearing and appearance as a defect a more original openness toward being. The seeming of every appearance of a being is not something that really should not be, but the appearance of such a seeming necessarily belongs to the way in which (a) being itself makes itself known to human beings. This seeming, then, need not be understood in a privative manner, as something that should not be. It is part and parcel of this more original truth—*aletheia* as the event of being—that tries to think through that which, according to Heidegger, Aristotle already understood, namely, that *Dasein* "can *either* conceal *or* unconceal" and that this double possibility is distinctive of the truthfulness of *Dasein*'s existence.[22] To return to our example: it is not that the seeming and the appearance of the table must be opposed to an adequate judgment, to, say, a scientific and 'correct' understanding of the table. It is, rather, the other way around: such a scientific understanding is only possible since (un)concealment is already in play. It is not the case that the judgment unconceals the 'essence' of the table and is 'more true' than all the rest we would like to say about tables, for instance in poetry. Both are possible only on the basis of authentic and inauthentic (un)concealment, which, in turn, is possible on the basis of *Dasein*'s being-thrown-in-the-world as concealing and unconcealing. What happens in the distinction between ready-to-hand and present-at-hand judgments is that in the latter the reference to this particular being, and to *Dasein*'s relation toward this being, is interpreted in a metaphysical way: when judgment becomes the locus of truth, this judgment is always and already an utterance about something that lies present (as objects lie present) for someone—the subject—to which this object always and already *only* can lie present. What is overlooked is that the 'truth of the truth of the judgment' lies in *Dasein*'s appropriating it in its own way—which always is both concealing *and* unconcealing, improper and proper. In short, that *Dasein* has to be—or, rather *is*—its own *Entdecken* from out of a particular world is no longer taken into view.

But can it be? Heidegger's own account of overcoming metaphysics is a complex one. On the one hand, it seems that one can only surmise what this 'overcoming' might be, if one understands metaphysics *from within*. The famous '*Schritt zurück*' tells us precisely that: the step back out of metaphysics occurs only when metaphysics is properly understood. However, whether this 'overcoming' can ever succeed is not clear. Not only is the appearance of 'ground,' the movement that seeks to found finitude in an infinite and unfounded instance, portrayed as a "perhaps necessary illusion of foundation,"[23] but it is also affirmed that "fallenness is a natural condition of *Dasein*."[24] Throwness and falling are constitutive for *Dasein's* being-in-the world. As such, they account for what Heidegger has called the "inauthentic manner" of being-in-the-world. I have already noted that this inauthenticity deals only with beings in their presence rather than with their becoming-present and that it therefore has lost sight of the being of this or that being. In other words, the openness toward being is closed off in favor of a disclosing of beings, which, in turn, is regarded as the only possible way of relating to being. It is, at least in *Being and Time*, not sure whether this inauthentic manner is something that can be overcome. Indeed, authenticity is not a permanent state of *Dasein*. Rather, it 'has its moments': for instance, angst, sickness, boredom, and death.[25] Here the tendency of fallenness to understand itself out of the world and out of beings disappears but only to show, or to make appear, that *Dasein* already has to be its world, that is has to be its openness toward the world and toward being; in short and more familiar terms, what is revealed is that this *Dasein* is the being that has to be its own being as a being-with others and entities within-the-world. The inauthentic tendency is not brought to halt, but what now appears is that its unconcealing is, in fact, at the same time, a concealing—a comportment toward beings. Angst and death, one could say, make *Dasein's* openness appear—its *Entdecken*, *Entwurf*, *Erschlossenheit*—as such, that is, as entailing the double possibility of concealing and unconcealing: its relation to (its own) being. But since this authentic way is not a permanent *Zustand* of *Dasein*, some have argued that angst and death only show the inevitable character of fallenness.[26] However, to look at things in this way *already* presupposes that this fallenness is a defect to be overcome. Rather, and instead of deploring the inevitability of fallenness as such, one should ponder whether the tendency to regard the appearance of beings to be a defect, that is, the tendency to regard fallenness and throwness to be a privation, as 'that which really should not be,' is inevitable.

It is not sure whether Heidegger, at least in 1927, succeeded in doing this. Indeed, if one can maintain that Heidegger was seeking to disclose another way of comporting toward being, it is highly disturbing as to how precisely he reached this conclusion. Thrownness is part and parcel of being-in-the-world, and it is characteristic of thrownness that it is disclosed "more or less plainly and impressively."[27] The disclosedness of thrownness thus admits of degrees: it is either disclosed totally or in a lesser manner. This point needs to be proven, and it is Heidegger himself who, though through a single occurrence, delivers this proof. Those instances that make our being-in-the-world appear seem like a sort of maximum of disclosed-ness. So, for instance, angst is accompanied by "the selfsame of the disclosure and the disclosed,"[28] which is, in both cases, (the possibility of) being-in-the-world as such. Indeed, that which is disclosed is the same as that which discloses, that is, being-in-the-world or *Dasein* as such. However, does not such a maximum intimate the return of truth as correspondence or at least the thesis that *Dasein's* facticity can be taken into view adequately?[29]

Remarkably, the theory of truth as adequation also returns in the works of Levinas and Marion. In Levinas' work, it is the Other who coincides with him- or herself and who, therefore, is able to tear the subject out of its situatedness—Levinas' term for *Geworfenheit*. In Marion, however, the gifted is, time and again, defined as the sum of his or her responses toward givenness.

Another Metaphysics: The Metaphysics of the Other (Levinas)

This section focuses on two issues: first, Levinas' insistence that all knowledge entails the correspondence theory of truth, that is, in his terms, the reduction of the other to the same; second, Levinas' concern that this primacy of the theoretical attitude devalues both human beings and God.

For Levinas, all knowledge exposes a will to power or a reduction of the Other to the same, and there is but one instance that supposedly breaks with this procedure: the face of the other. The transcendence of the human person resists all identification or adequation. The other's face is not reducible to some common characteristics, or 'form,' that this particular other would share with others. Hence according to what would be Levinas' account of racism:[30] racism reduces black persons to their being black, to their 'form' or visible attributes. This is to commit an injustice toward the black person's face, his or her being a unique individual. The black person is reduced to being 'nothing other' than his or her blackness. Note that, if racism proceeds thus, it almost automatically extends to all black men and women: since you, as a black person, would be nothing other than your blackness, all other black persons would also be merely instantiations and instances of this essence of 'blackness,' and thus one will be racist against these others as well. For, if one black person can be reduced to his or her participation in being black, the racist will also reduce all the other black persons to what they share with or have in common with this one particular other to whom he or she is being racist.

In a Levinasian vein, one can describe the 'end' of metaphysics as the end of thinking about anything or anyone in general, since the dignity of a human being, for Levinas, does not lie in being a member of a particular community, a determinate context, but precisely in his or her irreducibility to such a context. Thus, Levinas sets out an opposition between the (invisible) face and the (visible) form of the human person, between the manifestation, the revelation and the epiphany of the face, and the ordinary phenomenality of objects and beings, between the "pure signification" (OB, 143) of the encounter with the other and the 'impure' appearance of a form, already contaminated with the phenomenality essential to being. While the former is an inadequation par excellence, the appearance of the latter is conditioned by the correspondence between the concept and the phenomenon in question. While the former manifests itself "independently of every position we would have taken in this regard" (TI, 65), the latter is dependent precisely on the position that the subject assumes over and against the objective phenomenon (just as the table can only appear to a subject over and against the horizon of a table in general).

However, we need to examine how Levinas maintains this distinction. It might be that the nonadequation in the case of the face in turn is dependent on the correspondence theory of truth, since after all the manifestation of a face entails "a coinciding of the expressed with him who expresses."[31] What does Levinas mean? The face-to-face with the other originates, as we have seen, in language. In expression, that which is manifested coincides with the one manifesting himself or herself. On one condition, however: the one manifesting itself attends to its own manifestation, that is, is able to correct its own manifestation. According to Levinas, the Saying always differs from the said.[32] For example, if I see someone crying, it is not me who decides on the meaning of the tears of the other; the truth of these tears has to be communicated by him or her. It is only in discourse that the transcendence of the Other makes its appearance, but only to disappear, to leave its trace. The Other can tell me that his or her tears are faked, since he or she is rehearsing for a play, but he or she can just as well retrieve even this statement on a later occasion. Thus, it is not *what* the Other says that is the trace of transcendence, but the fact that he or she speaks and that he or she, in this way, is always able to retrieve *what* he or she has said. In short, the other is able to *teach* me in the sense of revealing to me something that I do not already know. Thus, the transcendence of the other lies in his or her being always other and always different from that which is said, in his or her irreducibility to the form of the said.[33] However, this difference is, in one way or another, subordinated to the possibility that the one speaking coincides with that which is said. Thus, if there is a difference between the face—the Saying—and the form—the said—it can only be so because the one instance that makes a difference—the other—is excepted from this difference: the other can coincide with himself or herself and is, therefore, able to point me to the difference between his or her saying and his or her said. It seems, therefore, that the difference between the Saying and the said can only be maintained if this difference is measured by the possible adequation between the one manifesting and that which he or she manifests: in order to condemn me of my inadequate response, the Other needs to be fully present and transparent to him- or herself! One might surmise therefore, that it is, at least for the Levinas of *Totality and Infinity*, not me who is the modern subject, but the Other. Here is not the place to tackle all these questions, but suffice it to say that the return of truth as merely more 'adequate to the same' might point to the fact that 'overcoming metaphysics' may not be as easy a task as it nowadays sometimes seems.

In the next section I will therefore point to a critique of Levinas that is encountered in the works of both Marion and Visker. Visker argues for a reconsideration of the relation between the face and the form. Marion is concerned with the individuation of the other over and against the neutral horizon of Levinasian ethics.

A Significant Other? From the Other to the Individual (Marion)

Levinas is quite clear on the distinction between the face and the form, both in *Totality and Infinity* and in *Otherwise than Being*. Consider the following passage, taken from the first mentioned book: "[T]he alterity of the Other does not depend on any quality that would distinguish him from me, for a distinction of this nature would precisely imply between us that community of genus which already nullifies alterity" (*TI*, 194). Hence there is a distinction between the transcendence of the other and the (Husserlian) transcendence of the object. For the difference between different objects is possible only on the basis of the (different) qualities that emerge from within a community of genus, just as we are able to distinguish between a brown and a black table from out of the shared horizon of a table in general. *Otherwise than Being* will underline the nonphenomenal character of the other as well: "[T]he neighbor does not stand in a form, like an object abides in the plasticity of an aspect, a profile or an open series of aspects, which overflows each of them without destroying the adequation of the act of consciousness" (OB, 87), for if he would appear in a form and be reduced to the *Abschattungen* and adumbrations the reducing I performs in face of the object, the glory of the face would become a phenomenon *as every other phenomenon* and enter into conjunction with the very subject to which it appears (cf. OB, 144). To be sure, the face *can* be treated as every other phenomenon, and it is precisely in this reduction of the other to his or her visible properties that the possibility of racism and sexism resides.

Although we will see Marion arguing for the individuation of the other later in this book, it is noteworthy that Marion, in his own way, rehearses Levinas' distinction between the face and the form. According to Marion indeed, one should distinguish between the flesh ('*la chair*') and the body ('*le corps*'): whereas I am exposed as an object in a medical examination or in surgery, the erotic flesh-to-flesh, according to Marion, is to be conceived of as the pendant of the ethical face-to-face.[34] This strict distinction between the face and the form or between the flesh and the body, however, might suffer from a similar spiritualization we detected earlier in Marion's phenomenology of the icon, for one could concur with Derrida here and state that "by putting the flesh everywhere, one risks vitalizing, psychologizing, spiritualizing and interiorizing everything, even there where one speaks of a non-possession and of an alterity of the 'flesh.'"[35] A similar question will concern us in that which follows, for if I really may not "notice the color of [the other's] eyes," not even that "his pupils are black as holes," how then can I 'see' his face?[36] The question can be posed in another way: is Levinas' account of the alterity of the other apt to encounter a *singular* other, that is, "able to welcome the Other in his or her ethnic identity"?[37] What if this particular other does not speak Greek or Hebrew and speaks, perhaps, only a "babbling language, like [. . .] the discourse of a stranger *shut up in his maternal language*" (OB, 143)?[38]

In this section, therefore, I would like to trace a few criticisms of Levinas' distinction between the face and the form, for, if it is correct to contend that the end of metaphysics implies that one should refrain from thinking of anything or anyone in general, then one should ask whether the Levinasian other indeed refuses all generalization.

Visker, for instance, develops the idea that a "more correct phenomenological description"[39] of the other would amount to a reconsideration of the relation between the face and the form, for the dignity of the human being might not lie in him or her being an abstract man without context but rather in his or her being *not without* context. This is why an African American "is angry not just with those who discriminate against him because of his color, [but also] with those who respect him notwithstanding his color."[40] It seems, therefore, that Levinas somewhat underestimated the attachment of human beings toward their form and visible being, and here is another reason why the axiom I traced from *Totality and Infinity* and *Otherwise than Being*, namely, the reduction of everything in being to being but an expression of an (unjust) *conatus essendi*, is itself, perhaps, an injustice toward the Other. To develop this claim, one might reconsider Levinas' argument that the face is strictly distinct from the works in which it expresses itself (*TI*, 66–67; 175–83). For the works *of* the other are, perhaps, not merely egoistic and economic reductions of otherness to the same, but rather seem to contribute to the other's otherness in a particular way. Just as African American women and men would be angry if I would say to them that I respect them regardless of their skin color, so too the other would be treated unjustly if I would pay no attention at all to that which he or she does to make a living or to persevere in his or her being. It is in this way that Levinas seems to disregard the attachment of human beings to that which they identify themselves with and does not even consider that the ontological enjoyment in 'making a living' might just as well "enter into the way of existing of the exterior being" (*TI*, 35).[41]

Such a sweeping claim that turns all identification into an egoistic complaisance of oneself also bears on that which one often praises as Levinasian ethics, for this ethics suffers perhaps from that which Finkielkraut remarks of the doctor without frontiers, who "is too busy filling the hungry mouth with rice, to still have time to listen to what it is trying to say."[42] Here an ethics solely based on an asymmetry between the Other and I seems to encounter its limits, for how could an ethics that does not concern itself with the other's movement toward me (cf. *OB*, 84) ever make room for Finkielkraut's objection? Indeed, what if the other demands water, and all my hands have to give to him or her is bread? One should ponder indeed whether an ethics appropriate to the individual is not another ethics than the one Levinas advances, which is almost exclusively focused on the relief of the other's basic needs. The signification that is supposedly before culture turns into an attending to the other that is an ethics *only* of "nourishing, clothing, [and] lodging" (*OB*, 77). But, to misuse a New Testament phrase, one does not live by bread alone. It is here, therefore, that the Heideggerian analysis of solicitude (*Fürsorge*) as a care for-the-other might be invoked to balance Levinas' ethics, not only because it incorporates the concern "with food and clothing, and the nursing of the sick body,"[43] but especially because solicitude in its authentic mode does not take away the care of the other for him- or herself—leaping in for him or her as when one, as a parent, would do the child's homework—but rather "gives it back to him authentically as such for the first time"[44]—as when one would take the time to teach the child the matter at hand so as to prepare it to do the homework itself. Most important for our concern here however is how Heidegger defines this authentic care for the other: it is an authentic care because it pertains to the care for the existence of the human being *in toto* and not only, as is the case in Levinas' ethics, to a 'what' or to the basic needs with which he or she is concerned.[45]

All this might entail that the encounter with the other is not so much "without context" as Levinas contends and that, if one wants to take singularity seriously, one best not dream of a "total transparence" (*TI*, 182) in these matters, for an ethics that wants to be truly an ethics might need to take into account not only that the care for the other is *in each case mine* but also that the ethics to be followed might be different from one ethnic group to another or from one individual to another and that, therefore, the appropriate response to the other is *in each case different*.

Marion, then, envisages a passageway to the particular other through the question of love. There are, of course, good reasons for this, because perhaps only love permits and demands the individuation of the other (*BG*, 324). In this way, love is always love of *this* particular other. Marion seems to open a pathway that goes beyond Levinas's almost exclusive attention to ethics. Already in *Prolegomena to Charity*, Marion manifests a certain reluctance toward the universality of Levinasian ethics and the Kantian resonances thereof.[46] Both the Kantian respect for the other as an end in itself and the Levinasian responsibility for the other concern the other human being in general. In this sense, ethics is always and already the neutralization of the particular other. I am not responsible for this rather than that other; I am responsible for every other human being to the extent that he or she is an instantiation of the face: "[P]aradoxically, the moral law—which states that the other man must always count as an end and not as a means—never uses the face of an individualized other except as a means for accomplishing the universal. The injunction of obligation toward the other leads, in reality, to the neutralization of the other as such."[47] The objection can be repeated in the face of Levinas' other, for "the face itself neutralizes unsubstitutable individuality: I do not find myself responsible for *this* other as much as this other admits of being reduced to a face *in general*."[48] One should ponder, however, whether this notion of a 'face in general' is not in itself a metaphysical notion, robbed from all things finite and temporal, for if this or that other can only impose an ethical claim on me because of his or her being an actualization of the face in general, how are we to determine the status of this face-in-general? Is it that one leaps from the particularity of this face to the essence of a face in general or—the other way around—that the concept of a face 'in general' determines beforehand how this or that particular other will appeal to me? Here again one finds reasons to doubt that the appeal is always and everywhere ethical and why ethics might be yet another usurpation of our particular being-in-the-world. It is because of these intimations of Levinas' inability to attend to the other as an individual that I fully subscribe to Marion's turn to the individual (*haeccitas*)[49] and to the conclusion of *Le phénomène érotique*, that, "strictly speaking, we ought not to speak of [. . .] the face in general, nor of the other in general, but only of *this* other, designated by *this* face—it being understood that I never envisage a universal or common face, but always *this* face which opposes me *this* alterity."[50] Given, however, Marion's insistence on an appeal in general that, because it is considered to be the 'pure form of the appeal' that incorporates all possible other appealing instances, whether it be God, the other, self-affection or difference (cf. *RG*, 202), one should ask whether the sketch of the other as an individual that one finds in Marion's thinking about love is not somewhat at odds with the abstract phenomenological project of *Reduction and Givenness* and *Being Given*. One should, therefore, take not only Derrida's claim 'that there is more than one appeal' seriously but also ask why and to what extent Marion's configuration of the *adonné* is incompatible with the turn to the individual evoked here, for why, first, assume that the appeal of God, of the other, of self-affection, and so on would correspond to and converge in one single, general appeal? For, second, the account of the *adonné* as the one who receives him- or herself from that which he or she receives makes no mention at all of the sexual difference between men and women and in this sense, seems to disregard all questions on the differences in the manner of receiving between men and women. Third, given the rather abstract classification of saturated phenomena in Marion's phenomenological project, one wonders whether or not Marion would put the human *haeccitas* simply on a par with every other phenomenon as it gives itself. If Marion indeed would not be able to distinguish between the appearance of a human being and givenness 'in general,' one needs to ask whether Marion—on a phenomenological level—takes sufficiently into account that the phenomenon's appearance is in each case different. In short, to mix all appearance into the one, single appeal of givenness might simply be a (phenomenological) injustice toward the manifold ways of making an appearance, of presencing.[51] There is no place to develop this here, but the question at least hints at the fact that Marion's phenomenology is substituting the face-in-general for the *adonné-in-general*, itself derived from an 'appeal in general.'

The next section, therefore, will focus on the *mathematical* metaphors with which Marion describes the *adonné* in order to point to the incompatibility of the human being as an *adonné* with the account of the human being from out of his or her *haeccitas*.

Responding *ad Infinitum?*

Marion presents a radicalized version of Levinas' philosophy: "[O]ne would have to extend the status of a beyond of beingness (*epekeina tes ousias*) to every being-given" (*VR*, 58). This is, in fact, what his *magnum opus*, *Being Given*, sets out to do. Givenness gives itself in every phenomenon as a nonmetaphysical present (gift). Phenomena come into being, but without that being determining essentially this or that particular being. Phenomena always exceed the gaze of the subject that tries to constitute it as an object; that is, it exceeds attempts to describe it adequately. Take, for example, the saturated phenomenon of the event. No one has seen the totality of the battle of Waterloo (cf. *BG*, 228–29). The event cannot be described adequately but appeals to a multiplication of views that altogether forbid constituting it as one single object. Saturated phenomena have no essence, no constant presence to which one can constantly and confidently refer but appeal to the subject to align itself to its appearance. This appearance is a gift: therefore, it cannot be, as was the case with the correspondence theory of truth, foreseen—the presence of this or that chemical element predicts that the table must be brown—its invisible present arrives as a surprise, unforeseen—as when one suddenly notices that the brown of this particular table here resembles the table in one's parents' house. This nonessential character of the gift extends to all phenomena: though to some extent everything that happens to the subject can be considered to be an object, this objectlike character never suffices to explain the unforeseeability of what come to us as a gift. An echography makes the birth of a child to a certain extent foreseeable, at least for the doctors, but this anticipation of its birth cannot annul the fact that this birth will be lived, at least by the parents, as unforeseeable.[52] According to Marion, all phenomena can give themselves as an event and can summon the subject to receive itself from that which it receives. Hence Marion's thought that, for phenomena to appear, they require an individuation: the phenomena give their selves when giving themselves. The birth of my child is, at least for me, a *singular* event. Moreover, this event singularizes me as the gifted; its happening happens to give me to myself as the one who is given, in and through the reception of the birth, to the child: I am now given to the child as a father, and this is what individualizes me. Therefore, the gifted plays a secondary role toward givenness: it is already a response to an appeal. However, it pertains to the gifted to show or to make appear what is given to him: the appeal shows itself in the response of him or her to whom it is given. However, the generalization of the *epekeina tes ousias* requires one to consider the appeal anew. Herein lies Marion's critique of Levinas.[53] It is, according to Marion, not clear whether the appeal of the face in Levinas comes from the other or from God. This *à Dieu* even risks naming that which cannot be named, to suppress the anonymity and ambiguity of the appeal, in short, "to dissolve the very thing [it was] to protect."[54] Hence there arises Marion's insistence on the pure form of the appeal which cannot be identified, that is, it is radically anonymous, and, if it was to be identified, it can only be named inappropriately, since pertaining to the limited and finite response of the *adonné*.

What concerns us here is, however, that there is an appeal and that one cannot not respond to this "always already there interpellation" (*BG*, 217, mod.). This is why Marion can determine human beings as follows: "[T]he history of the gifted is due to the *sum* of its responses" (*BG*, 295). Such a mathematical understanding of phenomena is by no means a single occurrence in Marion's phenomenology: not only the event, of which Marion insists so much that it resists all unification, seems to allow for a kind of teleology *ad infinitum* of which the *telos* nevertheless receives a determination as "the *sum* of the agreements and disagreements among subjects" (*BG*, 229), but the painting as well could in principle be adequately represented, if only one could make a "sum of all that which all have seen, see, and will see there" (*IE*, 72). It is, however, the definition of the human being as the sum of his or her responses that shows itself to be particularly revealing of the objectification of the subject I sketched in Marion's works. Indeed, *what is* this sum, and who or what is going to determine it? In any case, that such a sum of responses is possible shows that the overcoming of the metaphysical adequation may not have succeeded. Indeed, simply the fact stating that such a sum could be envisaged seems to imply the recurrence of a God's-eye point of view, that is, the thought that someone or something can oversee the totality of my responses. One could agree that this sum of my responses is obtained at the occasion of my death. However, since it is considered to be an endless hermeneutics, the responses of those that respond to my death would have to be included in the sum of my responses. This sum of responses is, therefore, in this world, always to be deferred and postponed. Therefore, one can surmise whether an instance 'not of this world,' distant from the world, could oversee the sum of my responses. A God's-eye point of view indeed!

The Consequences of Overcoming Metaphysics for Faith and Theology

We have seen that Heidegger, although keen to keep our openness to being open, has recourse to the concept of 'adequation' to define this 'proper' openness: there are moments when that which is disclosed is the same as that which is disclosing itself. Levinas responds that this openness toward being is already filled in by the other and that it is this other that coincides with him- or her-self, for that which is spoken is the same as the one speaking. And, if it is not the same, the being that speaks can at least correct itself, thus, pointing to a 'possible' adequation. Marion, in turn, responds to Levinas that this filling-in is too much of a filling in and that, therefore, there is no reason to prefer the other, instead of something without name.

It is well known that Heidegger had a somewhat peculiar relation to Christianity and that he, more often than not, claimed philosophy to be thoroughly atheistic. In *The Metaphysical Foundations of Logic*, for instance, Heidegger deals with the accusation in a way that is at least ambiguous: on the hand he concedes the atheistic character of his thinking insofar it concerns the ontic involvement of his fundamental ontology, but on the other hand, he asks, "[M]ight not [. . .] the presumably ontic faith in God be at bottom godlessness? And might not the genuine metaphysician be more religious than the usual faithful, than the members of a 'church' or even the 'theologians' of every confession?"[55] This conclusion hopes therefore to show that, 'after' metaphysics, the link between faith and atheism in all three thinkers is tightened to such an extent that one might even ask whether atheism does not genuinely belong to faith of any kind. In the later *Introduction to Metaphysics*, Heidegger develops a similar mode of procedure towards the question of faith: "Anyone for whom the Bible is divine revelation and truth has the answer to the question 'Why are there beings at all instead of nothing?' before it is even asked."[56] However, even here Heidegger kept open the possibility of an authentic questioning, even in matters of faith. For faith, of course, has no answers, only faith. For faith to be a mode of questioning, it must, according to Heidegger, rid itself not only of the answer that God as Creator answers for the existence of beings, not only of the agreement to adhere to a doctrine somehow handed down, but, most important, "continually expose itself to the possibility of unfaith."[57]

Surprisingly, we find Levinas saying something similar. For instance, in his *Entre nous*, he writes: "The ambiguity of transcendence—and thus the interplay of the soul going from atheism to faith and from faith to atheism—[is] the original mode of God's presence."[58] One might even surmise in Marion's phenomenology a similar critical stance toward dogmatics. It is indeed difficult to see how the emphasis on God's incomprehensibility can be reconciled with the church as the guarantee of truth.

The overcoming of metaphysics thus not only means that we cannot consider faith to be an object that is freely at our disposal, or as Marion would put it, an "idiotic prolepsis of a blunt certitude" (GWB, 71). It is worth noting that this supposed overcoming of metaphysics also entails not only the end of rational theology, as explained above, but also that of natural theology. This is obvious in, for instance, Levinas' rejection of theodicy. 'God' cannot be invoked to explain (or to justify) the suffering of human beings. God is no longer to be viewed as the 'reason' or 'cause' of humanity's violence and miseries, since God is transcendent to history. Every attempt to explain history on the basis of the will of God is, according to Levinas, an infliction toward precisely the victims of that history, and, most often, such an attempt cannot prevent this God from becoming "a protector of all the egoisms" (OB, 161). Heidegger would argue that developing a theology on the basis of, for example, the natural sciences disregards the fact that these sciences are already indebted to the metaphysical theory of truth as correspondence. These sciences are therefore ontic and deal with being only in terms of beings. Therefore, they cannot instruct us on what it means to be, and even less on how God might come into being.

This means that faith is not primarily dogmatic, but ethical (Levinas) and pragmatic (Marion), a faith moreover "in which it is no longer a matter of naming or attributing something to something, but of aiming in the direction of . . . of relating to . . . of comporting oneself toward . . . of reckoning with . . ." (IE, 144–45). It is not that this faith would become purely and solely pragmatic; it is the admission of the fact that the debate of whether or not a referent applies to this faith can only begin in and through precisely such a pragmatic stance, in which faith first and foremost has become a question. This is the reversal: theology can no longer start with the assertion that "God is . . ." It can only start in prayer or in ethics, as if a *fides qua* without the blunt certitude beforehand of *fides quae*, as if only in the faithful stance of the *fides qua* a genuine *fides quae* might be able to be discerned. This, therefore, seems to be the lesson to be learned from Heidegger, Levinas, and Marion.

But, then again, is it? Have I not shown how all three of them have recourse to the concept of a (possible) adequation to make acceptable their respective accounts of overcoming metaphysics? We have seen how both Levinas and Marion try to institute an invisible instance that accounts for our being-in-the-world. For Levinas, the other does not and cannot appear 'in' the world. For Marion, that which is shown of givenness through the *adonné* is not 'of' the world. For both, then, and to recall Lacoste's phrasing here as well, a certain distance from the world and its history is the condition of the correct interpretation of this world. That there is no metaphysical 'otherworldliness' involved does not mean, however, that the metaphysical mode of procedure has been surpassed. Indeed, both have recourse to the metaphysical theory of truth as correspondence to justify such an instance distinct and distant from the world. This might mean that we, philosophers and theologians alike, have not yet succeeded in thinking finitude otherwise than as a fall. For Marion, givenness 'arrives' in the world from a distance that is not of this world but that could only be given. This again seemed to imply that there is an instance that could obtain adequate sight of the *adonné*, that could oversee the sum of my responses, as if I were only an object, transparent to whatever kind of subject.

Chapter 8

Marion and Levinas on Metaphysics

In this chapter, I will consider Marion's and Levinas' account of the "ontotheological constitution of metaphysics." This will allow us to understand the reversal of the subject-object distinction at issue in the larger bulk of their respective works in greater detail. My overall question is to understand why there, after all, can still be some ontotheological residues detected in the works of the authors under discussion. One should indeed be wary when these authors, who are very much aware of the question concerning ontotheology, still succumb to the temptation of a clear and adequate description of the human being and its finitude. To explain these residues, I think it best not to go along with what one could call the "historical approach" to the problem of ontotheology, in which one identifies one or the other author as 'ontotheological' only to make sure that other authors are not—as Marion does with Suàrez and Descartes, and Radical Orthodoxy for instance with Duns Scotus.[1] For, just as ontotheology does not seem to have a clear-cut beginning, so too it might not have a clear-cut ending.

In the case of Marion, it is good to start with *The Idol and Distance* (1977). Here Marion tries to show that only a certain kind of theology, the discourse of the cross, is able to surpass metaphysics. "Perhaps," Marion writes, "it would be necessary to attempt to take this discourse up again, from out of the place where we are, ontotheology" (*ID*, 19, mod.). Marion then explains his mode of procedure: "We undoubtedly cannot get out of it, as if one could pass through the idolatrous mirror" (*ID*, 19), since "[w]hoever claims to jump outside of onto-theology in one leap is exposed to the danger of repeating it, by a slight, naively critical inversion" (*ID*, 20). Only one path, according to Marion, lies open, that is, "to travel through ontotheology itself along all its limits [. . .] to expose oneself to what already no longer belongs to it" (*ID*, 19).

Our question in this chapter will be whether Marion succeeds in doing this and if he, though keen to take up another path, has not himself

fallen into the trap of the first path, that of repeating metaphysics through
a simple inversion. At the time of *The Idol and Distance*, only a "non-onto-
theological theology" (*ID*, 20) was seen as able to expose the limits of
the ontotheological enterprise, since "[a]ny metaphysician [. . .] maintains,
within onto-theology, an oblique relation to [distance]. Distance works him
as unbeknownst to him" (ibid.). Admitting on the same page that he works
from out of "the insurpassable primacy of Christian revelation," Marion then
considers *ontotheology from a theological point of view*: "It is not a matter of
questioning Christianity starting from onto-theology, but of sketching out a
perspective on onto-theology [. . .] starting from [. . .] Christianity" (*ID*, 21).

Marion and/on Ontotheology

Nihilism, the Death of God, and the Persistence of Idolatry

The Idol and Distance aims at thinking through "the indisputably apparent
absence of the divine" (*ID*, 21). This absence has come about in the wake
of the death of God. But this death of God, according to Marion, is at the
same time the end of metaphysics. The latter coincides with its idolatrous
function being exposed. Discussing Nietzsche's announcement of this untimely
death, Marion asks which God is precisely dying here, for "the proclamation
of the 'death of God,' in order to be rigorously articulated [. . .] must attack,
that is, rest upon, a precise idol—the idol forged by the will to truth and
morals. Hence a paradoxical consequence [. . .]: the 'death of God' remains
a seriously thinkable event only by surrounding the 'God' who dies with
quotation marks. It maintains its power only over a vain idol of that which
God, if he 'is,' is not. Twilight falls irremediably only on an idol" (*ID*, 32).

In Nietzsche, then, it is the moral God, God as the rewarding father
and judge, who has died. For the same 'resentment' that has called God all
that which weakens will, in due time, exposes the weaknesses of this concept
of God. The fact that the moral God of Christianity is dead means the
following for Marion: "Over the 'God' who is an idolatrous mirror of morality
is superimposed the idolatrous function that metaphysics imposed [. . .] on
the Christian God" (*ID*, 34). What dies, but by coming to the fore, is thus
the idolatrous function of the idol itself: that is why the announcement of
the 'death of God' does not overcome nihilism, but rather inaugurates it
and makes it possible (*ID*, 33). The death of God *is* the end of metaphysics,
but this end shows metaphysics to itself in its idolatrous function. And it is

this idolatrous function that now, more importantly, no longer works: "[God and the gods] are dead in their idolatrous function" (*ID*, 34). "God," in metaphysics, found his place and his role "as the supreme being who, within the field of a discourse on the Being of beings [. . .] fulfills the function of concentrating its exemplary perfection [. . .] and of causally ensuring the coherence of a world" (*ID*, 35).

Far from liberating us from idolatry, the end of metaphysics and the death of God lead us to the persisting of precisely this idolatrous function, no longer aiming now at 'God' (whether or not between quotation marks) but at anything that satisfies the longing of the gaze. It is for this reason that, in Marion, "[t]he death of the idols frees up [. . .] an empty space, [. . .] the emptiness of a desertion, in expectation of a new presence. [. . .] Unlike others that opened up in the last resort, the question of an occupation of the divine does not at all have to mature for long in order to appear" (*ID*, 36).

The place of the divine will be occupied "not like an inheritance [. . .] but like a power falls to the one who takes possession of a territory that he does not know, but that he alone knew how to recognize, identify, and already invest" (*ID*, 37). This is what Nietzsche (and Marion) will name nihilism: "It falls to man to establish the value of every being without exception: this is [. . .] the establishment of man as the place of the production of beings in their Being. In order to reach their Being, beings must pass through valuation itself, through man" (*ID*, 41–42). Here is the (metaphysical) character of Nietzsche's eternal recurrence: "that nothing that is be excluded from one's perspective, such that nothing that occurs be subject to erasure or censure. The future has nothing better to do than to give again what passes" (*ID*, 42). Nothing genuinely new will and can happen. It is here that we, again, encounter 'postmodernism' as a lived reality of the eternal return of the same. One should note that the *rapprochement* I am forging here between Levinas' portrayal of the bad infinite as a *regressio ad infinitum* and Heidegger's claim that ontotheology cannot think being otherwise than jumping from beings to beings, is, in no wise merely floating in the air, devoid of any lived experience.

Indeed, in our postmodern age, everything appears from out of the subject's passed measurements and estimations to the point that any genuine newness comes to be mocked. 'After' metaphysics, therefore, in the contemporary situation, seems to consist in lacking all means to qualitatively differentiate between phenomena (of whatever kind). What is distinctive of postmodernism, I would contend, is that it only differentiates in a quantitative manner. Here postmodernism shows itself to be the heir of

Cartesianism: whereas Descartes inaugurated the possibility of a world-picture as a *collection* of finite substances (though appearing from out of the infinite) to the point that the extension of a piece of wax does not markedly differ from, say, the corpse of a human being, so, in our days, the world seems to appear as a *sum* of consumer goods, images, and texts to the point that one can no longer distinguish between the virtual and the real. It is in this sense that one needs to understand Marion's denunciation of, for instance, television as the production of images for which no original any longer exists. Rather, the image and the screen are such that nothing can be said to exist if it has not appeared on television (CV, 46ff). Note, in addition, that just as the announcement of the death of God does not equal the end of nihilism, but rather its inauguration, the death of the idolatrous function does not mean the end of all idolatry, but rather its beginning, or rather its *persistence in the cultural realm*. The disenchantment of the world occurring in and through metaphysics will leave no room for the divine but all the more for men and women to divinize themselves. Marion concludes that once the moral "God" is revoked, the "new gods" themselves also remain tied metaphysically to the will to power (cf. *ID*, 72).

Once the idolatrous function is laid bare, we seem to witness, therefore, an intensification of idolatry, as if the end of metaphysics cannot stop ending. Again Marion resorts to the terror of the televisual image according to which nothing really has happened if it was not televised: "[T]he technological possibility of being seen by an indefinite mass of viewers gives, today, a despotic power to the trivial (and Sartrean) adage: 'I am what the look of others wants (and sees) that I should be' [. . .] what I appear to be (the look) invests my identity bit by bit, and, in the end, completely" (CV, 52). Technological understanding, and its corresponding nihilism, thus pertains to the subject as well: one can appear to others only if one appears according to their own measures and expectations.

But all of this comes at a certain price, "the loss of nonmastery, or better, the inversion of mastery, shifting from the unseen to the anticipated [*prévu*]" (CV, 35). Unable to give ourselves over to someone or something, we are delivered to the mastery of the always and already anticipated and seen, thrown into a world where everything has already been said and has already been seen by someone. In light of this, the voyeuristic god we detected in Marion's work that sees 'with an eye that sees all' is all the more surprising. Nevertheless, Marion and Levinas' analysis of the postmodern world dominated by the despotic power of the already said and the already seen should not be underestimated.

Marion's Understanding of Ontotheology

I will now inquire just how Marion understands ontotheology and how it incorporates our contemporary nihilism. It is, as we have seen, the self-showing of the phenomenon that will allow Marion to proceed in his venture of overcoming metaphysics. But, whereas his early works conceive of such a self-showing only in relation to divine revelation, the later works will consider this self-showing as belonging to phenomenality in general.

What, then, for Marion, is ontotheology? Metaphysics is "[t]he production of a concept that makes a claim to equivalence with God" (*ID*, 13). Metaphysics has forgotten being in favor of a certain conception of beings. Indeed, it "thinks being, but in its own way" (*ID*, 13),[2] namely, in "that the thought of Being is obscured even in the question "*Ti to on?*" where the *on hē on* indicates more the beingness of beings (*Seiendheit, ousia, essentia*) than Being as such. Beingness thus transforms the question of Being as well into a question of the *ens supremum*, itself understood and posited started from the requirement, decisive for being, of the foundation" (*GWB*, 34).

Ontotheology thinks being from out of beings, that is, from out of that which is present in all beings. Subsequently, that which is present in all beings will be deemed to be the essence or the substance of the being. This substance will "present the achievement of Being" (*ID*, 14), what is most being-full in and of a being. Consider again our example of the table: what is essential to a table is not that it has this or that color but that it is produced as a plateau with four legs so that people can sit around and eat on it. The 'essence' of a being will thus be determined from out of what these beings have in common, what most determines their presence in the world. This essence is then constructed as the ground or the reason of the particular being: a table is what it is because it is a plateau with four legs. A being, for instance a table, *is* because it corresponds to the essence of a table (or any other being) that is determined in advance. But since such an essence still refers to the empirical existence of these beings (at least one of them), the essence of a being needs again to be founded in something else. "Hence, second, the movement to the supreme being. The supreme being in its turn delivers the most present figure of presence, which alone permits each—nonsupreme—being to remain already" as presence (*ID*, 14). This supreme being is then invoked to assure the unity of the essence of all the diverse, empirical beings and, importantly, to present the essence of a being independently of that of which it is the essence.

Marion's contribution to the question concerning ontotheology seems to consist in the thought that this ontotheological mode of procedure ends up in a "mutual grounding" (*ID*, 15) to the point that one must ask, hinting at Derrida, whether or not this foundational thinking has ever founded anything at all. Marion's point is that the supreme being can take up the role as first and founding being only because thought has, in advance, decided that being announces itself in presence (*ID*, 14). Because a being is considered to be founded only insofar as its essence (as permanent presence or as ousia) can be established, "God" can enter into philosophy only when God, in turn, is considered a foundation or the "most present figure of presence" (*ID*, 14). This mutual grounding is most clear in Marion's "Metaphysics and Phenomenology," an article that was republished in *The Visible and the Revealed*: "The inner unity of 'metaphysics' [. . .] stems from the fact that, between the science of being in general and the science of the being par excellence, the single institution of the ground is at work: common Being grounds being, even beings par excellence; in return, the being par excellence, in the mode of causality, grounds common being" (*VR*, 52).This is to the point that one can conclude that "each of them founds inasmuch as it lets itself be founded."[3] In the Cartesian case, where "being is [. . .] as much it is caused," this means that "this way of Being grounds beings by deploying them as *causata* and, inseparably, is itself grounded in a being par excellence, which is marked as *causa sui*" (*DMP*, 118).

The God of metaphysics must appear as *causa sui*, because philosophy has decided in advance that the divine must show up as that which gives reasons for finite beings: as much as each table appears as a table because it answers to the essence that thought has determined for it, so God can appear in metaphysics only as that being that assures (by founding precisely) the foundation or essence of all the diverse empirical beings. Once this mode of founding is questioned, metaphysics cannot not perish (Cf. *VR*, 53). *The Idol and Distance* insists on the compatibility of the idol and the ontotheological God as ground and moreover points to the political aspects of the problem of ontotheology: "The characteristics of the idol are equally suitable for a "God" who serves as ground, but himself receives a ground; a God who expresses supremely the Being of beings in general and, in this sense, reflects back to them a faithful image of that whereby they are and of that which they are supremely; a God who remains distant from common ontology only within a Conciliation (*Austrag*) that preserves a fundamental familiarity. Produced by and for onto-theology, this "God" is ordained by it like the idol by the city" (*ID*, 16–17). Marion makes mention of this political character of idolatry and ontotheology regularly (esp. *ID*, 6) but has, regretfully, and at least to my knowledge, never extended this claim with an effective political analysis. Therefore, I will now turn to Marion's depiction of ontotheology and ontotheologians.

Who's Afraid of Ontotheology? The Usual Suspects

In a certain sense, listing those who are labeled as ontotheologians is a bit of an awkward endeavor since such an enterprise in a text claiming the inescapability of ontotheology is indeed somewhat absurd. This list, however, serves only as a stepping stone to introduce ourselves into what seems like a deep ambiguity of contemporary thought, that is, the dividing line drawn between modernity and medieval times so as to safeguard (classical) Christian theology from the accusation of ontotheology.[4] Marion's position in this matter is somewhat ambivalent. In *God without Being* and earlier, Marion seems to have subscribed to the Heideggerian view that modernity merely was an intensification of the medieval paradigm: "[W]e will admit with Heidegger but also as a historian of philosophy, that this concept [that idolatry sets in equivalence with 'God'] finds a complete formulation [*une formulation achevée*], in modernity (Descartes, Spinoza, Leibniz but also Hegel)" (*GWB*, 35/*DsE*, 53). In this sense, what happened in modernity, with the concept of '*causa sui*,' was but the unfolding of a tendency already present in the philosophy and theology of the Middle Ages. In *God without Being*, this is most evident in Marion's attack on the proofs of God's existence (*GWB*, 32–33). Marion is perhaps again following Heidegger, who stated that "a god who must permit his existence to be proved in the first place is ultimately a very ungodly god. The best such proofs of existence can yield is blasphemy" (*GWB*, 64).[5]

Marion begins his exposition of ontotheology with the claim that concepts too can function as idols, as "the making available of the divine" (*ID*, 9) in that such "concepts [make] a claim to equivalence with God" (*ID*, 13). Marion thinks of the Greeks: the idea of the Good (Plato), the divine self-thinking (Aristotle), and the One (Plotinus) (cf. *ID*, 10). Then Marion discusses Aquinas' five ways to prove the existence of God and comments that "the question of the existence of God is posed less before the proof than at its end, when it is no longer a question of simply establishing that some concept can be called *God* [. . .] but more radically that that concept or that being coincides with God himself" (ibid.). Here Marion hints at the devastation that took place in the transition to modernity, when the

consensus that makes all proclaim that it is this being that we call "God"
is lost. Marion's answer is as unsettling as it is correct: "[T]he consensus of
'all' is replaced by the idiomatic phrase 'by [God] I mean . . .'" (ID, 11).
Understood in this way, the transition from modernity to postmodernity
might hint at an even more profound loss. For, just as Marion describes
the transition from the Middle Ages to modernity as the loss of consensus
in matters divine, the transition from modernity to postmodernity could be
described as the loss of consensus of precisely those postulates that Kant
used to redefine the limits of knowledge at the dawn of modernity. So, for
instance, whereas the modern subject was that instance that remained the
same despite the variations of its lived experiences, the postmodern subject
is shattered, schizophrenic, and, according to Levinas and Marion, in a
permanent state of alteration rather than remaining the same.[6] Whereas
the postulate of the world was, for Kant, used to assure the unity and
the coherence of the world amidst all the subject's diverse experiences,
postmodernity's plurality presupposes a multitude of worlds that altogether
seem to forbid the thought of a unity underlying all these different worlds.
Whereas the postulate of God's existence assured the coincidence of virtue
and happiness, it now sometimes seems as if happiness is what is to be
obtained at all costs, and perhaps especially that of virtue.

These remarks aside, it is clear that Marion did not adhere to a sharp
distinction between the Middle Ages and modernity with regard to the
question of metaphysics, the proof of which is that metaphysics, for Marion,
resides more in "the equivalence of God to a concept in general" (GWB,
29) than in the plain and simple "theological character of ontology" (ID,
16).[7] Metaphysics, therefore, and again, is not that God is used all too
easily in philosophical discourse, nor is it a "bad theological response to a
good philosophical question."[8] The theological character of ontology—here
as the need to invoke one or the other being as a supreme being—"has
[. . .] to do with the manner in which [a] being, from the beginning, is
un-concealed (entborgen) as [a] being" (ID, 16). In the words of Mabille, and
to introduce to the process that I will depict below: "the emphasis of the
[onto-theo-logical] constitution is not at all on the theos but on the logos."[9]
It is this representational or 'logical' character of ontotheology, aiming at
the mastery of the concept over the being, this "logic [as] but the discourse
that leads from a being to a being to the supreme being, [as] the vector by
which the ontic reduction [from beings to beings, JS] [. . .] has irreversibly
been accomplished"[10] that will come to think of God as being one more
object at human beings' disposal. More important, it is this domination of

the concept over the being and its culmination in the equivalence of God to a concept in general that, according to Marion, arrives at its acme in the modern era—especially, as we will see, with Descartes—and that explains our contemporaries' preference for naming only modern authors when it comes to the question concerning ontotheology.

The importance of this domination of logic and logocentrism and its consequences for our understanding of ontotheology should not be underestimated, for this domination of logic may already have been present in earlier times as well. At least this is what Marion hints at when stating that "the theological character of ontology does not have to do with the fact that Greek metaphysics was later taken up and transformed by the ecclesial theology of Christianity" (ID, 16)[11] nor with the fact that the god of Christian revelation has passed into Greek thought, "for this passage itself became possible only inasmuch as, first and foremost, [. . .] Greek thought [is] constituted [ontotheologically]" (GWB, 64). God has not entered philosophy because God has been thought on Greek terms, as an inappropriate hellenization of the Christian God. It is rather that Greek thought was *already* predisposed toward *to theion* that the God of revelation could be caught into philosophy's web. This is why Marion will state that the "ontotheological constitution remains the same where God, as Christian, disappears" *and* "why Plato, Aristotle, and Plotinus did not await Christianity in order to put the ontotheological constitution into operation" (ID, 16). In this way, Marion seems to subscribe to the Heideggerian hypothesis that the ontotheological constitution is not only, in Mabille's words, a historical ('*historique*') but also a historial ('*historiale*') and epochal phenomenon,[12] in that "'the metaphysical concept of God' has not become the 'causa sui' because of a contingent historical evolution, but in 'historial'' conformity with the determination of being as ground from out of the logos."[13]

This is also why Heidegger did not see any sharp distinction between the medieval and the modern period: "At the beginning of modern philosophy, which is readily passed off as a break with philosophy hitherto, we find that what is emphazised and held onto is precisely what has been the *proper concern of medieval metaphysics*."[14] Heidegger explains that the influence of the mathematical sciences on philosophy in modern times, especially with Descartes and Fichte, raised the question as to what extent the subject can attain absolute certainty. According to Heidegger, the whole of the traditional problematic is retained but is brought to light in and through aspects of the new sciences: "If metaphysics asks concerning the first causes, concerning the most general and highest meaning of beings [. . .], then this kind of knowing must be commensurate with what is asked about. Yet that means: it must itself be *absolutely certain*."[15]

That which is able to question the *alpha* and the *omega* of being must be absolutely certain (of) itself. The ego will now be the starting point of philosophy: no longer will the existence of God and its corresponding proofs be that which incites questioning but is not questioned itself; it is rather the I or the cogito that is able to interrogate all beings without letting itself be interrogated. The cogito is the starting point of philosophy only to the extent that it is absolutely certain of and through itself, and thus cannot itself be questioned as it becomes the "most secure and unquestioned foundation"[16] of philosophy and metaphysics. Here is the continuity between the medieval and the modern age: just as the medieval age self-evidently started from the existence of God, so modern times will take the existence and certainty of the ego as the starting-point of its reflection. It is worth noting that Heidegger elsewhere relates this concern for certainty in the modern period explicitly to the certainty of salvation and redemption that dominated medieval times. *Die Frage nach dem Ding*, for instance, mentions that the primacy of certainty, onto which modern mathesis would graft itself, stems from Christianity and its certainty concerning redemption and its guarantee of the individual's soul.[17] In his lecture on Parmenides, Heidegger divines that the Christian question concerning truth, namely, whether human being's beatitude is certain and the question of the relation between the just Christian life and justification, is the breeding ground for the just use of reason that will prevail in the modern period with Descartes and Kant.[18] And Heidegger concludes: "[T]his concern for ultimate certainty and the orientation toward the I and consciousness is meaningful only if the *old problematic is entirely maintained*."[19] Just as the substance of beings of nature in medieval times are thought from out of its persistence in presence, so too the modern subject will be thought of as a '*hypokeimenon*,' as that which remains unaltered by that which it experiences.

But if Heidegger did not draw a sharp line between the medieval and the modern age, we will have to ponder whether for example Smith's contention, not unlike many others in the Radical Orthodox series, namely, that "what Heidegger decried as ontotheology is a distinctly modern phenomenon,"[20] can effectively be held. It is indeed striking, for our problem of ontotheology, that different authors point to different thinkers to discern the ontotheological mode of procedure. It is for this reason that I will now turn to Marion's account of metaphysics as it came about in the modern period.

Marion's Understanding of Modern Ontotheology

In the previous section we have seen that in God *without Being* and earlier (i.e., 1982 and before), Marion seems to understand ontotheology as a structural rather than a mere 'historical' phenomenon. In his later works, however, Marion notes that one first and foremost must keep in mind the "original indetermination of the concept of metaphysics itself."[21] For, following a distinction of Aquinas, God remains beyond the scope of that which the majority of medieval authors designated as metaphysics. Avicenna as much as Duns Scotus, according to Marion, follows Aquinas' statement that it is only theology that treats the divine revelation as including God in its *subiectum*. In this way, God does not fall under the topic of metaphysics, dealing with the science of being-qua-being.[22] The second characteristic of the metaphysics of the medieval age that Marion notes is the indetermination of the concept of (a) being (*ens*) itself, for metaphysics there can only be if its subject, *ens qua ens*, receives an adequate determination. Marion, however, here accrediting the legitimacy of Heidegger's question that it remains historically undecided whether *to on* must be heard nominally or verbally, concludes that, since there was no definite concept of (a) being, there could not be a univocal science of being-qua-being. In this way, Marion can conclude that the "historical period usually recognized as the golden age of 'metaphysics' was characterized thus by an extreme reticence toward the use of the term, a term of which this period, more than others, measured without a doubt the eminent problematic character."[23]

According to Marion, it is only when a definite concept of (a) being is introduced that the ontotheo-*logical* constitution of metaphysics can hold sway. It is precisely this primacy of the concept over the being that came about in the modern period and above all with Suárez, for "a being becomes conceptual only when it can be reduced to it—*being* does not name primarily a determination of this or that being, but a mode of perceiving and representing [it]."[24] The concept of a being does not have its origin in a particular being itself, but merely in the "act of representation accomplished by the mind."[25] Keeping in mind that Heidegger traced the origin of metaphysics to the fact that encountering a particular being was, since Plato, to be conceived of as a fall over against and but an inferior copy of the more being-ful idea of the being, one should note that Marion, who has clearly seen the ways in which phenomenology resists the temptation of positing the phenomenon over and against the metaphysical construed *noumenon*, one should take seriously the question the end of metaphysics seems to pose to all of us: "[H]as the hypothesis even been taken seriously that 'ontology,' understood historically, never dared to confront a being as such [*l'étant comme tel*]?" (*VR*, 163n. 5, mod;*VeR*, 78 n. 4). It is in this sense that the turn from the other to the individual being might bear its fruits and why perhaps only phenomenology can overcome metaphysics, that is, if it would dare to look at the phenomenon in its naked contingency and finitude.

With this primacy of the concept over the being, according to Marion, the metaphysical turn of philosophy and theology comes to the fore, and metaphysics itself "is assured of its unity and of its rank as a science. Indeed, the irreducibility of *theologia* [. . .] to the science of being-qua-being [. . .] disappears as soon as one approaches these sciences no longer with regard to the beings they treat of, but with regard to the representation of the being reduced to a pure concept."[26] Historically, this move seems to be, to believe Marion, effectuated by Suárez. Only now, "and *almost* for the first time," Marion argues, "the adequate object of this science needs to include God."[27] Marion then comments upon the Heideggerian question of how God entered into philosophy:

> The entry of God in metaphysics plays not only, not even primarily in God's denomination from out of being. Thus Thomas Aquinas maintains God's transcendence with regard to metaphysics and with regard to the created [order] by differentiating between *ens commune*, representable through concept and imagination, and the *actus essendi* by which God, with regard to God's being, remains profoundly unknown. [This] equivocity (or at least the analogy) traverses being enough in order that God might be without falling into metaphysics. *This entry is accomplished only when God is named and thought from out of a univocal concept of beings, or of being* [. . .]. In each case [that of Malebranche, Descartes, and Spinoza], *God enters into metaphysics by giving into the metaphysical primacy* [. . .] *of the concept over the being itself.*[28]

This primacy of the concept over being is much commented upon in contemporary philosophy. One will encounter it in Hemming's genealogy of the sublime where the contemporary terror of the image and the imagination is discussed as that which can be held noetically independent *of which* it is the appearance; in Marion's musings on the technological object and the 'preseen'—to the point that I can know what a table is without ever having seen one.[29] Mabille notes this "noetization of ontology"[30] as well, and states: "[W]hat characterizes post-Cartesian modernity (*but which has been premeditated since the medieval period*) is, with regard to the question of the being of a being, the substitution of the being itself for the being-as-it-is-thought."[31] Mabille, finally, links this primacy of the concept over the being with the metaphysical thinking of beings in their essence rather than in their existence. For if the existence of a particular being no longer matters, the criterion for what it is to be comes to lie on the basis of whether it is thinkable or not. Only insofar as it is thinkable, at the disposal of thought, can a being in fact exist. "That which *can* exist is the possible [. . .]. At the moment when the term 'ontology' imposes itself, [ontology] is not the logos of the 'on' but the science of the thinkable."[32] Thus Mabille can conclude: "[T]o the forgetting of being accomplished by metaphysics since its instauration in favor of one sole being (ontic reduction) is added the forgetting of beings in favor of the thinkable.[33] This is why, finally, Marion will say that with this submission of beings to a concept in general the transcendental turn of metaphysics is necessitated, because "for the *ens* to be able to be reconducted to the *cogitabile*, a reference to a *cogitatio* is implied, thus a reference to a subject exercising a transcendental function."[34] Metaphysics will thus be redefined as the science of that which is thinkable, and all experience will have to comply with one or another condition of possibility. This is also why Marion agrees with Mabille's statement that philosophy's craving for a foundation stems more from its obsession with logic than from its theological or ontological nature: "the foundation stems from 'logic' that can unite ontology and the[i]ology only insofar as it works through both of them. [T]he missing of being by metaphysics as well as its onto-theo-*logical* constitution can be explained by the primacy of the concept over the being and the reduction of the being to what can be caused, founded, and represented."[35]

This general picture of 'ontotheology' is attested to in much of contemporary philosophy—from Plato to Aristotle, from Plotinus through the Middle Ages, and via Kant and Hegel, to us. But from whence this reticence to ascribe ontotheology to this author rather than that? And does this picture explain our statement of ontotheological residues in the works of Lacoste, Marion, and Levinas? Is it indeed not the case that when the human being is conceived of as 'without secrets' (Levinas), or as the object of a, divine or not, intentionality (Lacoste, Marion), this very human being recedes under the pressure of an adequate concept one has from this being? It is to these questions that I will now turn. But first I'll portray the rather peculiar look Marion has of Descartes.

A Metaphysical Schism? Marion and Descartes

We have just seen Marion stating that with Suárez God 'almost for the first time' entered philosophy and metaphysics. Such a quote, of course, makes one wonder who would be the first to do this and also who made modernity (and metaphysics) reach its acme. To answer these questions, it is suiting to have a look at Marion's description of Descartes' place in the history of metaphysics.

It is important to note that Marion, in *Descartes' Metaphysical Prism*, also affirms that, underlying all ontotheological figures is not so much this or that highest being but rather the emphasis put on the *logos*. This emphasis is such that this empirical being here can (and will) be substituted for its concept: "In the course of the development of metaphysics, the *logos* assumes the more and more weighty and powerful function of a foundation [. . .]. The 'logical' foundation, the *logos*, states being in an onto-logy only byduplicating *its own anteriority to being* in a theo-logy, where, still in the role of ground, *it also precedes the divine*" (*DMP*, 86). Descartes, then, is no stranger to this affirmation of the power of representations, for, Marion tells us, "haven't we emphasized over and over again that for Descartes the *cogitatio* precedes the *ens in quantum ens* precisely in order to ground it in terms of the criteria of certainty?" (*DMP*, 88). To stay with our example: as much as the essence of the table, that is, the representation and the concept of it, will determine just how a particular table can appear, so too the essence of the piece of wax, that is, its geometrical coordinates, precedes the particular way of appearing of the wax. Again: just as a designer table cannot appear once the essence of a table is determined as a plateau with four legs, so too philosophy will miss, once the wax cannot be anything other than its geometrical form, this particular and individual being here. It will, as Marion argues, never confront the *ens in quantum ens* and will, in Heidegger's words, "prescribe the world its being." One might also say: the concept thinks being, but in its own, whimsical, way. It is representational thinking that serves as a functionalization of being(s) and of God: of beings, it lets appear only that which it can understand of them, and it will put God in the place which it reserves for Godself.

Marion's analysis of Descartes results in a sort of redoubled ontotheology in which the ontotheology of the cogito is subsumed into an ontotheology of the *causa sui*: the very being that finds itself thinking will confess itself to be caused by a supreme being. This is the case to such an extent that even the thoughts of the cogito—its *cogitatio*, that which it is thinking of, and the very fact that it thinks at all—are implanted by the *causa sui* we all call God.[36] But when God is to be identified with the *causa sui*, Godself "does not make an exception to the pronouncement about the Being of beings as *causa* [. . .]. God appears here as a being subject to common law, and no longer outside this law. This situation can be described perfectly as a formal univocity" (*DMP*, 106). Marion concludes then that 'God,' as much as every other being, is, already by Descartes, dragged in—down?—by the principle of sufficient reason which, precisely, is a *dictat* of reason (*DMP*, 109, 257): God will occupy that place that reason and rationality will reserve for God.[37] But note that matters are more complicated still, for if such a formal univocity pertains to the ontotheological constitution, it is all the more questionable why Marion and Lacoste have, as I argued earlier, ascribed intentionality to God or why the Levinasian other *can* attend toward my being, as if I were a theme or a *noema*, of which everything can be exposed.[38]

This question of a redoubled ontotheology might just be one of the most important issues raised by Marion here. Marion is asking whether Heidegger's description of the ontotheological constitution of metaphysics might in fact be like a blueprint for many different forms of ontotheology (*DMP*, 118–19). Descartes' choice to let the *res cogitans* be overruled, 'overwhelmed and overdetermined' (Cf. *DMP*, 119n. 62) as it were by the ontotheology of the *causa sui* indeed gives food for thought. In this, Marion affirms Descartes' exceptional position: the turn to epistemology—what I can represent is what I can know and is what, thus, exists—"implies a revolution" (*DMP*, 37), and it is "Descartes, and Descartes alone, who defines the *scientia universalis* by the criterion of the order of knowledge" (*DMP*, 49).[39] Nevertheless, and especially considering the fact that Marion, in other writings, does not distinguish between the medieval and the modern age when it comes to matters of metaphysics, Marion's position in *Descartes' Metaphysical Prism* remains somewhat ambivalent. While it is affirmed that metaphysics ascends to power from Descartes onward (Cf. *DMP*, 335), Descartes' elevating of the *causa sui* to the rank of a highest being is still deemed to be a fact with an "(*almost*) total absence of genealogy" (*DMP*, 158). The question whether Descartes, or Suàrez, or anyone else for that matter, can figure as the starting point of ontotheology and stand out as a 'metaphysican par excellence' is still left hanging. My suggestion will be, with Levinas, that there *is* a genealogy of ontotheology but that it is not to be found in the history of philosophy. In its stead, it is to be found in the philosopher, that is, in yourself and, without a doubt, myself. But let us before developing this position consider Marion's stance more closely, since there is one instance in the book we are discussing where Marion abandons his somewhat ambivalent stance on the history of ontotheology.

When Marion considers the fact that Heidegger outlined the ontotheological constitution on the basis of primarily two authors, namely, Leibniz and Hegel, he advances: "[I]t seems to us that one has to admit an incubation period for onto-theo-logical constitution: less an effect in reverse allowing for a retroactive hermeneutic [. . .] in the sense that from Plato and Aristotle metaphysics gives itself to be read as an onto-theo-logy, than as a slow emergence, in often quite complex figures, of what in its Leibnizian and Hegelian achievements suddenly stands forth with a constitution that is simple because definitely accomplished" (DMP, 119). For Marion, then, it is less a matter of realizing that the ontotheological constitution, discovered by Heidegger primarily in Hegel and Leibniz, infected the entire metaphysical tradition from Plato onward, but that it is rather like a contamination whose symptoms break out in modernity especially. What Marion, then, is trying to convey is that these two ontotheologies to be found in Descartes—the ontotheology of the ens cogitatum leading to Hegel; the ontotheology of the ens causatum to Leibniz—might point to "a contradiction, a competition, or an incoherence due to something unconscious in metaphysics" (DMP, 120). The point is that if one would come up with a contradiction in the ontotheological constitution of metaphysics, one would simultaneously come up with that which, supposedly, breaks with, denies, or leaves metaphysics behind. In fact, this is what Marion's rhetorics often seem to indicate, since "it is a matter of understanding, verifying, and thus also 'falsifying,' the thesis, proposed by Heidegger, that there is an essentially onto-theo-logical constitution of metaphysics" (DMP, 6) and "if onto-theo-logical constitution strictly delimits the Cartesian constitution of metaphysics, it fixes its limits: therefore, by closing it, it opens the possibility of its overcoming" (DMP, 7). This opening, then, Marion will perceive in Pascal, which I will discuss below.

For now, it is important to understand that one will have to challenge Marion's historical approach to the problem of ontotheology: the hypothesis that there are more complex, and even multiple, figures of ontotheology than Heidegger indicated might not be "verified [. . .] only by works that seek out such a constitution in this or that thinker of metaphysics" (DMP, 121), for such an endeavor, I will show shortly, is itself ontotheological to the very core. The question of ontotheology must concern the nature of the contamination more than the incubation period it causes.

Intermediary Conclusions

In this intermediary conclusion, I would like to place the contemporary praise of the 'end of metaphysics as a possibility'[40] somewhat into relief by asking whether it is indeed possible for metaphysics to end as well as scrutinizingthe underlying assumption of whether an escape from ontotheology is possible at all.

First, if, for Marion, the ontotheological constitution of metaphysics reaches at peak in modernity, precisely because ontotheology resides not so much in the 'theological character of ontology'—taken as the need to invoke one or the other being as the supreme being— but rather in the fact that the emphasis of the ontotheological constitution might very well be on the *logos* rather than on the *theos*, then this means, of course, that it is not so much the fact that there, as we have seen in Marion's debate with Levinas, still can be a highest being that matters. On the contrary what matters is that, due to the representational thinking of our days, the place of the prime piece of being will time and again be occupied anew, and instead of focusing on this or that highest being, one should perhaps rather pay attention to how and why its place gets occupied time and again.

Second, if ontotheology occurs when God and beings are interpreted univocally from out of a concept in general, then this will allow us to understand our claim that the reversal of the subject-object distinction remains within the horizon Heidegger took ontotheology to be. I ascribed to the works of Marion, Lacoste, and Levinas a certain return of the transcendental subject, in that the reversal of the subject-object distinction presupposed the projection of a prior I that allowed for one or the other instance to take on the transcendental function. So, for instance, the very idea of a reversal of intentionality leads Lacoste and Marion to state that either God or givenness exercises an intentional aim over the believer or the *adonné* respectively as if human finitude can be represented clearly and distinctly after all. In Levinas, where the religious situation of human beings marks the end of all privacy, a similar concept is at work.

Finally, the definition of ontotheology acquired in the previous pages allows us therefore to state just where these authors fall into the ontotheological mode of procedure, for if the lesson of the critique of metaphysics was that, for instance, the concept of substance cannot be ascribed to God and to creatures in a univocal manner, the very same problem recurs when intentionality is allotted to both God and human beings. This is, it seems to me, the reason why these authors could not escape the vocabulary and modes of procedure of modern subjectivity.

At the same time, however, the limits of the mere historical approach to the problem of ontotheology, which I depicted above, are revealed. These limits are clear in Marion's approach when he argues the following: "Just as the onto-theo-logical definition of metaphysics directly implies the possibility of the "end of metaphysics," so the 'end of metaphysics' directly implies 'the end of the end of metaphysics.' There is no paradox in this: as soon as *"metaphysics" admits of a concept that is precise,* historically verifiable, and theoretically operative, it follows that this concept can undergo a critique proportionate to its limits, but, thanks to those very limits, it can also offer the possible horizon of its overcoming" (VR, 54).[41] But was not the presupposition of any enquiry into the history of ontotheology the claim that ontotheology occurs when a 'precise concept' substitutes itself for the (ontic) being of the entity? Did we not see that the very enterprise of ontotheology is that a concept takes precedence over the being itself? Here is the problem of any historical assessment of ontotheology and of all detectivelike enquiries into its nature: in any such endeavor, *ontotheology itself is objectified,* and its concept rules over the problem it poses. This is why every kind of 'who's who in ontotheology' is itself ontotheological in its very being. In this way, ontotheology is, so to speak, experienced from without and in enquiring into it as a spectator, it remains in the subject-object distinction in which the object recedes over and against the desires and the evaluations of the subject. When, therefore, will we be able to take seriously Heidegger's statement that, against wagers of whatever kind, metaphysics will not remain up for choice?[42] After all, Heidegger over and over stated that ontotheology or metaphysics is not a mistake of past philosophers. Ontotheology, therefore, is not something that occurs because this or that thinker has willed to entertain it (i.e., ontotheology is not one among many other possibilities that the subject does or does not choose). 'Metaphysics' as well as its overcoming might not be options. When philosophy wants to 'overcome ontotheology' it is not that it faces a dilemma: it is not that one either thinks ontotheologically, or one does not. Interpreting the problem of 'overcoming' as a dilemma is already to presuppose that ontotheology is a unified and simple thing, that it has an essence—as if it were an object that could be described adequately. If it were, the task of thinking would be easy: one defines this object in a clear and distinct manner, and then one acts accordingly, that is, one chooses for something other which, in this case, would be not to think ontotheologically.

Thus, the problem with the mere historical and ontic approach is that its comportment toward ontotheology is in a certain sense paradoxical: since, if ontotheology consists in the primacy of the being over the concept itself, then the historical approach identifies a concept of ontotheology in order to 'e-valuate' what or who is ontotheological and what or who is not by means of a purportedly adequate concept of ontotheology. The reason why a mere historical approach to the problem of ontotheology does not suffice is, however, that it treats ontotheology merely as an ontic phenomenon and thus misses the ontological (and therefore, always and already: existential) nature of the question concerning ontotheology. If ontotheology is an ontological and existential phenomenon, we must ask whether Smith's contention, namely, that ontotheology is a distinctly modern phenomenon—or can at least be reduced to one of its instigators—can effectively be held. Such an ontological approach to the question concerning ontotheology requires us to delve into the nature of the human being's contamination with ontotheological and representational thinking, by trying to pass by the symptoms with which it, after its incubation period, breaks out of in order to understand why the fluctuations of its fever can still occur even in the postmodern period. For this, it is perhaps necessary to face the question whether the ultimate cause of the contamination does not reside in the act and operation of thinking itself: it might be the case that whenever, wherever, and whatever we think, we think ontotheologically. When Levinas, for instance, states that "one should [. . .] neither underestimate the temptation nor misjudge the depth of the reign that [theodicy] exercizes over human beings and the *epochemachend*—or its *historial* [. . .]—character of its entry into thought,"[43] one might wonder whether, even in our postmodern era, such a theodicy can entirely be eradicated, for it might not be the greatness of this philosophical and metaphysical doctrine that has made it make its way into people's minds; it might on the contrary be that because of the nature of people's minds—because of thought and how it operates—such a doctrine can be *epochemachend* in the first place.

A better way to comport ourselves to the problem of ontotheology is perhaps to retrieve the vocabulary of authenticity and inauthenticity of *Being and Time*. For, just as authenticity is not the dialectical counterpart of inauthenticity, in that it is not the eradication of all inauthentic comportment, so too the problem of ontotheology, whether it is taken to be as putting God at our disposal or a mastery over being/beings, might allow for a proper and improper comportment toward it.[44] Just as authenticity in *Being and Time* is not the complete extrication of all things inauthentic, so too, then, our comportment toward ontotheology might point to both the unavoidability of ontotheology and a proper comportment toward it. After all, one should ponder that, for Heidegger, one can only surmise what the 'overcoming' of metaphysics might be, if one understands metaphysics *from within*, that is, from out of its most intimate questions. Therefore, just as one cannot surmise what authenticity might be without being implicated in inauthenticity, so too one might not be able to venture outside of ontotheology—if there is such a thing—if one has not been infected, contaminated, and affected by the very being and existence of ontotheology in the first place. Only by 'appropriating' metaphysics from within, one might understand, and perhaps assume, its position.

In this way, Heidegger's later writings on metaphysics might simply point to the fact that the human condition is, in fact, an ontotheological condition and that, in this sense, it is not a matter of overcoming metaphysics, but rather of comporting oneself toward it in an appropriate manner, if you like, to avoid idle talk (*Gerede*) as much as we can, and to go to the *Sache Selbst* as far as our *Selbst* allows.

Levinas and/on Ontotheology

I have stated above that it is only after *Totality and Infinity* and Derrida's "Violence and Metaphysics" that Levinas developed an interest in the critique of ontotheology. The reasons for this are philological. Heidegger's essay, *Identity and Difference*, was presented at a seminar in 1959, two years before the publication of *Totality and Infinity*. Heidegger's essay was therefore not widely known at the time of writing of *Totality and Infinity*. It is only Levinas' later writings, then, that acknowledge the significance of Heidegger's critique. This is evident from the famous preface of *Otherwise than Being* that to hear a God uncontaminated by being is no less important and precarious than to retrieve being from out of its oblivion "in which it is said to have fallen in metaphysics and onto-theology" (OB, xlviii). This much is admitted as well in *God, Death, and Time* where we hear Levinas saying that ethics both must account for the critique of ontotheology (GDT, 125) and aim at "God outside of onto-theo-logy" (GDT, 137).

The Said as the Birthplace of Ontology

Levinas starts his discussion of ontotheology with a succinct summary of Heidegger's principal thought on the subject (GDT, 121–25). For our purposes, only two of the six themes Levinas mentions are of importance. First, Levinas seems to subscribe to the thesis that, due to ontotheology, "European philosophy of being becomes theology" (*GDT*, 123), recalling that "for Heidegger the comprehension of being in its truth was immediately covered over by its function as the universal foundation of beings, by a supreme being" (ibid.). Levinas also seems to acknowledge, contrary to the well-known praise of technology in "Heidegger, Gagarin et nous," the persistence of metaphysics and ontotheology in our age of technology, for "the same movement that substitutes onto-theology for the thinking of being leads [. . .] to science, which pays attention only to beings [and] which wants to conquer and dispose of them, and which seeks power over beings [. . .]. The end of metaphysics, the crisis of the technical world, which leads to the death of God, is in reality *the prolongation of onto-theo-logy*" (*GDT*, 124).

Levinas proceeds by retrieving God from out of a different model of intelligibility than that in which the question of being is and is not—in the case of ontotheology—posed. Over against the craving for unity, adequation, and rest, Levinas proposes to inscribe into the heart of philosophy's questions an unrest that might point to a transcendence that cannot be reduced to the quiet contemplation of the divine that hitherto characterized Western philosophy and theology.

This different model of intelligibility is produced in the *contingent* relation with the other (*GDT*, 138). It is here, of course, that one finds again the idea of a human transcending "without aiming and without vision, a seeing that does not know that it sees" (*GDT*, 139), that goes into the open and toward the neighbor, "without any hope for oneself," a transcendence, therefore, that does not, like Odysseus, return to its point of departure. This transcendence, and we should take note of this for Levinas' understanding of ontotheology, cannot be "brought back to the models of negative theology" (*GDT*, 138). It is with respect to this difference with the modes of procedure of negative theology that we need to understand the two different appreciations of the ontotheological 'God of the gaps' at issue in the later works of Levinas.

In order to present Levinas' position toward ontotheology, it is important to recall Levinas' anarchistic account of transcendence. Levinas sought that which is outside the system, that which flees from concepts, namely, the individual human being. In order to make appear that which from out of the system and totality does not appear, Levinas will, in *Otherwise than Being* entertain a particular form of the Reduction. The Reduction, for Levinas, is that which allows one to bracket the omnipresence of epistemology, representational knowledge, cultural *mores*, and ontology. In short, the Reduction to the saying is what allows one to take a step back 'outside' the totality in order to let appear that which is prior to ontology and epistemology, namely, "the subjectivity of Saying" (OB, 45, mod.), or, in other words, the subject, the human being in its individuality. In *God, Death, and Time*, Levinas elaborates on the preference for vision and manifestation that belongs to the primacy of the Same. Levinas argues that the subject that is called to representation is but "a detour that the act of being takes, one that the essance of being takes in order to appear in truth" (*GDT*, 150). In this sense, the human subject is merely a 'personage' in the game of being. It is against such an absorption of the subject in the system of Being that Levinas protests, for it is possible that "the subject ha[s] another meaning, which could arise if we insisted upon the communication to another person of the manifested essance" (*GDT*, 151). Thus we are brought back to the superiority of speech: it is not because there is ontology that we speak; rather, since we speak there is ontology (or anything else). It is for this reason that I propose below to have another look at the difference between the Saying and the said and the relativization of the question of being that it incorporates.

Levinas' account is twofold: first, there is his critique of Heidegger's *Seinsfrage* and of the impersonal nature of being taken in its verbal sense; second, there is a confirmation of Heidegger's critique of ontotheology. The first is introduced to reduce the omnipresence of that which Levinas terms "the amphibology of being and beings," the second confirms this amphibology in order to relativize it. *Otherwise than Being* will indeed acknowledge the importance of what Heidegger called the "ontological difference for the determination of truth" but will, in a second phase, deny that this difference is the ultimate in and of being by displacing it with a nonindifference toward the other (OB, 23).

This amphibology of being/Beings not only implies, as Marion argues, "the ambiguity of beings in their Being and of Being always in a being,"[45] but also, as Kosky rightly shows, designates that the question of the ontological difference can only arise on the basis of the said of language and by admitting the precedence of speech and saying. "In the term 'said,'" Levinas captures, to follow Kosky's opinion, "what is called the apophantic function of the logos, its function of showing a being by making a predicative statement about it."[46] In order for the ontological difference to appear, therefore, it must comply to the said, to the '*logos apophantikos*': "in a predicative proposition, an apophansis, an entity can make itself be understood verbally, as a 'way' of essence, [as] a modality of essence" (OB, 38). To hear being verbally—*Das*

Sein west—it must be stated in a predicative proposition of the sort 'Being is some*thing* that "is" verbally.' Here is the real amphibology and perhaps the reason why Levinas will consider (the question of) being as mere play: "[A] noun can resound as a verb and a verb [. . .] can be nominalized" (*OB*, 42). Levinas gives the example of "red reddens" (*OB*, 39), but it is obvious that one must hear here all of the Heideggerian examples one can think of: "*Der Welt weltet*," "*Das Nichts nichtet*," "*Die Sprache spricht*" and so on. Kosky concludes that "'the birthplace of ontology is in the said.'"[47]

The Said as the Birthplace of Ontotheology

A point worth noting, however, is that the 'said' or predicative speech is the breeding ground not only for ontology but also for ontotheology. For not only is it in the said that every entity (noun) can be reduced to a moment of Being[48] (verb) but also that Being (verb) will be reduced to an entity or a being (noun). First, in what one might call the "verbalizing of the noun" or of the entity, ontology extends improperly to that which, supposedly, escapes ontology, namely, the human being, for in predication everything can be understood as modes of being: "[T]he very individuality of an individual is a way of being. Socrates socratizes [. . .] is the way Socrates is" (*OB*, 41). This is the point where the 'who' turns in an improper manner into a 'what': the question who Socrates is receives an answer by saying that Socrates is the being that 'socratizes.' This is, of course, an odd claim, but it is the way, according to Levinas at least, through which ontology proceeds. Ontology or being is, as I have indicated, what poses questions to human beings: "the question '*what* shows itself?' is put by him *who* looks" (*OB*, 23). To Levinas' mind, however, ontology is marked by the complete forgetting of this 'who' that is looking, for this 'who'—me, you—looks for the answer to the question, 'what is being?' not only in terms of being but will also understand itself in terms of being and will find a response to this question by not asking "about such a one or other, but about the essence of the 'who that is looking' *in its generality*" (*OB*, 27): "The logos as said [. . .] lets the 'who?' get lost in the 'what?'" (ibid.). This is why, for Levinas, transcendental philosophy misses the individuality of the individual by reducing the existence of all empirical human beings to be but an instantiation of the transcendental ego, which is common to all, and why, in the case of Heidegger, for Levinas, the subject is but a detour that being takes in order to show itself. In this way, the question of being would give way to the disclosing of the discloser itself and the subject becomes, for example, an object to be studied and dissected by the human sciences.[49]

In the second place, the said necessarily gives rise to *the nominalizing of the verb*. Here the verbal character of being is forgotten, and all language is reduced to its function of designating or doubling the entity designated. Language, then, will be considered as a mere code where signs serve to point an entity that is, supposedly, already there prior to language. Instead of interpreting language in its kerygmatic function where "[t]he noun [. . .] is necessary for [the] identity" of the being (*OB*, 40) or in any case is not "indifferent to [the] entity" (*OB*, 39) that it names, language as the said is turned into a "system of nouns identifying entities and then as a system of signs doubling up the beings, designating substances, events and relations by substantives or other parts of speech derived from substantives, designating identities—in sum, *designating*" (*OB*, 40). Instead of envisioning language as the way in which things come to presence through the ways in which we name them—what one might call the "Heideggerian approach"[50]—language as a code or a system of signs seems to be for Levinas *the birthplace of ontotheology* as well, for if it is in the said that essence can resound in the first place, it is similarly "on the verge of becoming a noun" (*OB*, 41). Just as the said risks verbalizing every noun or entity, so too, then, there is no "verb that is refractory to nominalization" (*OB*, 43). Here the verb par excellence—to be—will be taken to designate one more designating noun among others: "The verb *to be* in predication [. . .] makes essence resound, but this resonance is collected into an entity by the noun. 'To be' thenceforth *designates* instead of *resounding*. It designates then an entity having as its whole quiddity only the essence of entities, a quiddity identified like the quiddity of every other named entity" (*OB*, 42). The resounding of being is itself represented as the essence or whatness of being. By doing so, being in the verbal sense is itself represented as *a* being whose essence is predicated as that which makes possible the 'essencing,' so to say, of all other beings.

The origin of ontotheology for Levinas lies in the fact that, in the said, being in the verbal sense will inevitably be interpreted as a being par excellence which accounts for the resonance one might hear in all other beings. Therefore, even the verbal character of being, its ess*ance*, will be represented as a quiddity, a 'what' or essence of a being. In the words of Levinas, it is not only the phenomenon that appears in and as said, the phenomenality of the phenomenon (or the being of beings) will be stated in terms of beings—in the said—as well. Therefore, just as much as the appearance (of a phenomenon) resorts to the representation of a conscious subject, so too will the appearing of the appearing or the phenomenality of the phenomenon.[51] "The saying [correlative with the said . . .] names an entity, in the light or resonance of lived time which allows a *phenomenon* to appear. This light and resonance can in turn be identified in another said" (*OB*, 37). Kosky concludes by stating that "in this way, Levinas gives his own account of the onto-theo-logical constitution; the onto-theo-logy (or at least the theo-logy of onto-theo-logy) in which the verbal sense of Being is confused with a being par excellence arises not because the difference between Being and beings have been forgotten but because Being appears in the said of the apophantic logos."[52] Though Levinas seems here to relativize ontology and ontotheology by assuming the precedence of Saying over the said, we must note that Levinas might be interpreted to say that the theological character of ontology should be incorporated into the account of the transcendence of the other human being he envisions. For just as Levinas argues for the meaning of ontology (or knowledge and representation) from out of the Saying that is human subjectivity, so too he seems not only to accept the inevitable veering of ontology into ontotheology but also to endorse the theological character of ontology into his own account of the transcendence of the other. For this latter reading, I will return to the lecture course *God, Death, and Time*, but first I propose to dwell a little longer on Levinas' Saying.

With the term *saying* Levinas seems to query for a rationality proper to testifying, which is prior to ontology, although testimony incorporates it: "[O]n the hither side of [the] amphibology, Saying states and thematizes the said, but signifies it to the other, a neighbor, with a signification that has to be distinguished from that borne by words in the said" (*OB*, 45–46). The said is relativized because its signification is always and already dependent upon the Saying that communicates the thematized said to the other. "[T]he apophansis is a modality of saying" (*OB*, 47), but "[t]he essence of communication is not a modality of the essence of manifestation" (*OB*, 190n. 34). But the Saying or the testimony is neither to be taken as the "giving out of signs" (*OB*, 49) nor as "a simple transmission of a content or of a said" (*GDT*, 151), for speaking is not merely "a translating of thoughts into words" (*OB*, 48) as if a transcendental ego (sender) would always already have chosen to say something (message) to the other who would then in turn decipher the sign (receiver). Saying is, therefore, not a mere saying something about something but a seeking for "the condition of communication" (ibid.) that accounts for the fact that there is communication—predication, knowledge,and so on—in the first place. Saying is subjectivity, that is, in each case mine, and in each case my responsibility. It is, not a 'giving out of signs' but rather the sincerity of the one who "makes signs to the other of the very giving of signs" (OB, 144 et passim), the sincerity of the one who knows, therefore, that there is a salutation to the other in everything that has been said, that is said, and that is going to be said. Were it not for the other, nothing at all would be said, and absolute silence would reign (OB, 189n. 21). In the face of the other, however, a simple salutation cannot suffice, for not only does a salutation "not cost anything" (OB, 144), but it also answers as little as ontology itself does to that which Levinas names the question of questions,[53] namely, that ontology and knowledge itself in the final resort are questionable. Facing the other ohne warum: giving signs of a fraternity with/out God,[54] a fraternity that, therefore, suffers from not receiving any explanation and that turns ontology into "a demand and a prayer" and inserts "into the 'communication' of the given an appeal for help, for aid addressed to the other" (OB, 24).

In addition, it is noteworthy that Levinas' point of departure in the Saying as the very signifyingness of signification might be elucidated with a remark Heidegger makes in Being and Time, namely, that not all signification is dependent upon the apophantic logos. Indeed, in Being and Time, Heidegger points to the logic of the request and of prayer as a different manner of making manifest than ontological predication.[55] One might argue that Marion too both in the modes of procedure of the request as portrayed in The Idol and Distance and in the logic of love as it comes to the fore in his later writings is seeking to describe the rationality proper to human and theological address as well.

Halting the Regress, the God of the Gaps, and Ontotheology

In this last section I will look at another way in which Levinas incorporates the problem of ontotheology, for as much as the saying can supposedly do without a said,[56] one might think that this allows Levinas to conclude to the 'God without ontotheology' of which God, Death, and Time spoke. Levinas, however, seems to endorse the opposite view that this God without ontotheology can only appear if the ontotheological God is forever presupposed.

Throughout this text I have stressed Levinas' distinction between the beyond of being ('être autrement') and 'the'[57] otherwise than being ('autrement qu'être'). The former for Levinas seems to play the role of a Hegelian bad infinite, in that it invokes a regress ad infinitum of the mathematical infinite of n+1 possibilities obtained by the negation (and somewhat Platonic depreciation) of all things finite. The latter is supposed to convey to us the 'good' infinite, in that it communicates the transcendence of human beings—you, me, us—that is irreducible to, indeed "intolerable for" (OB, 199n. 21), any operation of thought. And yet, we think.

The critique of ontotheology, I contended, is precisely an awareness of the shortcomings of the former line of reasoning. Was there a time in which it was not illicit to endorse the view that one could pass from all things which are moved to an instance that moves but does not move itself and that, in turn, is not moved by that which it moves? Surely there must have been a time when one could and must pass from all things caused, chained together by all sorts of causes, to an instance that first caused but is not caused itself and that, conversely, is not caused by that which it causes? And was not there a growing consensus that this unmoved and uncaused being must be called God? Except, perhaps, that this otherworldly Highest Being turned out to be not unlike all 'worldly' beings after all, and, therefore, not all that divine. In fact, this 'otherworldly' foundation of the world might be, to use Marion's words, invisibly mirroring and reflecting the needs and desires of this finite world here. This, at last, is what Levinas has in mind when stating that the negation of the imperfections of this world, thus of finitude, do not suffice for a genuine otherness (cf. TI, 41): since the negation of something takes refuge in that which it negates and thus forms a system, the otherness or divinity of the Highest Being "is still within the same" (ibid.). The ontotheological God, then, is the Infinite reduced to the negation of the imperfect and in this sense remains indebted to the logic of finitude. It is, perhaps, such a mode of procedure that has come to the fore with the end of metaphysics and which justifies the indictment of the ontotheological God as a 'God of the gaps' or as a 'deus ex machina' or as an improper appropriation of the divine there where it can be used to fill in the system's blind spots.

Nevertheless, one must note that Levinas gives a very peculiar ring to this exigency to stop or to what is most often seen as an improper halting of the infinite regress proper to dialectics and negation. For this, we must first recall how Levinas interprets the relation between being and otherwise than being or between the same and the other.[58] Levinas has argued that the same and the other, insofar as we can think the other in the same, properly belong together as in an arpeggio. At the same time, however, when thinking starts to thematize or reflect on this relation between being and that which possibly escapes it, a contradiction appears between the statement of being's beyond and the condition of this statement, that is, its being uttered by a being from out of being. The ambiguity and ambivalence of the infinite signaling itself to thought is only then turned into a dilemma and logical opposition: the face is at the same time an epiphany *and* as any other phenomenon showing itself to the subject and its representations. Levinas argues that only when thinking starts to think and reflect on the 'immemorial past' of the otherwise than being, as such distinct from the infinite regress of the bad infinite, the nonrepresentable and nonontological unlimited responsibility stemming from this immemorial past is brought back to the order of representation and ontology, which subsequently declares itself to be the ultimate: "the immemorial past is intolerable for thought. *Thus there is an exigency to stop*" (OB, 199n. 21). This is to say that thinking thinks the divine (or what Levinas calls "the immemorial past" or illeity) inevitably *as* an infinite regress and that thinking *itself* configures the 'exigency to stop' or the halting of the regress in the matter it thinks appropriate. Thinking converts the otherwise than being into an *être autrement* or into a (mathematical) series of beings explaining being/s, into "an extrapolation of the finite" (OB, 78), of which thinking *itself* will grasp the halt or stop. The God of ontotheology is indeed an idol, but it is one that shall not die. Levinas, importantly, adds: it is only "in this reflection, that is, only after the event, *contradiction* appears [. . .] between a statement and its conditions" (OB, 156). Thus, it is between the statement of 'the' otherwise than being and its condition, that is, being and language, that a contradiction appears: it is impossible that 'the' otherwise than being be said from out of being. Levinas' point is that this contradiction only appears when thinking starts to reflect upon the (finite) conditions from out of which the infinite gives itself to thought. Levinas could thus be interpreted to say that thinking and thought are structured ontotheologically, that, whenever and whatever we think, thinking construes an egoistic and unjust 'ontotheological' God of the gaps

It matters little here that Levinas regards this 'stop'—this everpresent invocation of the 'God of the gaps'—as concretely produced by the advent of the third party—Levinas' reduction of ontotheology to politics. It matters that it *is* produced in a concrete manner[59] for this manner is what allows one to take the problem of ontotheology into view in a thorough phenomenological manner. Let us then turn to the third party, for just as the indirectness of the infinite is kept in check with the concrete straightforwardness of the face, so too is the occurrence of ontotheology balanced and attested to by a direct, concrete, and empirical 'production'—the fact that there are others besides the Other. Indeed, for Levinas, the infinite must appear (in being) and leave its ambiguous trace by betraying itself in and through its very appearing in being, that is, on being's terms. It is here that Levinas advances toward the mysteriousness of that which appears as twofold, and at the same time: "a face makes itself an apparition *and* an epiphany."[60] It is this doubling that thought reflects upon, reduces to the form of a dilemma or choice, and makes thought subsequently veer into an ontotheological direction.

In a concrete manner, this thus happens with the advent of the third party. For Levinas, "the relationship with the third party is an incessant correction of the asymmetry of proximity [. . .]. There is weighing, thought, objectification, and thus a stop in which my anarchic relationship with illeity is betrayed" (OB, 158).[61] The other's face becomes a phenomenon to be dealt with as if it were any other object. It is here as well that, according to Levinas, the Infinite is *necessarily* interrupted, halted, and fixed "in structures [and] totality" (OB, 160). Moreover, because this relation with the third party is at the same time "the turning of the I into 'like the others,' for which it is important to concern oneself" (OB, 161), the fixing of the divine into a structure and totality can and will give way to the "permanent danger of turning [God] into a protector of all the egoisms" (ibid.), to the politics of a *Gott mit uns*.

All of this would seem far-fetched if Levinas had not explicitly linked this political 'God of the gaps'—*mis à l'oeuvre* precisely there where the subject or the system stands in need of it—with the theme of ontotheology. For "it is only in an exacted stop (*arrêt*) that the movement beyond being [. . .] become[s] ontology and theology" (GDT, 203; OB, 199n. 2/AqE, 191). This appearance of the two tentacles of the problem of ontotheology, moreover, "thereby [marks] a halt [*un arrêt*] in the halt-less quality [*nonarrêt*] of the relationship in which the infinite is traced. From this halting flows an idolatry of the beautiful in its indiscrete exposure [. . .]. Here, the gaze substitutes itself for God. With theology, which is linked to ontology, God is fixed in a concept" (GDT, 203–04/DMT, 233). This stop, then, is always and already there: there are others besides the Others, being is in the neighborhood of otherwise than being, and ontotheology is haunting theology.

Conclusion

It is thus that Levinas makes room for the ontotheological mode of procedure, assuming that, taken in the sense of an improper appropriation of the divine, ontotheology is inevitable and belongs to the thinking of transcendence. Ontotheology, then, would amount to the *unsurpassable* idolatry of all conceptions of transcendence, whether it be on the part of an individual or a community. Furthermore, one should not pass easily over the fact that in the account of the third party, ontotheology is linked to politics, for is it not in the latter that divine power is all too readily turned into a power over the divine?

It remains to be seen just how or even if Levinas differs from Heidegger on this matter of the ontotheological operations of thought and thinking. Let me just note a few striking similarities. First, just as we have seen Heidegger contending that metaphysical thinking—a pleonasm—separates that which properly belongs together, for instance being *and* time, so for Levinas thinking, when and if it thinks, will separate between being and otherwise than being to the point of irreparable cleavage: it is impossible, contradictory even, to speak of something else than being from out of being—as if *es kein Anderes als Sein gibt*. Second, when Levinas comments upon the nominalization of the verb *to be* to such a point that being (in its verbal sense) becomes represented and thought of from out of *a* being that, in a way, distributes beingness to all beings, one might again be reminded of Heidegger's interpretation of Plato's 'error,' for this nominalization seems to correspond exactly to how Heidegger understands the 'beginning' of metaphysics in Plato. According to Heidegger, Plato interpreted the presencing of a particular being as something present-at-hand, which is the same for (and present in) every particular being. Presencing as a mode of being—verbal—is then itself taken as a present-at-hand property of any particular being. This is why I will discuss such a phenomenology of presencing in the conclusion, for it is precisely such a phenomenology that seems compatible with the turn to the individual being. Insofar as such an attentiveness to the appearing and presencing of a particular being would elude the permanent presence characteristic of all metaphysics—since presencing is in each case different—it remains to be considered whether an overcoming of metaphysics would be a possibility.

When it comes to the ontotheological operations of thought, Levinas' account of what thought *does* when it thinks might give us the opportunity to answer the question I raised earlier against Marion: for if it is, for Marion, with the anamorphosis really a question of 'two phenomenalities in a single phenomenon,' and if Levinas states that the Other is always and already— simultaneously—an apparition and an epiphany, the correction I would like to advance against Marion would be simply this: it is not a matter of the object *or* the saturated phenomenon; it is rather that one should try to understand how, when confronted with a saturated phenomenon, objectness nevertheless remains there. The question, then, is how diverse appearances can appear *at once*. For this, I would suggest returning to Heidegger's account of the worldling of the world—after all, it is a good philosophical question to ask in consideration of whether things might actually exist outside the (my) ego or even why the worldling of the world did not await me for its actual happening and occurs independently of every position we all would take in its regard. In a certain way, we might be back at square one, back to Heidegger that is, for Being, in Heidegger, is named already in its difference with beings; we come across, and encounter beings always out of the twofold ('*Zweifalt*'), the between of being and beings.[62]

To conclude, then, it might not come as a surprise that Marion's account of Pascal does not answer the question of the recurrence of the subject-object distinction in French phenomenology. In fact, it simply prolongs the problem. Marion's account of Pascal seems to be, first, a theological usurpation of the question of metaphysics, and this usurpation, second, seems to proceed in an entirely metaphysical manner. This is obvious in Pascal's portrayal of what looks like Descartes' version of the bad infinite. Marion comments that "the infinite requires an absence of limits in an infinity of parameters and not simply in just a single one of them. In the latter case, nonfinitude results directly from the conditions for the exercise of our finite mind, which privileges this or that parameter" (*DMP*, 290). This latter case, then, is what Descartes would name 'the indefinite'—as opposed to the 'good' infinite—and resembles the mathematical infinite of n+1 possibilities, which produces something like infinity, by privileging one, single parameter, namely, the set of numbers. Marion then notes that Pascal "annul[s] the indispensable distinction between the infinite and the indefinite" (*DMP*, 291). And while this solution might seem suitable for the theologian, it troubles, as I will show, the philosopher, for the solution Pascal proposes to Cartesian metaphysics, relies upon Christian theology to such an extent that the metaphysical vocabulary it employs unsettles even those befriended and concerned with God. Let me state clearly what I mean: when Pascal 'overdetermines and overwhelms' Cartesian metaphysics, by arguing that the "ultimate question is no longer [. . .] the relation between God, the being par excellence, and existence in general [. . .] but between man and charity (Jesus Christ)" (*DMP*, 297), it remains to be seen just how such a relationship is conceived in Pascal, and even in Marion, for Pascal's "step back from metaphysics does not go back to the nonmetaphysical origin of metaphysics; it attempts to reach a land other than metaphysics itself" (*DMP*, 307). It might just be this latter option that will turn out to be impossible.

Over and against Descartes, then, Pascal will posit and postulate a "reduction to charity" (*DMP*, 337). Again the whole field of finitude, immanence, and knowledge is swallowed, so to say, by another order, be it the order of love. The problem here, again, is not that this is a theological usurpation *per se*; the problem is rather the way in which such an usurpation takes place. According to Pascal, there are three orders, namely, flesh, mind, and will, and God, purportedly, transcends them all. What matters here is the relation between these orders: the will knows what the mind and the flesh know, while the mind only knows what the flesh is about. The relation between the order is thus entirely hierarchical. In the words of Marion: "the superior order remains invisible to the inferior order," while, nevertheless, "a relation [. . .] reconnects the orders by fixing them in an hierarchy—the gaze" (*DMP*, 315, 314). This gaze, then, not only "evaluates and judges" (*DMP*, 315) the inferior orders—as did Marion's givenness, Lacoste's God, and the face in Levinas—it also controls it as if it were a mere object. Indeed, what happens to the *ego* when it is "suffering from [this] gaze" (Cf. *DMP*, 323)? It undergoes and passively registers the "counter-experience" (*DMP*, 324) of its being decentered by the loving (?) gaze: for this "inverted gaze" dispels me from my egoistic ego into my self, which "demands love [and] that the *self* serve as addressee and receive the love of others, who are thus defined as subjects. And it is precisely this which calls for *the inversion of the subject ego/I into the object me*" (*DMP*, 326).[63] To conclude from this—and I hope that this is clear by now—that "if one considers metaphysics' ascent to power from Descartes to Hegel [. . .] metaphysics must from now on [with Pascal, JS] recognize the irreducibility of *an order that it does not see, but which sees it, grasps it, and judges it*" (*DMP*, 335), is perhaps not simply to beg the question, it might even be that the question concerning ontotheology has not yet been properly posed as long as one has not reversed the reversal in French phenomenology.

Conclusion

Toward a Phenomenology of the Invisible

Theological Turnings

This text started with the commission, so to say, to study the so-called theological turn of phenomenology (Janicaud). It would be an exaggeration to say that I have found no such turn. However, it would not be totally incorrect to say that identifying such a turn is a somewhat vain effort. Indeed, such an identification might perhaps only arise from a desire to keep things simple and clear-cut. But this work will hopefully show that such a desire presupposes that there is an 'essence' to philosophy or to theology for that matter. It would also presuppose that we can 'represent' this essence in order to be able to distinguish one essence from another, for example 'philosophy' and 'theology.' A second reason why one might deem Janicaud's targeting of all things 'theological' as insufficient is the very manner with which he distinguishes between the two disciplines. If phenomenology is to be taken as the study of the phenomenon as it appears and insofar as it appears, Janicaud argues, phenomenology is restricted to visibility: it describes the manifold ways in which a phenomenon appears to human beings. Since phenomenology is in this sense a description of visibility, Janicaud says, it is unable in any way whatsoever to have something to say of things invisible, whether this be God in the phenomenology of Marion or the transcendence of the other person as it appears in the works of Levinas. Thus, the essence of philosophy, on the one hand, is the description of visible things; and, on the other hand, the essence of theology is the presupposition of faith in that which is unavailable to sight.

However, things are not as simple as Janicaud wants us to believe, since phenomenology has not only dealt with invisibility from its very beginnings, but there would perhaps not even be such a thing as phenomenology if human beings were not surrounded by things which are not visible. First, a philological argument: already in Husserl's works, one can find elaborate descriptions of, for instance, ghosts. Husserl was examining how the body of the other person appears to us, and in order to describe this he compared it to ghosts, who, as you know, do not have bodies.[1] Second, and though it is perhaps not obvious at first sight, in everything we perceive there is an element of invisibility. Just as we do not perceive all four legs of a table at the same time, or even the back side of the television we are watching, so the transcendence of the object conveys something of an invisibility, intrinsic to the visibility of an ordinary object. Without phenomenology's investigation into the 'how' of the appearing of an appearance, such an invisibility would not even be noticed. Similarly, were it not for this difference between what is visible of the phenomenon and what is not, the phenomenological reduction perhaps never would have found any impetus for it to be operative at all. Thus it seems that one can safely conclude, and without further ado, that "Janicaud made a major phenomenological blunder when he assumed that phenomenology deals only with the visible (the audible, etc.)."[2]

The instigator, however, of such a 'theological turn' might once again be Heidegger. In his later works Heidegger developed the idea of 'a phenomenology of the unapparent,' a phenomenology of the invisible.[3] In everything that appears, Heidegger argues, there is an element that does not appear or, in more technical terms, that appears by precisely not appearing. This nonappearance is not nothing. In fact, for Heidegger, it is a thing of utmost importance. To give one of his examples, when looking at the blossoming of a tree one usually does not notice that for this blossom to exist, the leaves that preceded it disappear. So, when looking at the blossom of a tree, what appears to us is not only the blossom but also the loss or absence of the leaves. Such things are revelatory of how being appears to us.[4] In this sense, it is via Heidegger that 'revelation' once again provokes philosophical minds, and the thought of Marion and Levinas is precisely an attempt to think the possibility of revelation rationally. However, to think revelation in this way all these thinkers try to avoid theology. Contrary to Janicaud, it would be better to say that these thinkers display a certain *reluctance toward theology*.

Although it is perhaps not a turn to theology that we are witnessing, we are encountering a philosophy that searches for a contemporary form of the Absolute. What is happening in contemporary continental philosophy is thus perhaps not a turn to theology, but a philosophical move that finds itself persuaded to think an appeal that does not derive from one's own preferences, or from one's own limited vision. In contemporary philosophy, what is at stake is the possibility of finding an instance that is beyond the grasp of the subject, that is, to find, among all historical constructs, an instance that cannot be reduced to being merely a historical construct. 'Otherwise than being'—if it would be possible to take this term as indicating one clearly determinable reference—means the search for a 'signification' or 'meaning' that is irreducible to the subject's *Sinngebung* (Husserl). It is in this sense that 'a phenomenology of the unapparent' is not a contradictory statement. Phenomenology, in this way, is concerned with what the French now call "*l'apparaître de l'apparaître*" or even the experience of experiencing. Note that, while we may fashion our experiences in whatever way we find appropriate, be it through *Sinngebung* or one or the other will-to-power, the very fact *that* we experience the world is one that is given to us without our consent.

Our approach to this 'absolute' has certainly been critical. The reason for this lies in the very manner with which Marion, Levinas, and Lacoste construct their relation to the Absolute. Over and over again, the immanence of this world is seen in distinction with a vague nonmundane signification that is supposed to 'transcend' the world, and we are led to believe that this world must be seen as an immanence closed in on itself and is to be portrayed as an "egg in its shell" (Levinas), a "visual prison" (Marion), or a "world without God" (Lacoste). However, it is here that the unquestioned assumptions of much of contemporary philosophy is revealed, for such a distinction shows itself to be yet another subjectival operation inheriting, perhaps, its modes of procedure from Descartes and German idealism. Just as for Descartes the world was to be conceived of as a collection of finite substances, so the monolithic understanding of immanence at issue in the authors under consideration stands in need of a clear and distinct insight into this logic of immanence: it seems thus that if we want to hail the advent of the other, the excess of givenness, or God's coming, we must first agree that the immanence in which we act, move, and live is but a collection of epistemological operations that reduce the other to the same or the world to a sum of constituted objects or to an always and already improper appropriation of being-in-the-world. Only if such an axiom is granted can one then conceive of an instance that—supposedly—forever escapes this devouring logic of immanence. And yet it seems that such an operation not only resembles Descartes' dualism between the world and the subject, but it also—as Derrida hinted at—seems to borrow, despite its proclaimed aversion of the transcendental subject, its line of reasoning from precisely such a subject. For, if we are to believe Levinas, this subject configures every encounter with that which is not the subject (Fichte's 'nicht-Ich') from out of a positing of the subject itself in order that every encounter can emanate from and return neatly to this subject. Insofar as immanence obeys the logic put forward by these authors, however, one must ask whether an operation that delineates immanence in such a way is not itself indebted to a prior positing of the subject, for the dichotomy of immanence and transcendence that they endorse seems again to be valid if and only if one or the other subject distinguishes in a transparent manner, and without residue, between an 'impure,' monadic immanence without doors and windows and a 'pure' transcendence. In short, the very fact of positing immanence as an egg in its shell betrays a subjectival operation that is too close to the logic of the transcendental subject to be able to speak of genuine decentering here. This is, finally, the reason why I spoke of an ontotheological turn in the works of Lacoste, Marion, and Levinas.

And yet one should not simply brush aside their attempts to think transcendence, because the transcendence evoked in the works of Lacoste, Levinas, and Marion might nevertheless insinuate a genuine account of something/someone transcendent. And although a historical assessment of the problem of ontotheology matters for the simple reason that one still needs to answer Marion's question on the extension of the concept of ontotheology, it is similarly forever on the verge of evoking a 'precise concept' of ontotheology. Then the question concerning ontotheology would again be reduced to a dilemma and to the logic of exclusion inherent to every concept and representation. Indeed, the historical approach to the critique of ontotheology reduces the problem of ontotheology to the terms of a choice, as if thinking metaphysically or not shows itself to be up for choice after all.

Yet the pattern of transcendence as occurring despite one's will should be examined, on the condition, perhaps, that it is somehow 'existentialized.' Not only because it seems to counter the Nietzschean diagnosis of our times where one values whatever one wills, and in the manner one wills, but also because the thought of such a 'despite oneself' might be evoked to describe those moments which most concern us *in* this world of immanence. Despite oneself, thus, these moments are birth, death, and love:[5] birth, in that one has been thrown into a world without one's consent; death, because the moment of our deaths (even in the case of euthanasia) is never something chosen; love, because love occurs most often as if it could not have happened otherwise. It is for such a reflection that one might wish to retain the title of 'metaphysics': not only because metaphysics (in the Heideggerian sense) seems inevitable, but as a reflection on what those moments precisely have in common, despite differences in race, culture, age, and so on. But such a metaphysics should proceed in a proper manner, that is, without its questions starting from axioms that one takes over from mere hearsay. Here is the advantage of the return to *Jemeinigkeit* I perceived in Levinas and Marion: there are no axioms that one should receive without questioning, and, similarly, there are no questions if one did not, previously, attend to the question in one's ownmost manner.

The Privation of Immanence

Why counter the closure of metaphysics with a phenomenology of the unapparent? Perhaps because metaphysics never properly inquired into the particular appearance of a phenomenon. Indeed, we have seen Heidegger decrying the cleft that constitutes metaphysics and out of which the beings in and of this world can only appear as a fall over and against the perfection of the Platonic Ideas or of the theological '*ens increatum.*' It is in this way that one might agree with Levinas' saying that, throughout Western philosophy, beings were never able to appear in the light proper to them. For indeed, if we are to believe Heidegger, it is since Plato and the sophists that all seeming ('*Schein*') was reduced to mere semblance over and against the more being-full *idea*: "The chasm [. . .] was torn open between the merely apparent beings here below and the real Being somewhere up there. Christian doctrine then established itself in this chasm, while at the same time reinterpreting the Below as the created and the Above as the Creator."[6] Though the changes in this transition should not be underestimated, the similarities between these two accounts are all the more striking: just as the beings of this world were to be conceived of as mere semblance over and against the suprasensible realm, in Christian doctrine the immanence of this world is to be conceived of as a diminution and privation of the transcendent creator. We have seen Levinas struggling with this 'ontological' and paradoxical concept of creation where the Infinite admits of an inferior creature besides itself. This inferior creature, then, could not be conceived of otherwise as one craving for its return to the Infinite as that instance in which its limitations are supposedly undone. It is of importance to note that in this way creation not only appears as a diminution or as a degradation of the Infinite but also that the creature itself necessarily appears as dependent, qua being, on the being of the Infinite. Creation, to use Levinas' words, is configured from out of a logic of need rather than out of a logic of desire. For a creature to truly be, it tears its being, not from itself, but from its (necessary) relation to the Infinite. As a consequence, the Good is understood from out of a finite conception, that is, "*by relation to* the need to which it is lacking" (*TI*, 103 mod.). Similarly, the finite can only be understood in relation to the Infinite, and its independence and separation as a finite being are never taken into view. Immanence is supposedly to be understood from out of its relation to the Infinite, in which all of the imperfections of the finite being are resolved by the perfection of the Infinite, as if the need that is the finite being is to be countered with the satisfaction that is the Infinite.

Oddly enough, for all of the Platonic echoes in Levinas' thought, Levinas' main target here is the Neoplatonist One. It is in Neoplatonism that, according to Levinas, 'the relation *with* relation' takes form: if time is but the privation of eternity, the relation of the finite being to the infinite is conceived of as a return to and union with the One. The relation with the infinite is "understood itself from out of the unity of the One where the relation is consummated and consumed, but of which the relation signifies the privation."[7] It is important to note that, for both Levinas and Marion, the turn to transcendental philosophy is necessitated by the ontotheological constitution of metaphysics. Levinas for instance describes the *exitus-reditus* scheme of Neoplatonism as a foreshadowing of the domination of the theoretical attitude of the transcendental subject.[8] For Marion, the primacy of the concept over the particular being necessarily veers into transcendental philosophy: if the One or the '*ens increatum*' loses its credentials, then another instance will take up the role of the *alpha* and *omega* of that which is thinkable, possible, and visible.

The reason why the relation without relation remains without satisfaction entails a thought of love different from a Neoplatonism in which love of the infinite "extends only to the term that it seeks."[9] The love of the neighbor that Levinas seeks to describe, therefore, is an attachment to other human beings that must not be confused with any default of privation of the unity of the One whatsoever.[10] It is here that one might imagine God's descent toward human beings in another way as a diminution of God's divinity, for insofar as this metaphysical relation with the infinite determines both the infinite from out of a logic of need on the part of the finite and the finite from out of its privation of the infinite, it is open to question whether thinking the infinite by relation to the need to which it is lacking or the finite by relation to the privation of the infinite is the wrong way of thinking about the infinite or the wrong way of thinking about the finite. For indeed, what is lost in this metaphysical line of reasoning is both God's independence toward human beings and the human beings' separation from the infinite, since not only, as Levinas argues, is the Good no longer Good in itself, but it is only Good in relation to the need to which it is lacking, but the finite also cannot be thought on its own terms, but only from out of its relation to the infinite, of which it is the lack. It is in this sense that finitude as the privation of the infinite intimates a total adequation between the immanent and the transcendent realms.

Privation understood as a lack seems to operate always and already within a dialectical system wherein the presence of perfection, that is, an instance that resolves the lack of privation, is *presupposed*. Indeed, in the metaphysical statement where finitude is but a privation of the transcendent, both a subject and an object genitive must be heard: the finite is the lack aspiring for the infinite as much as the infinite is the plenitude that satisfies this lack. In this sense, the transcendent realm is configured as the adequate fulfillment of the finite being's needs, that is, from out of a complete overlap between infinitude and finitude. Just as the infinite is adequate to the finite being's needs, so too the finite being's lack is adequate to its satisfaction through the infinite. Whereas from out of the ontotheological constitution of metaphysics, the finite being appeared *in relation to* the infinite being of God, in the ontotheological constitution of transcendental philosophy the infinite will always and already appear *in relation to* the finite being. In the former case, one might say that immanence is reduced to playing a role in the designs of transcendence; in the second case, transcendence is reduced to the designs of immanence. Though the outcome of these thoughts is different, the mode of procedure remains essentially the same. Whereas in metaphysics, the perfect model of this particular being in one or the other suprasensible realm took precedence over the appearing of this particular being itself, in modernity the concept of a particular being took precedence over the being itself. If this is the case, it seems that we lack a proper account of the immanent appearing of the being of beings. The proper way to proceed 'after' metaphysics, therefore, is to turn the phenomenological gaze toward immanence, to confront it head-on and refrain from any improper spiritualization or vitalizing of our finite world in order to advance toward a phenomenology of the presencing of the world.

In Lacoste, for instance, the world and its finitude are not only interpreted as the limit (im)posed on our finite existence and with which human beings are permanently and brutally confronted, but the transgression

of these worldly limits in and through liturgical experience is also conceived
of from the outside, as it were: theology and liturgy hold the key to the
vague 'sketch' that the world is to such an extent that the world no longer
can conceive of itself as even a sketch. When, thus, it is true that 'facticity
cannot interpret itself' (NT, 84), facticity and immanence are entirely
overdetermined and overwhelmed by the nonexperience that liturgy imposes.
Immanence on the whole disappears without a trace—without residue—in
the register of the Infinite. Something similar is at issue in Marion's portrayal
of Pascal in Descartes' Metaphysical Prism: for just as we wonder whether
the human being, as adonné, is not merely an epiphenomenon of the event
of givenness, so too one can ask whether all things finite are not merely
an epiphenomenon of the infinite, when the latter is to be interpreted as
"the a priori horizon [of the finite] and precedes the finite in that it makes
experience and the objects of this experience possible" (DMP, 228, 229). One
can thus ask whether the finite here is taken up entirely by the infinite, is
robbed of every substance it would have of its own. In any case, one seems
to be stuck with a sort of monism when the infinite "oversees the relation
between the infinite and the finite" (DMP, 234). The problem, however,
is then that theology obfucscates the problem that finitude poses to such
an extent that finitude and immanence, now devoid of any substance, are,
well, 'overlooked.'

But whereas Levinas, Lacoste, and Marion are primarily concerned with
God's independence or freedom toward (the human) being, it is thus perhaps
equally important to affirm human beings' independence from the infinite
and to examine whether the relation with the infinite could be conceived
as simultaneously respecting God's freedom to relate to human beings and
the freedom of the human being to relate to God. To save God from an
all too human conception of the infinite might therefore at the same time
mean that one tears the finite being from the clutches of its participation
in the Infinite, in which the finite is merely playing a role in a drama of
which it would not be the author (cf. TI, 79). The suggestion is that a
transcendence irreducible to immanence can be discerned inasmuch as we
are able to conceive of immanence in its irreducibility to transcendence.
Hence there is Levinas' endeavor to reinterpret the traditional 'ontological'
concept of creation, in which it indeed remains incomprehensible as to why
a superior being would create an inferior world. This is also why, in Marion,
despite God's indifference towards ontic and ontological differences, God is
not indifferent towards a being as such ('l'étant comme tel'). Therefore, the
turn to the individual over and against the (Levinasian) face in general is a

move of which the importance should not be underestimated. Our contention is, however, that it is precisely this latter move, namely, to conceive of immanence in an other than metaphysical fashion that has remained largely unexplored. In this way, we have seen Marion laying the blame for the nonappearing of the excess of givenness (and a fortiori of God), in good metaphysical fashion, on account of an ill will, a '*vouloir défaillant*' of human beings: *All* nonappearing of the excess is due to a lack of willingness to receive that which gives itself of itself. However, such a line of reasoning not only presupposes that an adequate and transparent view on immanence can be obtained, in that immanence is a closed region in which *all* responses or nonresponses signify from out of the 'horizon' of givenness, such a line of reasoning is also unable to make intelligible the response of finitude to any 'nonfinite intuition' otherwise than in a privative fashion: the ill will is the absence of that which, properly speaking, ought to be there, the will to see the given. The point is that finitude here is immediately taken as part and parcel of an infinite register in such a manner that it cannot ever be thought of on its own terms. Here is the limit of a single appeal that one cannot not hear: every nonhearing (of the appeal of givenness or of the other) will need to be conceived of, first, as unable to escape the logic of appeal-response (and thus a hearing of the appeal anyway), and, second, such a deafness toward the appeal cannot be conceived of otherwise than in a privative fashion as the absence of a hearing that properly speaking should be there. It is in this sense that all recourse to privative reasoning has the appearances of a cover-up operation, since any role that the finite being would want to play for itself remains unthought.

One can put this in a Derridean fashion: there is nothing outside the appeal. Finitude cannot be conceived of as a genuinely other *from* the appeal. The comportment of finitude will always and already have to be configured *in relation to* the appeal to which it is the response. The usurpation of immanence by the excess of givenness or by the responsibility of the other, in short, the thinking of a transcendence that is irreducible to immanence, inevitably leads Levinas and Marion to reducing immanence (or the finite being) to a privation of the infinite (or the excess or whatever one wants to call it). Everything that supposedly falls outside of the appeal—every nonhearing—cannot be given any ontological (or otherwise) weight and is, to put it in classical terms, a *nihil privativum*.[11] This concept of the lack of an object can only understand this lack from out of its relation to the object to which it is lacking, like shadow is understood as the absence of sunlight. Just as the Ideas of Plato are that which really 'is,' and by relation to which the particular beings appear as something that should not be, and that 'are' not either, so too in Levinas and Marion responsibility toward givenness and toward the other is construed as that by relation to which all irresponsibility appears as a lack of responsibility, that is, as something that has no intelligibility of its own and therefore must be understood from out of its relation to 'responsibility.' This is why Visker states that, contrary to appearances, Levinas is not so much taking us out of the tradition that sees evil as a privation, but rather reformulating it. If the appeal of the Good is an appeal from which no escape is possible, one can indeed wonder "whether Evil, which involves precisely such a distancing and slipping away can occur at all under these conditions?"[12] Even more so, *if* evil occurs under these conditions, how is it to be understood? The answer is plain and simple: evil or indifference toward the other can be interpreted only in a privative fashion as the absence of that which ought to be there, namely responsibility. "As soon as the order of being is disturbed by the Good, it can only *act as if* this is not the case. The so-called irrevocable lie of Evil is thus actually already refuted."[13] In this sense, Visker argues, what Levinas cannot receive is an irresponsibility toward (or nonhearing of) the other that is not immediately the lack of something that ought to be there, but rather an 'irresponsibility' *sui generis* that needs to be understood in an otherwise than privative fashion.[14] The conclusion Visker draws from this is, however, all the more surprising. Given the fact that Levinas wanted to think the subject without being, because, in the realm of being "every game that it would play for its own account would only be a veiling or obscuring of the being's esse" (OB, 132), this privative account of irresponsibility merely seems to substitute the role the subject would play in the drama of being for a role in the intrigue of the infinite: "if the subject refuses such responsibility—which it cannot do except by being irresponsible—then it cheats, and once more falls outside the role provided for it. But it remains inserted in the script of the Good [. . .]. In neither case could the subject therefore 'play for its own account'—whatever it does takes its place in the balance of a *different* accounting, *whether it is that of Being or that of the Good.* One may ask what it has thereby gained."[15]

Thus the deficient status of the particular being over and against its idea or its creator, seems to be merely transposed to the phenomenology of givenness and into the 'phenomenology' of the other. Just as for Marion the reason for the nonappearing of givenness is due to a failing of the will on the part of the subject, so too all nonattending to the other is for Levinas merely to be accounted for as a lack of responsibility on the part of the subject. In both cases, therefore, the immanence of the subject is conceived of as an obstacle or impediment to the appearing of transcendence. The quest for a transcendence that cannot be reduced to immanence can be thought of only at the expense of finitude and immanence. It is only when immanence is thought of as an impediment or obstacle to transcendence that an excess 'en tant que tel' or the Good 'for itself' can be maintained. However, did not Levinas himself advance that precisely by evoking such a lack the Good can appear only in relation to this lack? Thinking the Good as the Good (or otherness as otherness) seems to stand in need of precisely such a privative reasoning. But, paradoxically, by the same token the Good can only appear by relation to this lack, and the 'relation without relation' is turned into a relation where "terms [. . .] complete one another and consequently are reciprocally lacking to one another" (TI, 103). The affirmation of God's independence toward being(s) can only be done, it seems, if one denies the independence of being(s) toward the Infinite, for, from the very instant that one affirms the dependence and deficiency of being(s), God can only be conceived of as the plenitude that satisfies this lack and thus appears in relation to immanence. Again, it is not certain whether thinking the infinite in relation to the need to which it is lacking or the finite in relation to the privation of the infinite is the wrong way of thinking about the infinite or the wrong way of thinking about the finite.

Heidegger and the Phenomenology of Presencing

To otherwise understand immanence and finitude and its possible opening to transcendence, it seems fitting to turn to Heidegger. For Heidegger as well noted that the immanence of beings in and of this world appears from out of the (Platonic, Christian, etc.) cleft between the sensible and the suprasensible world, not only as that which really should not be but also as that which, properly speaking, is not either. Immanence is interpreted in a privative fashion as an obstacle or an impediment of transcendence that ought not to be there: the beings in and of this world sink to the level of nothingness and can be said to exist or 'be' only insofar as their actual existence here corresponds to and participates (by degrees of imitation) in the real being somewhere up there. It matters little if beings are interpreted by relation to their likeness to one or the other Platonic idea or by relation to their prior causation in the mind of God, for both lines of thought share the tendency of regarding the appearance of a particular being in the world as an imperfect shadow of that which this particular being ought to be.

Is the appearance of a particular being condemned to the rank of a mere semblance? Let us consider a Heideggerian example: "We may say of a painting by Van Gogh, 'This is art.' [T]his manner of speaking reveals something essential. *When* do we say so emphatically, 'This is art'? Not just when some piece of canvas hangs there smeared with dabs of color, not even when we have just any old 'painting' in front us, but only when a being that we encounter steps forth preeminently into the appearance [*Aussehen*] of a work of art, only when a being *is* insofar as it places itself into such an appearance [*Aussehen*]."[16] This placing itself into the appearance of being as a mode of becoming present is the sense of '*eidos*' that Heidegger wanted to retrieve through a phenomenological interpretation of Aristotle in his difference from Plato. This '*eidos*,' then, is "the appearance of a thing [. . .] in the sense of the aspect, the 'looks,' the view, idea, that it offers [. . .] because the being has been put forth into this appearance and, standing in it, is present of and by itself—in a word, *is*."[17] Heidegger comments: "Plato, overwhelmed as it were by the essence of *eidos*, understood it in turn as something independently present and therefore as something common (*koinon*) to the individual 'beings' which 'stand in such appearance.'"[18] Leaping ahead one might say: Plato interpreted the presencing of a particular being as something present-at-hand, which is the same for (and present in) every particular being. Presencing as a mode of being is itself taken as a present-at-hand property of any particular being. When, for instance, the appearance *kat'auto* of this painting of Van Gogh is to be equated with the appearance of an ordinary, mediocre painting, say, a Dutch painting from the end of the seventeenth century, the presencing of a particular being is itself taken as a present-at-hand process. With this move, Heidegger adds, "individuals, as subordinate to the idea as that which properly is, were displaced into the role of non-beings," and it is precisely such a view that Heidegger sought to overturn by returning to Aristotle, for "Aristotle demands that we see that the individual beings in any given instance (this house here and that mountain there) are not at all nonbeings, but indeed beings insofar as they put themselves forth into the appearance of house and mountain and so first place this appearance into presencing."[19] Only then, Heidegger concludes, can we avoid seeing in the appearance of a particular being merely a fall over against whatever 'full-presence,' and only then, in addition, are we able to address this or that being—"a this and a that *as* this or that, i.e., as having such and such an appearance."[20] Therefore, phenomenology's pathway might address the being in its very being as much as it can approach the human being in its very *haeccitas*, if and only if it would dare to admit not only *that the appearance of a particular being (human or otherwise) is in each case different but also that the very manner of the becoming present of a particular being differs from being to being.*[21] It is here, perhaps, that the end of metaphysics can be at the same time a beginning. Having lost the means to chain beings together from out of one or the other common horizon (whether infinite or otherwise), beings might finally appear to one another as this or that particular (and finite) being. It is here as well that one might envision the encounter between God and human beings as an encounter between singularities, rather than laying the blame for God's nonappearing, in good metaphysical fashion, on the account of an ill will of human beings.

The phenomenologies of the invisible of Marion and Levinas,[22] I contend, take their cue precisely from this phenomenology of presencing as sketched in the later Heidegger. We have seen how Marion wanted to overcome the privative mode of invisibility in the idol and how Levinas portrayed the encounter with the other as an escape from epistemology, for which all nonknowledge points toward a knowledge yet to come. Though we have seen Levinas and Marion return to such a privative line of reasoning, it is important to note the stakes of such an overcoming. The phenomenology of the invisible, which Marion seems to endorse from the early theological to the later philosophical works, can indeed be understood from out of the Heideggerian 'presencing' that is irreducible to the constant presence of the essence of a being. Marion and Levinas indeed seem to conceive of the 'appearance' of Christ or of the other in terms structurally similar to what Heidegger describes as the 'presencing' of a being. If, for Marion for instance, Christ's appearance is such that "the appearance coincides exactly with the apparent disappearance" (*ID*, 119)[23] in order that "God's present is not inscribed in a presence" (*ID*, 119), and if, for Levinas, the Other leaves but a trace in his or her way of "passing, disturbing the present without allowing itself to be invested by the arche of consciousness" (*OB*, 100), then we must learn to appreciate otherwise this disappearance or nonappearance (to consciousness) rather than relegating it to the nonexistent or nonbeing, where the nonappearance is merely the privation of a full-fledged appearance. In this sense, Marion's phenomenological enquiry into the rationality of revelation, and its quest for a rational account of this "present without presence" (*BG*, 79), can help us to understand how there can be after all a relation between immanence and transcendence.

Amidst all of this metaphysical reasoning, then, with its abundance of privative terms, and its relegation of everything seemingly lacking reason and visibility to the realm of the nonextant, it is of great importance to affirm the rationality of phenomena that, at first sight, escape the realm of the rational in order to value the immanent opening toward transcendence otherwise. It is again to Heidegger that we need to turn to understand this appearance in being (of beings) in a proper manner, that is, in his retrieval of the presencing process of being/beings in its irreducibility to the presence and the representation of a being by a subject. Heidegger endeavored to think a nonappearing that is not simply the privation of the full-presence of the object (where that which does not appear 'is' not), but a nonappearing that *belongs* to the order of being (where the nonappearing 'is' as much as that which appears). Heidegger thus examines whether an absence, or, to put it in more fashionable terms, an invisibility, belongs to the realm of the visible. This invisibility would be an invisibility *sui generis* and is not thought in relation to the subject to which it appears. On the contrary, it would appear independently of any production and fabrication on the part of human beings. To understand this, we need to understand the presencing of a particular being as a "self-placing into appearance [that] always lets something be present in such a way that *in* the presencing an absencing simultaneously becomes present."[24] As always, the simplest things are the hardest to say. Heidegger therefore elucidates this with the following example: "When today, for example, we say, 'My bicycle is gone!' we do not mean simply that it is somewhere else; we mean it is missing. When something is missing, the missing *thing* is gone, to be sure, but the *goneness* itself, the lack itself, is what irritates and upsets us, and the 'lack' can do this only if the lack itself is 'there,' i.e. only if the lack *is*, i.e., constitutes a manner of being."[25] Heidegger is here retrieving the Aristotelian notion of '*steresis*' in its difference from the Latin translation of it by '*privatio*.' 'Steresis,' according to Heidegger, is the becoming-present of the becoming-absent and therefore differs from the mere absentness with which we define '*privatio*.' It is the appearing of the unapparent, not as nonbeing, but as belonging to the very manner in which being presences. The becoming-absent is therefore an integral part of the presencing of a particular being, and it is this 'presencing' of an absence—an absence that is not nothing—that will be lost and will inappropriately be reduced to nothing in subsequent metaphysics.[26] Heidegger adds that our contemporary addiction to thinking beings as objects makes it so that "today we are all-too inclined to reduce something like this presencing by absencing to a dialectical play of concepts rather than hold on to what is astonishing about it."[27]

Metaphysics and Society: More Ado about Nothing

Why should we hold on to the wonder of this? Perhaps because it allows us not only to reinterpret some of the peculiarities of our contemporary time and contemporary philosophy, and its silent equation of visibility and reality but also because this wonder might allow us to confront the overabundance of negative theologies with one of those instances that is central to Christian understanding, namely, God's incarnation as God's coming toward (human) beings. Levinas has clearly seen this eradication of wonder at work in modern epistemology. In the short but important article "Transcendence and Intelligibility," for instance, Levinas accuses epistemology of its satisfaction in and through the plenitude of adequation. This plenitude, according to Levinas, "implies the unintelligibility of that which surpasses its measure."[28] Everything that remains outside the scope of knowledge will be deemed to be 'irrational.' Or, to take a phrasing from everyday life: "I only believe what I can see with my own eyes." Remarkably, Levinas concludes his survey of the scope of this epistemological operation as follows: "Nothing ever comes to unseat this intentional will of thought or fails to measure up to it."[29] The scope of the epistemological reduction of the other to the same is literally limitless, and therefore a leap can and will be made from the statement 'Everything outside the grasp of knowledge is irrational' to the statement 'There is nothing outside knowledge's grasp,' or, to return to everyday parlance again: 'That which I cannot see, does not exist.' Such a mode of procedure is at work, for example, in the method used by the natural sciences. These sciences operate according to the great metaphysical principle that nothing happens without a reason. So, in evolutionary biology for instance, even the smallest spot on a frog's hide has a function. Since such a spot is the result of natural selection, it must have a reason in this great survival of the fittest. So biologists, wondering why this frog has this or that spot on its hide, will explain the spot in a privative fashion: it is something that really should not be and therefore needs an explanation and further investigation. The spot cannot appear as lacking all explanation: if everything happens for a reason, such a lack of explanation is not only something that should not be, but it is also something that *is* not. Therefore, such a lack of explanation will be undone by further investigation, for that which cannot be explained, cannot exist.

A phenomenology of the presencing of the invisible thus counters the contemporary technological reduction of beings to their being visible and intelligible (i.e., captured adequately in our representations of them). It is only when we understand the presencing of being(s) *in* being in a proper manner that theology might find the means to speak of the presence of God again. Over and against Marion's and Levinas' attempts to retrieve the invisibility of transcendence in givenness and the face of the other at the expense of the ordinary visibility of objects and phenomena, I contend that it is only from out of an examination of precisely this ordinary visibility in being and in the world, the coming-to-presence of beings *in* immanence, that a genuine phenomenology of the invisible might be developed. The phenomenologies of the invisible of Levinas and Marion operate within the assumption that immanence is somewhat like a cocoon that no genuine transcendence can penetrate. In this sense, in Levinas, Lacoste, and Marion, the complaint that in *this* monadic immanence all things transcendent are reduced to immanence is merely countered by the reduction of all things immanent to the absence of transcendence. It is in this sense that the solution Levinas and Marion propose to the eradication of wonder in our contemporary technological understanding of beings still adheres to the problem it wants to resolve and that it can revel in this immanence *here* over and against an unrepresentable, invisible transcendence *there*, while it, by doing so, simply reiterates the subject-object distinction. Therefore, one might ponder, first, whether such a phenomenological description of immanence suffices, and second, in what sense the question whether we can still say the transcendent from out of immanence is even addressed in a proper manner. It seems that a genuine account of immanence should rather try to speak of the wonder of an absence or invisibility *belonging to* the realm of 'presence' or the visible. In this way, the phenomenological gaze can be pushed to explore its limits and try to trace, within the realm of immanence that is ours, what there is to transcendence.

In short, I hope to have deconstructed somewhat Lacoste's, Levinas', and Marion's assumption that the immanence of this world can and must be described as a cocoon devoid of all transcendence, an assumption that causes one to tirelessly juxtapose transcendence and immanence in a clear and distinct way ('without perturbation'). Therefore, it seems, following Heidegger, phenomenologically more appropriate to blur the boundaries between immanence and transcendence and to try to speak of an invisible *within* the visibility of the world. It can no longer be simply taken for granted, or at least we cannot take for granted as Marion, Lacoste, and Levinas do, that immanence is *merely* the absence or privation of transcendence. It is only from out of the presencing of this or that particular being, as an ambiguous interplay of presence and absence, that we might be able to glimpse the presence or absence of the divine within the realm of being. In any case, the ambiguity of immanence here does not preclude the appearance of God. Immanence, then, is no longer reduced to a realm that, in principle, can be described adequately, but is rather the place where one might again be able to hold onto the wonder of both the presencing of particular beings and the recognition that this presencing cannot be reduced to a one and simple presence. Immanence *here* is the *condition* of the appearance of anything transcendent. But the immanence that is the condition of the possible appearance of the divine allows for no overlap between two distinct realms of transcendence and immanence. In this way, in immanence is intimated a lack that cannot be resolved—*Aufgehoben*—by a positive instance that is supposed to be represented as the absence of all lack. Over against the privative negation that I saw recurring in the works of both Levinas, where all irresponsibility is merely the absence of responsibility, and Marion, where all nonseeing of givenness cannot but be the absence of a will to see, it seems important to ponder what is excluded in this line of reasoning and to ask whether the total transparence of immanence that the privative negation in this way installs is not in itself a metaphysical move.

Perhaps it is necessary to affirm that immanence does not allow itself to be fully signified by whatever 'infinite instance.' This should not mean that we must resign ourselves to abandon the infinite altogether, but rather that we must learn to think the encounter between immanence and transcendence otherwise and perhaps to speak of the lack in the absence of the *plenum*, or, as Jean-Luc Nancy has put it, of sense without providence.[30] It is here that we would follow Heidegger's account of the immanent presencing of being(s) as unfolding with 'lack,' 'gaps,' 'holes' that resist both the resolving of these lacks to a superior presence or sense through a dialectical negation, and the domestication of these lacks through the privative negation.[31] Again, it is only when we learn to appreciate the presencing of being(s) in immanence in a proper manner that we might be able to speak of the presence of God again. We should be reminded that Heidegger's account does not dismiss all presence but rather seeks to retrieve the presencing of being(s) in another manner than the metaphysical tendency to describe beings from out of their permanent presence to the subject's gaze. This presencing, then, does not describe the finite being from out of its supposed fall out of one or the other realm but seeks to understand the very movement of presencing in being and in time.

It must be understood that a different conception of the nothing than the *nihil privativum* is at issue here. For the *nihil privativum* remains in any case at the ontic level:[32] it construes the nothing either as the negation of a positive quality of something (like blindness) or as the negation of beings as a whole (which in itself only leads to more being), but in both cases the absence or the nothing remains intelligible through the presence of that which it is supposed to be the privation. The lack is thus not intelligible in itself, but receives its signification only as diminished presence. In this sense, the constant presence remains the norm and the criterion to understand all nonpresence or nonappearance. Therefore, in order to understand 'presencing,' a different concept of the nothing is needed. This nothingness resists any clear and distinct signification and is not relative to the (constant) presence of which it is the negation; in short, it is not the privative nothingness in which the negation delivers the absence of a positive instance, but rather a nothingness wherein *the presence* of something negative is delivered.[33] To speak of presence again, therefore, seems to be accompanied with a renewed attention toward nothingness as if we can speak of that which 'is' only insofar as we can affirm the presence of that which, at least at first sight, 'is not.' It seems that only when we speak of the presence of this 'lack' and 'gap,' which cannot be reduced to a full-presence that resolves and satisfies it, can immanence be taken in a proper manner. It is of importance to note that this attention to nothingness must not be confused with a nihilistic revelling in the nothing as such. On the contrary, it is only via an appreciation of nothingness other than the *nihil privativum* that one might be able to speak of beings in an other than privative manner. An example will perhaps make this clear: if one looks at the 'health hype' raging through contemporary societies, one should note that health is here defined most often negatively. The strangest thing is that this well-being, which is supposed to be something *positive*, is merely stated in a privative manner: it is only through the absence of alcohol and nicotine, for instance, that the positivity of this well-being can be stated to the point where one might wonder whether anything positive about the presence of health is being said at all.

For Heidegger, it is only when one refuses to let the negation do its dialectical work that one can confront both the nothing otherwise than as *nihil privativum* that will be resolved in a superior mode of presence and that one can interpret the presencing of beings *in* being without that the lack accompanying this presencing can be relegated to the realm of the merely nonapparent or nonexistent. Such a nothingness without the negation necessary to any *Aufhebung* is what allows Heidegger to take into account the way in which being unfolds and presences while *at the same time* remaining itself in retreat. It is only when this absence (of being) is interpreted as a negativity that lends itself to dialectics that the movement of presencing will itself be interpreted from out of ontotheology's obsession with objects as a permanent presence and will therefore itself be taken as a permanent presence. *All* absence or invisibility will henceforth signify from out of a full-presence established beforehand. *All* invisibility will then merely obey the norm of the visible that establishes, prior to any encounter of any particular being, what is visible and what is not. All disorder, to use Levinas's phrasing, will then be interpreted from out of the transparent presence of the order, as an absence of order or as another order. In this sense, Heidegger's enquiry into nothingness and Levinas' otherwise than being ('appearing' in being while remaining irreducible to it) might converge in trying to think a negativity that resists all synthesis, as "moments of negation without any affirmation" (OB, 194n. 4), in which the disturbance or disorder of the trace of the infinite in the order of being is not merely another or diminished order (privative negation: the meaning of the disorder is reduced to its being 'another order'), but precisely takes on a positive meaning *as* "the refusal of synthesis" (ibid.). Similarly, it seems, for Heidegger the absence or nonappearance of being in particular beings seems to exceed this interplay of privation and negation. Whereas the metaphysics of Plato regarded the appearance of a particular being as the privation of the more being-full idea of the being relegating the particular being to the role of instantiating but another diminished form of the full-presence of the idea, Heidegger's account of the retreat of being in and through particular beings seeks to understand this nonappearance, not merely as another or diminished form of the full-fledged appearance of (a) being, but precisely *as* the lack(s) through which being unfolds.

Turning to Theology? Of the Unredeemedness of the Human Being

In this sense, the critique of ontotheology would give rise to a reconsideration of phenomena that from within ontotheology's obsession with permanent presence or from within the totality and system that Levinas has exposed could not be taken properly into view. Among those is, of course, the phenomenon of evil as the *privatio boni* and the theodicy that issues from it. If evil is merely the absence of the good, then all evil is understood in relation to the good: privative terms are, as we have seen, only understandable in relation to their positive counterpart and presuppose therefore the perfection of the good. In this way, evil receives an explanation and justification: evil is something that should not be, and really *is not* either, since it is understood with reference to the good. Evil is not evil in an absolute sense; it is only a

lesser good. It is important to note that these kinds of 'explanations' come
naturally to us. In the wake of 9/11 in New York, for instance, public opinion
seemed sometimes to agree that, though what happened was surely a bad
thing, it nevertheless has some good consequences: the solidarity expressed
among New Yorkers after the event was greater than ever. Yet this kind of
theodicy, giving an explanation and justification to something so evil that
it precisely resists all explanation, is what Levinas vehemently rejects. Evil,
for Levinas, is not a lack of something (good) but the presence of an excess
that cannot be understood with reference to something else: "Evil is excess
in its very quiddity. [. . .] The rupture with the normal and the normative,
with order, with synthesis [. . .] already constitutes its qualitative essence."[34]

The point is, however, that this critique applies to other theological
concepts as well and that, therefore, ontotheology may very well have also
slipped into theology's constitution. Original sin is thus defined by Augustine,
Anselm, and others as the *privatio justitiae*, as the absence of justification
or grace. Though Adam and Eve possessed all that was necessary for their
salvation or beatitude, the original sin itself is defined as the lack of that
which is needed for salvation. While Adam and Eve are created immortal,
sinners are mortal; while Adam and Eve had perfect knowledge of their
beatitude, sinners are condemned to ignorance about the goal of earthly life;
while Adam and Eve were in a state of innocence, sinners are condemned
to concupiscence and are therefore, whether they like it or not, generators
and transmitters of sin.[35]

Now, if one considers ontotheology from a theological point of view,
one of the questions of theology is whether or not the concept of redemption
is constructed in an ontotheological way, since, as we have seen, privation
over privation yields adequation. Therefore, redemption in and through Jesus
Christ is, according to these classical authors, the grace and gift of precisely
that which was lacking to conceive of salvation—redemption as *privatio
peccati*, the absence and lack of sin. So Christ liberated us from mortality
in and through the promise of eternal life, from ignorance by revealing the
way to (and the truth of) eternal beatitude.[36] Ontotheologically, the pair
sin-redemption would appear as a perfect fit, an *adequatio rei et intellectus*
if you like, and changes into a system where the relation between terms
complete and complement one another. The point is that such a privative
manner of conceiving sin and redemption would remain stuck in an immanent
and negative conception of transcendence and would yield a false sense of
certainty with regard to salvation: salvation as the adequate fulfilment of a
certain need for redemption.

In its stead, one should perhaps conceive of an unredeemedness *sui generis*, not as the absence of grace and justification, but as the presence of the nonredeemed that precisely escapes redemption, as if there is something in human beings that even Christ cannot reach—or could not reach when descending to this finite world. But this nonsignifying 'element' of the facticity of human beings can at the same time be that which allows for human freedom with regard to God, for such unredeemedness might be what incites (but does not necessitate) faith as a struggle with God and at the same time allows immanence and finitude to be a genuine other than God. As is the case in Marion, faith would then be primarily pragmatic, and signifies, not as an 'idiotic prolepsis of a blunt certitude,' but rather from out of the performance that the human being undertakes (or not) with regard to God.[37] The decision to believe is one that the believer time and time again has to take. One might say that it is, in this desertlike experience, not sure at all whether or not this God who the faithful see appearing is or is not a fata morgana. Referring to Jacob's struggle with the angel, Marion writes: "I give the blessing to God only after having struggled enough to understand that that struggle itself was blessing me" (*ID*, 198–99). So, faith for Marion means that the faithful perform their faith in face of God while not relying on the false comfort that this performance—where the very act of performing functions as a signifier—would reach its intentional aim or attain its referent (signified). Faith, then, operates according to the logic later brought forward in, among other texts, *Being Given*, where the gifted or the *adonné*'s response toward givenness is his 'response' in a performance close to the Heideggerian *Jemeinigkeit*: my response toward whatever appears depends on me, and only on me. But this is not to say that the response of faith (and its referent) is floating in the air. It is rather to say that it is only in and through this faithful performance or auto-conversion that a hetero-conversion might occur, in short, that something other than myself might be encountered: in assuming a faithful stance or in the making one's own of faithful gestures, the faithful finally give themselves over to God and recognize that the very act of struggling with God is, perhaps, initiated by God.

To make matters more concrete: when I earlier put some question marks around both Marion's account of Pascal for its theological usurpation of facticity and Lacoste's somewhat Barthian description of the liturgical experience, it was obviously not a matter of dismissing all things theological. It is rather that, since the rise and fall of ontotheology and the fluctuations of its fever in our postmodern days, the turn to theology surely has been severely complicated. When one asks for instance, "Who is afraid of postmodernism?" one could argue that it might not be those who fear that in postmodernity "a being's ratio to the infinite" or its "referability to God" is lost, but those who see that it is precisely this referability, which makes individual beings part and parcel of an infinite register, which has been long questionable.[38] But again, it is not the referential nature of the mirroring of creation toward the Creator that is questioned here; it is rather that this referential nature of creation does not come into view when one merely *assumes* that the finite is always and already part and parcel of an infinite register. It is thus a matter of how to configure, in our postmodern times, such a reference and how one might account for the fact there might be more to the finite than finitude.

One of such ways might be to develop Lacoste's concept of 'the nonexperience' of the believer along the following lines, for this nonexperience is precisely that which *interrupts* the cheerful and pleasant belief in and feeling of dependence toward the Creator. The nonexperience is thus a painful *night* in which the feeling of dependence *itself*, or in any case the assumption of 'a ratio to the infinite,' is put into question.[39] Recall that this nonexperience, for Lacoste, is christologically motivated: it is an imitation of Christ's nonexperience on the Cross. But one might want to cling onto a different liturgical experience than the one Lacoste has in mind by pointing, not to the verification of faith's knowledge, but rather to the everpresent possibility of its *falsification*. It is in this sense that one might apply Lacoste's description of "an ignorance proper to the Messiah" (*NT*, 174), for it would indeed not be unwise for a liturgical experience that wants to be an *imitatio Christi*, to learn a lesson or two from the ignorance that accompanied Christ during his mission. This ignorance, as Lacoste suggests, is precisely an ignorance of the exact nature of God's coming (*parousia*): "[H]e expected the apocalypse, but the history of the world continued; he expected the Kingdom, and it is the Church that has come" (*NT*, 174). Such a falsification is not without consequences for the question of salvation, for if one avoids the (ontotheological) adequation of the grace received and the grace to come, one could understand the demand that arises from out of the world, not as something still standing out toward its fulfilment, but rather as an unredeemedness *sui generis*—as if something in the human being is not and cannot be redeemed. This concept of an 'unredeemedness' of the human being is in consequence of an immanence that might understand itself as a cry, a protestation and even a *lament* towards the Creator. Moreover, such a lamenting of one's unredeemedness differs from the traditional pair of sin-redemption, in that it does not assume a privative relation between these two instances. Whereas in the traditional account, all sinful behavior is countered by Christ's generous and graceful offer of redemption, it is something else altogether to imagine an unredeemedness that even Christ cannot reach. Here then the ignorance of Christ with regard to Christ's mission might meet not only with my (and our) freedom toward God but also with the ignorance of the human being with regard to his or her own vocation. It goes without saying that to imagine a point that even Christ cannot reach requires one to reconfigure the theocentrism that the thinkers of the Enlightenment have burdened us with. Such a theocentrism is still present in Lacoste's work as well, for God's nonparousiacal presence in the believer can be united "with an affirmation of a divine omnipresence" (*EA*, 45). The concept of an unredeemedness, however, would be willing to consider a nonpresence or an absence of God more seriously, for instead of taking God's presence as something present-at-hand, it would perhaps be good to speak of revelation as the *presencing* of God which precisely is God's appearance and incarnation in being as every other being, namely as a being in being. But just how phenomenology might speak of the presence of God from within the realm of being and how the presence of God could relate to the presencing of a particular being is, it seems to me, still an open question.

One can thus question whether Lacoste's affirmation of God's omnipresence is really compatible with the statements of his later work where it, for instance, is stated of God's presence that it is a "gift that arrives here and not there, at this time, and not at another" (*PP*, 28). It is *this* gift—the gift of presencing—that indeed "can appear as beneficial for our liberties" (ibid.). But it is likewise open to question just where such a presencing might lead. Therefore, it is, to my mind, not wise to confine God's presencing to God's presence in the Eucharist, as all too many Catholic theologians are doing today. To be sure: the liturgical experience is a sacramental experience, but it is not certain whether all sacramental experiences are of the liturgical kind Lacoste has in mind. Let us, to conclude, briefly consider Lacoste's account of the communal aspect of liturgy: whereas *Experience and the Absolute* could be considered as describing a singular, individual, monadic experience, *Présence et Parousie* delves into the community insinuating itself in liturgy more deeply.[40] Pickstock, for instance, has argued that "while we exceed the world through our liturgical trangression of lateral limits, the world [. . .] continues to exceed *us*. We remain with the other in praise."[41]

We remain with the other in praise. This is a phrase that Lacoste would not deny. Likewise, Lacoste would not and has not denied the validity of Pickstock's objection, "but, in order to proceed [. . .] let's say that one ought to describe a co-affectivity."⁴² This concept is already present in *Le monde et l'absence d'œuvre*, where Lacoste writes that in liturgical experience "angst is not annulled but undergoes a metamorphosis: it is no longer the revealer par excellence of one's solitude, but co-angst, *Mit-Angst*, angst that is lived from out of a community and is thus subordinated to joy" (MO, 75 n. 1). The concept of coangst is, however, in Lacoste's latest substituted for a community of love: the other appears in the liturgical experience not as an other Dasein whom I have to awaken for his or her ownmost possibility, but as my neigbor, as the one who "deserves to be loved" (PP, 53). The liturgical experience thus requires a "phenomenology of love" (PP, 160).

    The problem now is whether the liturgical experience is to be considered as a correction and an extension, as Marion is suggesting, or rather as a rival and repetition of Heidegger's existential analytic?⁴³ If the liturgical experience is to be interpreted as a correction and an extension of the existential analytic, if, as Lacoste suggests, it supplements Heidegger's analytic because this analytic did not let appear the whole of human existence, then it would be necessary to integrate the liturgical experience into the human being's factical existence, and thus to speak of a 'facticity otherwise than Heidegger' if you like. If, however, the liturgical experience posits itself as as a rival of the existential analytic, in that it would be able to make appear the truth of existence, then one would have to agree that the liturgical experience poses an entirely different version of the Heideggerian world and facticity, an 'otherwise than facticity' as it were. In short, the first option would leave the Heideggerian account intact, and would inaugurate (merely) the validity of the liturgical experience *next to* the Heideggerian 'experiences' of world and earth, whereas the second option would invalidate Heidegger's conceptual analysis and would install the liturgical experience *in place of* the existential analytic. Whereas Lacoste undoubtedly would prefer the first option, there are some indications that he nevertheless veers into the second option. If this is true, however, then Lacoste commits the same hermeneutical error as he advances against Heidegger, namely, that is not clear why one should value in phenomenology one experience over the other—in Heidegger's case 'anxiety' (Cf. PP, 313)— it is equally possible to ask why in theology one experience, liturgical or otherwise, is to be valued over another. The question indeed is whether the liturgical experience is to be valued over all the other experiences in the world, for instance as revealing the truth of those experiences, and what the relation might be between the different liturgical experiences, and even if there can be many liturgical experiences at all.[44] Thus when stating that "there is an overflowing of metaphysics by theology" (*PP*, 28), a similar "desire for hierarchization" (*PP*, 148), similarly "without phenomenological foundation" (ibid.), might be at issue, for, in fact, we not only remain with the other in praise; the other can also have many ways of praising.

The problem thus seems to consist in configuring an experience that experiences both the provisional and the eschatological, or, in more philosophical terms, in configuring the simultaneity of both the world and liturgy. Instead of forging the liturgical experience *into* the existential analytic or configuring a space for this experience *next to* and even *in place of* this analytic, it might be useful to imagine liturgy *in* and *out of* the world. But which world?

Perhaps the one that Lacoste is seeking after in the margins of *Présence et Parousie*. My thesis is that there exists a sort of discrepancy between this philosophical aspect of community—being-together-in-the world—and the one which, as we have seen earlier, gets excluded from the liturgical experience. Quite central to this philosophical concept of community is an aside that Lacoste inserts amidst his meditations on the possible differences and similarities between the philosophical and the mystical experience: "[T] his proposal takes its cue from, and tries to think a unity of experience—and a unity of the subject of experience" (*PP*, 203). This seems to say that whatever one experiences, this experience in principle could be shared by others. Likewise, this unity of experience seems to imply that whoever experiences could in principle communicate this experience to others. In any case, here, and, as we will see, elsewhere, Lacoste attempts to "think the unity before the distinction" (*PP*, 203), and it is precisely this principle which will allow Lacoste to settle the disputes between for instance different language games, different 'worlds' and thus perhaps between different 'liturgical experiences.' In fact, it seems to be the world that needs to be taken as the unity underlying our aptitude to experience, for "by world [. . .] we understand the profound structure of all human experience as such" (*PP*, 91). The world is thus that underlying and unifying structure in which all are in one way or another directed towards all: "in any case, *the* world, understood phenomenologically, is essentially *our* world: there is no human being that one can exclude from it" (*PP*, 91).

These thoughts are for Lacoste, however, more than an aside. This is obvious from the way in which these remarks come to the fore in the article *Philosophie, theologie et vérité* (*PP*, 85–116). The article responds vehemently to the Wittgensteinian way of separating ways of life and language games by

appealing to human beings' "totality of experience" which does not allow
for "the natural border one wishes between language games" (*PP*, 114). As
Lacoste considers the problem of evil: "to reduce the question of evil [. . .] to
the problem of evil and its metaphysical solutions [. . .] is to not even notice
that Job's question does not call for a solution, but for a word in return" (*PP*,
113). In face of evil and of pain, the presence and the speech of another
human being is required, for, and although philosophers and Job's friends
have debated the question of evil for centuries now, "it is on a common
terrain—the common terrain of experience—that there is hurt and debate
here" (*PP*, 114): evil and pain are experiences which are in principle shared
by all, and which for that very reason call for a human community that lies
prior to all differences in race, language, and philosophies one can imagine.

All this incites Lacoste to posit an "ethics of discourse" in which
indeed a strange conflation of philosophical and theological concepts seems
to take place and that seems to render problematic the supposed distance
and rupture liturgy takes from the world. A philosophical ethics of discourse
is concerned not so much with the distinction between true and false
statements, but rather with that which is important and that which is not,
for such an ethics of discourse knows that it is because of our finitude that
that which we decide to speak about is accompanied with a certain *urgency*.
This urgency, then, concerns both what needs to be spoken about and that
which needs to be listened to. It is important to note, however, that whatever
needs to be said and whatever needs to be listened to arises from out of the
world that is common because of "the common fact of existing" (*PP*, 115).
It is because of this common fact—one might risk the concept of a *shared
facticity*—that "to understand the questions of the other is never a Quinean
matter of 'radical translation' in which everything starts from scratch" (*PP*,
115), because "that about which it is important to speak [. . .] all that is a
common thing within a common world" (*PP*, 116). The urgency accompanying
all (meaningful) language is thus, according to Lacoste, founded upon the
universality and the commonality of a shared world. It is in this sense that
one might perceive in Lacoste's most recent work a renewed interest in
immanence.[45] It is to the truth of this universality that Lacoste points and
that for him, significantly, is not without theological significance, for such
a universality will allow the human being's needs to appear and "to notice
these needs is not little. The theologian will without a doubt add that their
apparition [. . .] will lead toward a theory of redemption" (*PP*, 116).

This nontheological account I am advancing here with (but perhaps
also against) Lacoste thus need not be confused with an antitheological

manner of looking at being-in-the-world, for such a nontheological account might be the appropriate way to configure the encounter between God and human beings as a *free and singular, that is, in each case mine,* encounter. Such an 'unredeemedness' might spring from the restlessly dwelling in and the impatience of being thrown, despite oneself, into a world. The liturgical experience which accompanies such an 'unredeemedness' might be the *lamenting prayer,* a mere vocative, that is uttered as a sort of cry for an of being-in-the-world. In this sense, it is worth noting that is precisely the being without God of the unredeemed that incites one to freely turn to God with one's lament. For, perhaps, it is only when the believer turns to God with his or her nonexperience and unredeemedness that Christ might turn to the human being. One could gather a few biblical credentials for such a line of reasoning. First, one could point to Rev. 3, 20: "Here I am! I stand at the door and knock. If anyone hears my voice and opens the door, I will come in and eat with him, and he with me." This might also be the reason why an election by Jesus is, though accompanied with an urgency, never prompted by force (Mt. 8, 22; 2 Cor. 5,14).

The Bible, of course, is never anything but good news: this is how the concept of 'unredeemedness' might elucidate Jesus' outrage against those of little faith (e.g., Mt 3,7). It is thus equally necessary that the concept of unredeemedness is accompanied with a radical affirmation of sin. This sin, then, might not be conceived as a *privatio iustitia,* always and already awaiting its redemption. It is in this sense that one could apply Nancy's concept of evil as pure wickedness, and affirm "that there is a pure 'positivity' of evil [. . .] in the sense that evil, in its very negativity, without dialectical sublation, forms a positive possibility of existence."[46] Thus, there is a sin or two: the ones that come to mind are murder and rape. Such a being without God would call for a reflection on various contemporary theological stances, for just as Smith argues against the Radical Orthodox omission of sin and the fall, because, according to their doctrine, everything "always and already is graced,"[47] so too one could argue against Levinas, Lacoste, and Marion that their failing to take a radical abandonment into account is the result of always and already dialectically sublating this abandonment toward admiration. One could argue against this by again following Smith and state that sin inhibits not only the human being's inclination to virtue, but also the powers of the soul, that is, the power to know—in a clear and distinct way?—about the infinite.[48] Again, such an account is not antitheological, it rather tries to configure the *imitatio Christi* from out of the ignorance that was proper to the Messiah. This contamination of the power to know, then, is finally what necessitates one to take leave of the Barthian stress on revelation and explains why understanding the extent to which one is in the dark about the divine should paradoxically fall to philosophy. To return to Marion's account of Pascal one last time: if Pascal can really ridicule Descartes and even qualify him as being 'blasphemous' because Descartes "would deal in a strictly philosophical rigor with what belongs first of all to charity" (*DMP*, 300), then this is, of course, for Pascal, to assume that Descartes would already assume what Pascal has in mind when speaking of theology and blasphemy. In either case, a dialogue between them would not be possible, and Pascal would preach to deaf ears. Instead of resorting to the primacy of love over knowing,[49] it is thus perhaps better to know how to love: for as much as there is no need to 'demarcate the rigid boundaries of the community' so too *is* there an urgent need both to pass beyond this theological speaking for the natives, for "the redeemed and the believers only,"[50] and to rid ourselves of not being on speaking terms with those who do not belong to the same flock in order to be reminded, again, that Christ's message was to the entirety of nations, to the unredeemed precisely, and that the theologian's task thus is indeed "to include rather than exclude."[51]

Notes

Chapter One. Some Notes on a French Debate

1. See *Phenomenology and the Theological Turn: The French Debate*, ed. D. Janicaud, J.-F. Courtine and J.-L. Chrétien (New York: Fordham University Press, 2000).

2. Levinas, *TI*, p. 299: "[T]he Being of the existent is a *Logos* that is the word of no one," which translates the French '*l'être de l'étant*.' Throughout this text, I will translate '*étant*' or the existents from Levinas' earlier works with 'beings' and '*être*' with 'being.'

3. For Heidegger on technology, see Merold Westphal's account in his *Transcendence and Self-Transcendence: On God and the Soul* (Cambridge: Cambridge University Press, 1998), (Bloomington: Indiana University Press, 2004), pp. 15–40.

4. Heidegger, "On the Essence and Concept of Physis in Aristotle's Physics B, 1," in Heidegger, *Pathmarks*, trans. T. Sheehan, ed. W. Mcneill, p. 192.

5. See Heidegger, *Being and Time*, trans. J. Macquarrie and E. Robinson (New York: Harper and Row, 1962), pp. 98–99.

6. See Lacoste, "De la technique à la liturgie," *Communio* 9 (1984), p. 29.

7. Catherine Pickstock, *After Writing: On the Liturgical Consummation of Philosophy* (Oxford: Blackwell, 1998), p. 250.

8. Compare his CV, p. 39.

9. Heidegger, *Brief über den Humanismus* (Frankfurt am Main: Klostermann, 2000), p. 20.

10. Levinas, "The Trace of the Other," in *Deconstruction in Context: Literature and Philosophy*, trans. A. Lingis, ed. M. C. Taylor (Chicago: University of Chicago Press, 1986), p. 351.

11. See J. K. A. Smith, *Speech and Theology: Language and the Logic of Incarnation* (London: Routledge, 2002), p. 169.

12. *God, the Gift, and Postmodernism*, ed. J. Caputo and M. Scanlon (Bloomington: Indiana University Press, 1999), p. 165.

13. Heidegger, *The Question concerning Technology and Other Essays* (New York: Harper and Row, 1977), trans. W. Lovittp. 14.

14. Ibid., pp. 18–19, trans. mod.

15. Heidegger, *The Question concerning Technology*, p. 19.

16. Heidegger, *Being and Time*, p. 129.

17. See also, Heidegger, *Zollikon Seminars: Protocols—Conversations—Letters*, ed. M. Boss, trans. F. Mayr and R. Askay (Evanston: Northwestern University Press, 2001), pp. 30–31.

18. See ibid., pp. 69ff.

19. Heidegger, *Being and Time*, p. 141.

20. Ibid., p. 140.

21. Heidegger, "The Question concerning Technology," p. 27.

22. Iain Thomson, *Heidegger on Ontotheology: Technology and the Politics of Education* (Cambridge: Cambridge University Press, 2005), p. 56. On such an objectification of the subject, see also Maurice-Merleau-Ponty, *The Visible and the Invisible* (Evanston: Northwestern University Press, 1968), p. 19: "We apply to man as to things the conviction [. . .] that we can arrive at what is by an absolute overview, and in this way we come to think of the invisible of man as a thing."

23. Heidegger, "The Question concerning Technology," p. 26.

24. Thomson, "Ontotheology? Understanding Heidegger's *Destruktion* of Metaphysics," *International Journal of Philosophical Studies* 8 (2000) 297–327, p. 302. Compare his *Heidegger on Ontotheology*, pp. 14–15.

25. Smith, *Speech and Theology*, p. 5.

26. Levinas' insistence that "knowledge remains linked to [. . .] the grasp even in the *concept* or the *Begriff* [and that] these metaphors are to be taken seriously and literally" is well known. See Levinas, "Transcendence and Intelligibility," in *BPW*, pp. 149–59, p. 152. Similar remarks can be found in Heidegger; see *Zollikon Seminars*, p. 129–32, where Heidegger states that phenomenology is concerned precisely with those instances that lie before all "*Begrifflichkeit*." On this topic, see also Marion's analysis of the Cartesian subject in Marion, *DMP*, pp. 92–94.

27. Heidegger, *The Question concerning Technology*, p. 61.

28. Ibid.

29. Ibid., pp. 61, 54.

30. Thomson, *Heidegger on Ontotheology*, p. 20.

31. Ibid., p. 8.

32. Ibid., p. 12.

33. Heidegger, "The Onto-theo-logical Constitution of Metaphysics," in *Identity and Difference*, trans. J. Stambaugh (Chicago: University of Chicago Press, 2002), pp. 70–71.

34. Heidegger, *Was ist Metaphysik?* (Frankfurt am Main: Vittorio Klostermann, 1998), p. 20. My translation.

35. Jean-Marc Narbonne, *Levinas and the Greek Heritage* (Leuven: Peeters, 2006), p. 75.

36. See Bernard Mabille, *Hegel, Heidegger et la métaphysique: Recherches pour une constitution* (Paris: Vrin, 2004), p. 131.

37. Heidegger, *Introduction to Metaphysics* (New Haven: Yale University Press, 2000), trans. G. Fried and R. Polt, p. 210 (my emphasis). I substitute the Greek 'idea' for 'essence.' The reason for this will become clear in chapter 7.

38. Westphal, *Transcendence and Self-Transcendence*, p. 22.

39. Cf. Merleau-Ponty, *Sens et non-sens* (Paris: Gallimard, 1963), p. 309.

40. Heidegger, *Introduction to Metaphysics*, p. 111.

41. Mabille, *Hegel, Heidegger et la métaphysique*, pp. 122, 130 et passim.

42. See Westphal, *Overcoming Onto-theology: Toward a Postmodern Christian Faith* (New York: Fordham University Press, 2001), pp. 1–27.

43. Westphal, *Transcendence and Self-Transcendence*, p. 18.

44. Heidegger, *The Question concerning Technology*, p. 69. My italics.

45. See "Jean-Luc Marion: Entretien du 3 décembre 1999," in Janicaud, *Heidegger en France II. Entretiens* (Paris: Albin, 2001), p. 217.

Chapter Two. Phenomenology, Liturgy, and Metaphysics: Jean Yves Lacoste

1. Lacoste, "*En marge du monde et de la terre: l'aise,*" in Lacoste, MO, pp. 5–22. As for Heidegger, see *Being and Time*, p. 42, "[T]he inquiry into being [. . .] is itself characterized by historicality."

2. Heidegger, *Being and Time*, p. 298. The last three words are italicized in Heidegger's text.

3. See, EA, 133, 183, 226; NT, 44; MO, 101; and PP, 163 et passim.

4. Note that Lacoste is not thinking here of Heidegger's (in)famous *Kehre* but of a turning in Heidegger's work with the emergence of the concept of the 'earth,' from "The Origin of the Work of Art" (1935) on. See Lacoste, EA, pp. 13–18.

5. A similar topology already emerges in Lacoste, NT, p. 124.

6. See Lacoste's article "Petite phénoménologie de la fatigue," in PP, pp. 309–22.

7. Although Lacoste only considers the 'project' in NT, it is not difficult to notice the structure of the project in the liturgical experience of EA; see pp. 33, 161, 163, 189.

8. Lacoste, *Carmel*, p. 15. Compare with EA p. 105.

9. Lacoste, BHP, p. 383.

10. Due to creation, the liturgical experience instructs us of our responsibilities to the cosmos as well; see Lacoste, EA, p. 187.

11. Lacoste, "Perception, Transcendence and the Experience of God," in *Transcendence and Phenomenology*, ed. C. Cunningham and P. Candler (London: SCM, 2007), p. 20

12. For this joy, see Lacoste, "Présence et affection," in PP, pp. 17–43. Hence, also, see Lacoste's description of liturgy as "the anticipated space of a resurrection," in Lacoste, "The Work and Complement of Appearing," in *Religious Experience and*

the End of Metaphysics, ed. J. Bloechl (Bloomington: Indiana University Press, 2003), p. 92.

13. See also *EeA*, p. 214, "l'ascèse inquiète légitimement . . ." and p. 222, "le fol nous inquiète . . ."

14. Ignace Verhack, "Eindigheidservaring en absoluutheid," *Tijdschrift voor Filosofie* 58 (1996) 142–53, criticizes Lacoste for not being able to show some sort of philosophical mediation between the world and the liturgy.

15. Lacoste, "The Work and Complement of Appearing," p. 70.

16. Note the continuity with *NT*, p. 93. Jean Greisch rightly wonders why these experiences devoid "of any eschatological meaning, still merit being qualified as 'sabbathic experience.'" See *Le buisson ardent et les lumières de la raison. Tome 2* (Paris, Cerf: 2002), p. 284.

17. Heidegger hints at this in "The Origin of the Work of Art," in *Basic Writings*, ed. D. F. Krell (London: Routledge, 1994), p. 151.

18. Lacoste, "The Work and Complement of Appearing," pp. 77, 80.

19. An intriguing exception, of course, is Heidegger, *Being and Time*, p. 358.

20. See Jacques Derrida, "Restitutions: On the Truth in Painting," in *The Truth in Painting* (Chicago: University of Chicago Press, 1987), trans. G. Bennington and I. McLeod, pp. 255–56, as cited in Lacoste, "The Work and Complement of Appearing," p. 93.

21. Cf. Lacoste, "The Work and Complement of Appearing," p. 84.

22. Ibid., p. 86.

23. Ibid., p. 88.

24. Ibid., p. 84.

25. Greisch, Le buisson ardent et les lumières de la raison. Tome 2, pp. 283–84.

26. Lacoste, "Sacrements, Ethique, Eucharistie," *Revue Thomiste* 84 (1984), pp. 227–28.

27. I will expand on this point in chapter 4. See on this also Merleau-Ponty, for what indeed has become of "the intermundane space ('*l'intermonde*') where our gazes cross," *The Visible and the Invisible*, p. 48?

28. Cf. Lacoste, *PP*, p. 134.

29. Greisch, *Le buisson ardent et les lumières de la raison*, p. 269.

30. Ibid., pp. 269, 274.

31. The point is taken from Laurence Paul Hemming, *Heidegger's Atheism: The Refusal of a Theological Voice* (Notre Dame, IN: University of Notre Dame Press, 2002), p. 50.

32. Compare Jeffrey Bloechl, "Dialectical Approaches to Retrieving God after Heidegger (Lacoste and Marion)," *Pacifica* 13 (2000), p. 293.

33. Compare also Lacoste, *EA*, p. 151 and *NT*, p. 171.

34. Lacoste almost literally confirms this hypothesis when saying that "we would not understand what is played out in the night if we did not perceive the reversal that lets God be affirmed as the only I, and by which, to repeat, man becomes nothing but the object of an aim he cannot take measure of in consciousness." *EA*, 152.

35. See Lacoste, *EA*, p. 144; *NT*, p. 165; and *PP*, 142.

Chapter Three. From the Subject to the *'Adonné'*: Jean-Luc Marion

1. Contrary to Derek J. Morrow, "The Love 'Without Being' that Opens to Distance Part Two: From the Icon of Distance to the Distance of the Icon in Marion's Phenomenology of Love," *Heythrop Journal* 46 (2005), p. 508. For further references to this "phenomenological distance," see Marion, *BG*, pp. 123, 124.

2. See for instance Marion, *BG*, p. 116.

3. See also Robyn Horner's discussion of this in *Re-thinking God as Gift*, p. 133. Horner furthermore notes that Marion here "manifests a strong tendency toward personifying the gift" (p. 136).

4. Marion refers to Husserl, *The Idea of Phenomenology*, trans. William P. Alston and George Nakhinian (Dordrecht: Kluwer Academic, 1990), p. 14.

5. See Marion, *BG*, pp. 68, 64.

6. Compare also Marion, *BG*, p. 68, "the given, issued from the process of givenness, appears but leaves concealed givenness itself, which becomes enigmatic."

7. In my citation, I take these two passages on the technological object together.

8. See also Marion, *BG*, 5.

9. See Heidegger, *Being and Time*, p. 57. Marion considers this definition already at work in Husserl, see Marion, *BG*, p. 184.

10. Recall that for Marion the ultimate question is not "to be or not to be. "

11. This role of the senses is even clearer in *VR*, pp. 127–33, where he describes the saturated phenomenon according to each of the senses.

12. Here is an important difference with what Marion first called "the receiver," the one who receives the given phenomenon: where the receiver is still "determined as a thought [*une pensée*]" (*BG*, 266/*ED*, 366), the *adonné* is defined by a complete loss of knowledge.

13. See, for Marion on birth, *BG*, pp. 289–90; *IE*, pp. 41–44.

14. See Heidegger, *Zollikon Seminars*, p. 120, "The appropriate French translation of Da-sein should be: Etre le là," literally 'being the there.'

15. Other 'slips of the tongue' are noteworthy too. While trying to reverse the classical scheme of cause and effect, Marion writes that "the event thus attests its nonconstitutability by constituting me, myself, its effect," *BG*, p. 170. Compare also *BG*, p. 146, "[the fait accompli of the phenomenon] is a fact made on my account; by it, I am made" with his *IE*, p. 34, and *BG*, p. 276.

16. Marion later elaborates on this judgmental character of the saturated phenomenon by retrieving Augustine's *"veritas redarguens"*: the saturated phenomenon judges me in that "I undergo the obscure obligation of letting myself conform to (and by) the excess of intuition," See Marion, *VR*, p, 140. Levinas adheres to this figure of truth as well; see his "Notes on Meaning," in his *Of God Who Comes to Mind* (Stanford: Stanford University Press, 1998), trans. B. Bergo, p. 170. See for

this also my critical study "In (the) Place of the Self: A Critical Study of Jean-Luc Marion's 'Au lieu de soi. L'approche de Saint Augustin,'" *Modern Theology* 25 (2009), pp. 661–86.

17. Marion, *IE*, p. 26. Compare his *CV*, p. 44, "the painting [. . .] gives *itself* [. . .], and the pictorial act is restricted to [. . .] *recording* and being undergirded by the support of a gift" (my emphasis).

18. Cf. Marion, *GWB*, pp. 19, 129, et passim. Compare with *CV*, p. 60.

19. Marion, "The Phenomenality of the Sacrament—Being and Givenness," in *Words of Life: New Theological Turns in French Phenomenology*, ed. B. E. Benson and N. Wirzba (New York: Fordham University Press, 2010), p. 100.

20. See also Marion, *BG*, p. 60, "[Givenness] must therefore be understood as an act."

21. Cf. also Marion, *BG*, p. 47, where Marion argues that a reproduction of a painting does not diminish the effect of the painting at all, since "in each case, the *power* of the original appearing is fully exercised for whoever knows how to see it in conformity with the intentional aim it requires," and p. 200.

22. For this resistance, see Marion, *IE*, pp. 49–53, and also already in Marion, *BG*, p. 314.

23. "To decide on the gift" renders "se décider au don"—the 'se' refers here to the *adonné* who has to decide on himself or herself. See Marion, *ED*, p. 159.

24. See Heidegger, *Being and Time*, p. 233. For Heidegger, however, this is but the first step to an authentic being-with others, see *Being and Time*, p. 344.

25. Horner, *Jean-Luc Marion: A Theo-Logical Introduction* (Aldershot: Ashgate, 2005), p. 7.

26. See also Marion, *CV*, p. 37 and, again, *CV*, p. 44.

27. Jocelyn Benoist, *L'idée de phénoménologie* (Paris: Beauchesne, 2001), p. 102.

Chapter Four: On Miracles and Metaphysics: From Marion to Levinas

1. See the entry on 'Miracle' in *Dictionnaire critique de la théologie*, ed. J.-Y. Lacoste (Paris: PUF, 2002), pp. 737–42. For Rahner's definition, see the entry on "Wunder," in *Kleines Theologisches Wörterbuch* (Freiburg: Herder, 1961), hrsg. K. Rahner and H. Vorgrimler, p. 389.

2. Caputo and Scanlon, "Introduction: Apology for the Impossible: Religion and Postmodernism," in *God, the Gift, and Postmodernism* (Bloomington: Indiana University Press, 1999), p. 9.

3. Caputo, "The Hyperbolization of Phenomenology: Two Possibilities for Religion in Recent Continental Philosophy," in *Counter-Experiences: Reading Jean-Luc Marion*, pp. 85, 83.

4. Westphal, "Transfiguration as Saturated Phenomenon," *Journal of Philosophy and Scripture* 1 (2003), p. 3. Note that Westphal is indeed responding to the, at the time, unpublished paper of Caputo I am discussing here.

5. Marion distinguishes between phenomenology and theology, in the sense that the first can only describe the possibility of revelation, while the latter examines the actuality or reality of this Revelation, see also BG, p. 367 n. 90.

6. Caputo, "The Hyperbolization of Phenomenology," p. 83; Caputo's italics.

7. Ibid., p. 87.

8. Ibid.

9. Marion, "They Recognized Him and He Became Visible to Them," *Modern Theology* 18 (2002), pp. 145–46.

10. Marion, "A Dieu, rien d'impossible," *Communio* 14 (1989), p. 56. All translations of this article are mine.

11. Westphal, "Transfiguration as Saturated Phenomenon," pp. 1–2.

12. Marion, "A Dieu, rien d'impossible," p. 49. See also p. 46.

13. Ibid., p. 46.

14. Falque, "Larvatus pro Deo: Jean-Luc Marion's Phenomenology and Theology," in *Counter-Experiences: Reading Jean-Luc Marion*, pp. 194, 193. Marion's earlier dealings subscribed to the objectivity of revelation, though: Falque cites Marion's "Ce mystère qui juge celui qui le juge," *Résurrection* 32 (1969), p. 55.

15. See also the reference to Augustine's *"interior intimo meo,"* in BG, p. 343n. 4.

16. Falque, "Phénoménologie de l'extraordinaire," *Philosophie* 78 (2003), pp. 73–74.

17. This decisional and volitional aspect thus runs through *Being Given* in its entirety: not only, as we have seen, in face of the gift but also in face of givenness itself. Even the work of art "demands an act" (BG, 42) to see it as given.

18. Falque, "Phénoménologie de l'extraordinaire," p. 74.

19. Consider also Marion, BG, p. 305, "there is no worse blind man than the one who does not want to see," and the parallel in GWB, p. 117, mod., "there is no worse deaf man than the one who does not want to hear." Instructive in this respect is also Thomas Carlson's article "Blindness and the Decision to See: On Revelation and Reception in Jean-Luc Marion," in *Counter-Experiences*, ed. K. Hart, pp. 153–70.

20. See Marion, BG, pp. 293–94.

21. See also Marion's response to this objection, in VR, pp. 123–24, 178n. 41.

22. Falque, "Phénoménologie de l'extraordinaire," pp. 55, 75.

23. Ibid., p. 71.

24. Contrary, then, to what Falque seems to think, a number of questions arise with regard to Marion's rather abstract classification of saturated phenomena. Since, while Marion asserts that these phenomena are "strictly distinct" (BG, p. 297), it can easily be shown that the saturated phenomenon of the event is implied in all the other saturated phenomena. See IE, pp. 43, 98 (birth as saturated phenomenon of flesh *and* of event); IE, p. 122 (icon and event); IE, p. 72 (idol and event). Thus

the event seems to be privileged in Marion's account of the saturated phenomenon. The question regarding the abstract classification has, to my knowledge, been raised first by Jean Greisch, "Index sui et non dati: Les paradoxes d'une phénoménologie de la donation," *Transversalités* 70 (1999), p. 45.

25. Marion, "They Recognized Him," p. 148, "the miscomprehension [of Christ] even appears *inevitable*," and Marion, "A Dieu, rien d'impossible," p. 56.

26. Levinas, *TI*, p. 65.

27. I deal at length with this remarkable book in my review in *Louvain Studies* 28 (2003), pp. 67–71.

28. Caputo, "Apostles of the Impossible: On God and the Gift in Derrida and Marion," in *God, the Gift, and Postmodernism*, ed. J. D. Caputo and M. Scanlon, p. 211.

29. Caputo, "Apostles of the Impossible: On God and the Gift in Derrida and Marion," p. 211.

30. Ibid.

31. Ibid.

32. See, e.g., Marion, *VR*, p. 136.

33. See for instance Marion, *BG*, p. 46: the given phenomenon of the painting "remains indifferent to its character as a thing."

34. What else would explain the grief when one loses one's wedding ring or whatever thing that symbolizes one's relationship? If it were merely an interchangeable item, buying another one would solve the problem, and no harm would be done. Thus, the question that Marion could not answer in *EP* could be answered only if it entailed a reappraisal of visibility. If Marion's account of love suffers from the absence of the durability and visibility of the oath between my lover and me, it would have found these (but not as the 'visibility of the invisible as such') in granting these visible formulations its status as 'presenting' and conditioning the 'invisible' bond between us. The distinction between, for instance, the 'pure' gift of power and the physical counterpart of it (the key to the city, etc.) would disappear, but the presence of the latter would not, in any way whatsoever, *inhibit* or *impede* anything to appear as a gift (perhaps not even revelation), although its presence would be ambiguous, and its signification never pure, present, or transparent.

35. On Levinas' refusal of dialectics, see especially Jean-François Bernier's "Négation et Révélation: L'ontologie et la question de l'au-delà dans la philosophie d'Emmanuel Levinas," *Les Études Philosophiques* 54 (2000), pp. 333–53, and his "Transcendance et manifestation: La place de Dieu dans la philosophie d'Emmanuel Levinas," *Revue Philosophique de Louvain* 94 (1996), pp. 599–624.

36. Cf. Rudi Visker, "De Goede Ander? Hoe vreemd is de multiculturele Ander?" in *De Vreemdeling*, ed. L. Jansen and N. Oudejans (Budel: Damon, 2003), p. 94.

37. This is not to say that the 'context' or 'form' is meaningless. It is not *because* the context is meaningless that the face signifies, nor is it because the face's signification that the context *becomes* meaningless. These dialectical lines of reasoning

are precisely what Levinas wants to avoid. My context and my form do have meaning, but they would have this signification only *for me*. The other precisely *disturbs* this natural egoistic comfort in one's own possibilities and orients it toward the other.

38. Cf. the analysis of 'enjoyment' in Levinas, *TI*, pp. 109–74.

39. Levinas, *GP*, p. 141. Compare *OB*, p. 123, "[The Good] preserves its 'illeity' *to the point of letting it be excluded from the analysis.*"

40. Cf. *OB*, pp. 149, 145.

41. One should ponder to what extent this basic epistemological operation and in consequence thereof Levinas' denunciation of Western philosophy's craving for unity is influenced by Heidegger's critique of ontotheology. Indeed, for Heidegger, the discourse on what and how a being is (*Ontologik*) is, most often, simultaneously the question of the highest being (*Theo-logik*). 'Onto-logik' is described by Heidegger as that discipline that "thinks of beings with respect to the ground that is common to all beings as such.'" See Heidegger, "The Onto-theo-logical Constitution of Metaphysics," p. 70. It might be that Heidegger and Levinas on these and other questions are much closer than we usually assume, or are used to assuming.

42. See Marion, *BG*, pp. 293–94. For indeed, does a responsibility toward the other (in his/her destitution) *in due time* make any sense at all? On this urgency, see Levinas, *OB*, pp. 88, 89, 91, 101.

43. Recall the *exitus-reditus* scheme so pervasive in Ancient philosophy. For an account of the coming about of such a fall or diminution, see Heidegger, *Introduction to Metaphysics*, pp. 190ff.

44. See Verhack, "Eindigheidservaring en absoluutheid," pp. 147–51, 148, citing *EA*, p. 10.

45. Marion sketches this debate briefly in his "A Note concerning the Ontological Indifference," *Graduate Faculty Philosophy Journal* 20 (1998), pp. 25–26.

46. Marion, "A Note concerning the Ontological Indifference," p. 28.

47. Marion, *ID*, pp. 232, 233.

48. The term is taken from Marion's *DMP*, pp. 273, 279.

49. Marion, "A Note concerning the Ontological Indifference," p. 34, "the destruction of the ontological difference is indeed effected in and through a being," and p. 36.

Chapter Five. Levinas: Substituting the Subject for Responsibility

1. The reader is reminded that, for the sake of clarity, I substitute Levinas' use of "existents" for "beings."

2. See also, *TI*, p. 44.

3. Maurice Merleau-Ponty, *Phenomenology of Perception* (London: Routledge and Kegan Paul, 1981), trans. C. Smith, p. 57.

4. See Heidegger, *Being and Time*, pp. 42, 37.

5. See Heidegger, *Being and Time*, pp. 179–82 (fear), 228–35 (anxiety). Whereas fear is fear for an object of any kind, anxiety, according to Heidegger, is not determined by any object whatsoever. "That in the face of which one is fearful," can be anything (fear of snakes, heights etc.). The point is that anxiety does not have such a determinate object: "that in face of which one has anxiety [. . .] is not this or that [. . .] it is rather the possibility [. . .] of the world itself." Whereas fear fears the very being or object of which it fears, the 'why' of anxiety coincides with "that in face of which one has anxiety": I am not only anxious *for* the fact of being-in-the-world, this being-in-the-world is also *why* I am fearful. But this being-in-the-world is not an object or a being. On the contrary, "The pure 'that it is' shows itself, but the 'whence' and the 'whither' remain in darkness" (*Being and Time*, p. 173). Thus, when 'being-in-the-world' shows itself nothing really appears, except the fact that I have to be this being in face of which I am anxious.

6. Cf. Levinas, "De la description à l'existence," in *En découvrant l'existence avec Husserl et Heidegger* (Paris: Vrin, 2001), p. 148.

7. Levinas confirms this in " 'Totalité et Infini: Préface à l'édition allemande," in Levinas, *Entre Nous*, p. 249.

8. See also Marion's phenomenological analysis of ageing in, *IE*, p. 95.

9. See also Levinas, *TI*, p. 88.

10. See Levinas, *TI*, p. 198. For the concept of a phenomenological reduction in Levinas, see Visker, *Truth and Singularity*, pp. 255–60.

11. Given the stress on language and 'Saying,' such a "reduction to silence" (*OB*, 197n.) is all the more surprising. After all, how do we attend to the other if "the ascendancy of the other is exercised upon the same to the point of [. . .] leaving it speechless" (*OB*, 101)? Why indeed relegate all "said" immediately "to the babbling utterance of a word" (*OB*, 151)?

12. See for this Levinas *TI*, pp. 172, 197,198, 203.

13. Jacques Derrida, "Violence and Metaphysics: An Essay on the Thought of Emmanuel Levinas," in *Writing and Difference*, trans. A. Bass (Chicago: University of Chicago Press, 1978), pp. 313n. 21, 117.

14. Ibid., pp. 112, 92.

15. See Levinas, *TI*, pp. 67, 210, and especially *Time and the Other*, trans. R. A. Cohen (Pittsburgh: Duquesne University Press, 1994), pp. 81–84. For Husserl, see *Cartesianische Meditationen: Eine Einleitung in die Phänomenologie* (Hamburg: Felix Meiner Verlag, 1995), pp. 120–23, 125–27, but also the concept of 'empathy' in *Ideas Pertaining to a Pure Phenomenology and to a Phenomenological Philosophy: Second Book: Studies in the Phenomenology of Constitution* (Dordrecht: Kluwer, 1989), trans. R. Rojcewicz and A. Schuwer, pp. 99–102, 171–78.

16. Derrida, "Violence and Metaphysics," p. 123; Derrida's italics.

17. Ibid., p. 124, mod.

18. Ibid.; Derrida's italics.

19. Ibid., p. 125.

20. Ibid., p. 126, mod.

21. Ibid., p. 133.

22. Ibid., p. 125, mod. This entails, according to Derrida, that "the movement of transcendence toward the other" would imply "that in my ipseity I know myself to be other for the other" (p. 126). Oddly enough, Levinas *does* mention this possibility but dismisses it by saying that "this comes about only across very complex structures." *TI*, 84.

23. Derrida, "Violence and Metaphysics," p. 128.

24. Christine de Bauw, *L'envers du sujet: Lire autrement Emmanuel Levinas* (Bruxelles: Ousia, 1997), p. 71.

25. Ibid., p. 73.

26. Ibid., p. 79.

27. Horner, "The Betrayal of Transcendence," in *Transcendence: Philosophy, Literature, and Theology Approach the Beyond*, ed. Regina Schwartz (New York: Routledge, 2004), p. 68; italics mine. Horner refers to Milbank, *The Word Made Strange* (Oxford: Blackwell, 1997), p. 38.

28. Apart perhaps from Marion, *Prolegomena to Charity* (New York: Fordham University Press, 2002), trans. S. E. Lewis, pp. 96–97. However: in the preface to the American translation of this work, written in 1999, Marion explicitly notes the compatibility of the *adonné* and the alter ego; see p. xi.

29. See also Levinas, *TI*, pp. 66, 84, 214, and 215.

30. Derrida, "Violence and Metaphysics," p. 141.

31. Ibid., p. 142.

32. Ibid., p. 318 n. 70.

33. Ibid., p. 141.

34. Ibid., p. 142.

35. Ibid., p. 148.

36. Ibid. See also p. 144, "Being not existing before beings—and this is why it *is history*"; Derrida's italics. See, however, also Levinas' 'reply' in *HAM*, p. 22.

37. Derrida, "Violence and Metaphysics," p. 136.

38. Ibid., p. 143.

39. Ibid., p. 142.

40. Ibid., p. 318 n. 77, quoting Nicholas of Cusa, *Of Learned Ignorance* (London: Routledge and Kegan Paul, 1954), trans. G. Heron, p. 79.

41. This is, in fact, what chapter 7 will try to show.

42. The closest *OB* comes to repeating the critique of the alter ego is in its mention of *Einfühlung* at *OB*, p. 125. But here again such an *Einfühlung* or empathy is not condemned, but understood from out of the substitution for another. At one time, *OB* even refers to the other as an "other than myself [*autre que moi*]" (see *OB*, p. 55; *AqE*, p. 70).

43. Note that this hunger underlying intentionality will be for Levinas the occasion to retrace intentional consciousness to "a desire outside of the simple consciousness of . . ." (see *OB*, p. 66, also pp. 72ff).

44. Cf. Levinas, OB, p. 56, "there is nothing that is named I."

45. See Marion, "A Note concerning the Ontological Indifference," p. 34.

46. Derrida, "Violence and Metaphysics," p. 316 n. 44.

47. For Levinas on Hegel's bad infinite, see also OB, 193 n. 34: "[T]he wrong or negative infinity [is] only a negation of a finite: but the finite rises again the same as ever, and is never got rid of and absorbed." In the 'relation without relation,' then, "the end is not reborn, but moves off, at each stage of the approach" (ibid.).

48. Note, however, that just as TI already uses the vocabulary of the trauma (TI, 73), so too does OB at times downplay this violence (cf. OB, 116).

49. TI finds this 'transubstantiation' in fecundity, since my child is at the same time an other and me: "I do not have my child; I am my child" (p. 277).

50. See also OB, p. 59, 166, 193 n. 33.

51. See also Levinas' Difficile Liberté (Paris: Albin, 1983), p. 120, "Le Messie, c'est Moi, Etre Moi, c'est être Messie."

52. Rodolphe Calin, Levinas et l'exception de soi (Paris: PUF, 2005), p. 205, translation mine.

53. To be sure, more often than not Levinas rejects statements like these. See for instance, OB, p. 117: "[I]n this analysis we do not mean to reduce an entity that would be the ego to the act of substituting itself that would be the being of this entity." I am, however, doing nothing more than taking seriously Levinas' thought of an alternance of meaning when it comes to matters transcendent, for in a note following this passage Levinas again suggests that "one could be tempted to take substitution to be the being of the entity that is the ego. And, to be sure, the hither side of the ego lends itself to our speaking only by referring to being [. . .]. The said of language always says being. But in the moment of an enigma language also breaks with its own conditions, as in a sceptical saying, and says a signification before the event" (OB, p. 196 n. 20).

54. Heidegger might be concerned with a similar question: the distinction between the 'ontic' human sciences and the 'ontological' realm of Dasein is precisely introduced to retrieve from the former's concept of the human being as a being (as psychological, biological, etc.) that can be studied scientifically (which is to say: objectified) an understanding of the being of the human being, which, in this latter case, seems to be Dasein in its difference with being merely a being, to make appear that the human being is not a 'Menschending' or "human-Thing." See Being and Time, p. 86.

55. Enigma is the term Levinas has used since the 1965 article "Enigma and Phenomenon," in BPW, pp. 65–77. See also Levinas, OB, p. 187n. 7.

56. Else how to speak of it at all? Levinas is, of course, conscious of this fact, see OB, p. 155.

57. Cf. OB, p. 154, "There is a dilemma in the said, but an ambivalence in the signification of saying."

58. Italicized in the French text; see Levinas, AqE, p. 88.

59. Levinas, "Enigma and Phenomenon," in BPW, p. 70.

60. Levinas, "Hermeneutics and Beyond," in *Of God Who Comes to Mind*, p. 108.

61. Levinas, "Enigma and Phenomenon," in *BPW*, p. 70.

62. Derrida, "Violence and Metaphysics," p. 110; Derrida's italics.

63. See, Levinas, *OB*, pp. 43–45. The reduction of the human being to Saying, to the point where he or she is capable only of signifying and bearing witness to the 'for the other,' starts from out of the Said—the realm of being, knowledge, and immanence. Obviously, Levinas sees, here too, an ambiguity rather than a certitude. For just as the reduction of the said to the saying "retains an echo of the reduced said" (p. 44), so too the absorption of the saying in the said is not without residue of the saying itself, since "the plot of saying [. . .] is not exhausted in this manifestation [in the said]" (p. 46). There is no clear and distinct reduction of the said to the saying, just as the said cannot fully absorb the signifyingness of the Saying.

64. Calin, Levinas et l'exception de soi, p. 238n. 1.

65. Levinas, "Philosophy and Awakening," in *Who Comes after the Subject?* trans. M. Quaintance, ed. E. Cadava, P. Connor, and J.-L. Nancy (New York: Routledge, 1991), p. 211, mod.

66. Ibid., p. 212, mod.

67. Derrida, "Violence and Metaphysics," p. 109.

68. Levinas, "Philosophy and Awakening," pp. 212–13, mod. Compare also Levinas, *OB*, pp. 32–34.

69. Ibid., p. 213.

70. Levinas, "Notes on Meaning," in *Of God Who Comes to Mind*, p. 161.

71. Levinas, "Philosophy and Awakening," p. 213.

72. See also Levinas, *OB*, p. 67.

73. See for instance the "Questions and Answers," in *Of God who Comes to Mind*, p. 93, "in knowledge there is a return of the I to oneself, but if there is, in the current of consciousness, a center toward which the return is possible, the core of this return originates in another plot. It is through ethics, through the emphasis of my obligation that the I is I."

74. Italics are Levinas'.

75. R. Calin, *Levinas et l'exception de soi*, p. 239.

76. Levinas, "Philosophy and Awakening," p. 213.

77. Ibid., p. 213, mod.

78. Levinas, "Questions and Answers," in *Of God Who Comes to Mind*, p. 92.

Chapter Six. Intermediary Conclusions and the Question concerning Ontotheology

1. Heidegger, *Being and Time*, pp. 67–68.

2. Raffoul, *A chaque fois mien: Heidegger et la question du sujet* (Paris: Galilée, 2004), p. 15.

3. See also Levinas' conclusion of "Un Dieu-Homme?" in *Entre Nous* p. 76.

4. Marion, "Notes on the Ontological Indifference," p. 35.

5. Ibid., p. 36. Of course, one should question this distinction between the hostage and *Dasein*, for one should keep in mind that the instances (angst, boredom, death) through which such a putting into play occurs entail a passive element as well: after all, one does not *choose* to be anxious, to be bored, and so on.

6. Compare Marion, BG, pp. 123, 174.

7. See also Marion, EP, p. 47, "the *illusion* of persevering in one's being."

8. Calin, *Levinas et l'exception de soi*, p. 237.

9. Visker, *Truth and Singularity*, p. 242.

10. Levinas, "The Trace of the Other," p. 353.

11. Visker, *Truth and Singularity*, p. 129.

12. Visker, *The Inhuman Condition: Looking for Difference after Levinas and Heidegger* (Dordrecht: Kluwer Academic, 2004), pp. 129–30.

13. For further references, see Visker, *The Inhuman Condition*, pp. 112–41, and *Truth and Singularity*, pp. 115–43, 235–73.

14. Levinas, "Transcendence and Height," in BPW, p. 17.

15. Visker, *Truth and Singularity*, pp. 266–67.

16. Ibid., p. 268.

17. Ibid., p. 272.

18. Ibid., p. 263; the last words refer to Levinas, "Transcendence and Height," in BPW, p. 29.

19. It is good to recall here Horner's comments that Marion 'manifests a strong tendency toward personifying the gift' and, in his early works, "moves to a more evident personification of distance," Horner, *Theo-logical Introduction*, p. 58.

20. Jocelyn Benoist, "Les voix du soliloque: Sur quelques lectures récentes du cogito," *Les Études philosophiques* 43 (1997), p. 546. All translations of this article are mine.

21. Ibid., p. 548.

22. Ibid., p. 552; his italics.

23. Ibid., p. 553.

24. Ibid., p. 551.

25. Ibid., p. 546.

26. See GWB, p. 85; DsE, p. 126. "[This] difference [is] indifferent to ontological difference, but above all *not to being* [*l'étant*]." See also GWB, p. 85; DsE, p. 127.

27. If earlier a solipsistic moment in *Being Given* was described when the *adonné* needed to decide on 'the great reason of things,' such a return of solipsism might point to the fact that, precisely by intersubjectivizing this originary alterity, Marion has *already* taken this decision. Yet there seems to be no philosophical reason here for preferring the personal nature of this call.

28. See Marion, RG, p. 202; BG, p. 266, and esp. pp. 296–97.

29. See Levinas, *Otherwise than Being*, p. 147, "The command is stated by the mouth of him it commands. *The infinitely exterior becomes an 'inward' voice.*"

30. For the disqualification of "*thaumazein*," see Levinas, "Philosophy and Awakening," p. 214.

31. See Marion, *BG*, 269, on wonder, which translates 'admiration.' Also *ED*, 371; *BG*, 200, and 363n. 44, where amazement ('*l'étonnement*' or *thaumazein*) is linked to admiration. See also *BG*, 219, on the idea of the infinite and the "surprise of admiration" it provokes.

32. Jean-Paul Sartre, *Being and Nothingness: An Essay on Phenomenological Ontology* (New York: Philosophical Library, 1956), p. 290.

33. Cf. Levinas, *GP*, p. 200 n. 29; *OB*, p. 115, 129 *et passim*. For Marion, see *BG*, pp. 56–59.

34. Levinas, *Existence and Existents*, trans. A. Lingis (Pittsburgh: Duquesne University Press, 2003), p. 67.

35. Derrida, "Violence and Metaphysics," p. 109.

36. Ibid., p. 94.

37. An example will make this clear: when I represent a table as a table, this act of identification simultaneously serves to distinguish the ego from the table because it indicates that the ego is *not* the table.

38. Derrida, "Violence and Metaphysics," p. 94.

39. Ibid., p. 114.

40. Cf. Marion, *BG*, p. 304, "the uninterrupted [. . .] series of its responsals."

41. Levinas, *Existence and Existents*, p. 4. See also Levinas, *Time and the Other*, p. 49.

42. Levinas, *Time and the Other*, p. 50.

43. Levinas, *Existence and Existents*, p. 60.

44. Visker, *Truth and Singularity*, p. 266.

45. For Marion, see *GWB*, p. 55, "a refutation remains within the field of predication." See also *DMP*, p. 228.

46. Compare Visker, *The Inhuman Condition*, p. 13, where such a transcendence "loses its platonic prestige and becomes vulnerable, in need of the particular which it is unable to fully take up into its absoluteness."

47. See for instance Levinas, *TI*, p. 147.

48. See also the reference to birth, in Levinas, *TI*, p. 144.

49. I am paraphrasing here Heidegger, *Being and Time*, p. 271. See also p. 329.

50. Ibid, pp. 426–27; italics mine; see also ibid., pp. 442–43.

51. Heidegger, *Einleitung in die Philosophie*, p. 331.

52. See ibid., p. 324. See also *Being and Time*, p. 237.

53. Heidegger, *Einleitung in die Philosophie*, pp. 324–25; translation mine. For such an element of mission in *Being and Time*, see note 38 of chapter 3.

54. Dastur, *La phénoménologie en questions* (Paris: Vrin, 2004), p. 127.

55. Heidegger, *Einleitung in die Philosophie*, p. 139.

56. Heidegger, *Being and Time*, p. 173.

57. J. Derrida and J.-L. Nancy, "Responsabilité—du sens à venir," in *Sens en tous sens*, p. 184.

58. See Nancy, *L'intrus* (Paris: Galilée, 2000).

59. Ibid., pp. 29–30; my translation.

60. Heidegger, *Einleitung in die Philosophie*, p. 334. See also *Being and Time*, p. 264.

61. Nancy, *Etre singulier pluriel* (Paris: Galilée, 1996), p. 52.

62. Heidegger, *Being and Time*, p. 213.

63. See for this point Raffoul, *A chaque fois mien*, pp. 58, 65, 77–83.

64. Heidegger, *Being and Time*, p. 350.

65. Heidegger, "The Onto-theo-logical Structure of Metaphysics," p. 51.

Chapter Seven. "And There Shall Be No More Boredom": Problems with Overcoming Metaphysics

1. Levinas, OB, p. 124: "Substitution frees the subject from ennui."

2. Heidegger, *Being and Time*, pp. 262ff.

3. Ibid., pp. 263ff.

4. Ibid., p. 263.

5. Ibid., p. 213.

6. Compare ibid., p. 217.

7. Heidegger, *Einleitung in die Philosophie*, p. 334; *Being and Time*, p. 264.

8. Heidegger, *Being and Time*, p. 266.

9. Ibid., pp. 153–68, 210–24.

10. Ibid., p. 267.

11. Ibid.; my italics.

12. Ibid., p. 267.

13. Heidegger, *Introduction to Metaphysics*, p. 198.

14. Heidegger, *Being and Time*, p. 129.

15. Heidegger, "On the Essence and Concept of Physis in Aristotle's Physics B, 1" p. 200.

16. For that which follows, see Heidegger, *Introduction to Metaphysics*, p. 192.

17. Ibid. p. 193.

18. Ibid., p. 196. The German has "das Seiendste am Seienden"; see Heidegger, *Einführung in die Metaphysik* (Tübingen: Niemeyer, 1958), p. 140.

19. Ibid.

20. Ibid.

21. Ibid., pp. 148, 123.

22. See Heidegger, *Being and Time*, p. 268; Heidegger's italics.

23. Heidegger, *Introduction to Metaphysics*, p. 3.

24. See Heidegger, *Vier Seminäre* (Frankfurt am Main: Klosterman, 1977), p. 100.

25. For sickness, see *Being and Time*, p. 291. For boredom, see *The Fundamental*

Concepts of Metaphysics: World. Finitude. Solitude, trans. W. Mcneill and N. Walker (Bloomington: Indiana University Press, 1995).

26. As Visker does in *Truth and Singularity*, pp. 23–46, 55ff.

27. Heidegger, *Being and Time*, p. 315.

28. Ibid., p. 233; see *Sein und Zeit*, p. 188, "die existenziale Selbigkeit des Erschließens mit dem Erschlossenen."

29. One should not too quickly object that such a return loses its sense in a philosophy where the '*intellectus*' is substituted for the affective *Befindlichkeit*. The thesis that an object can be represented adequately by the subject is as questionable as the thesis that our affective states would be available to us in a transparent manner.

30. The example is taken from Visker, *Truth and Singularity*, pp. 328–29, 349.

31. See Levinas, *TI*, p. 66, with parallels on pp. 296 and 262.

32. Levinas, *OB*, pp. 45–51, 153–62.

33. The frequent recurrence, for instance, in quarrels of formulas such as 'Did I say that?' or 'I did not say that!' might be elucidated thus.

34. Cf. Marion, *EP*, pp. 112–20.

35. Derrida, *Le Toucher, Jean-Luc Nancy* (Paris: Galilée, 2000), p. 267. For a confrontation of Derrida and Nancy, see also my "*What Comes after Christianity? Jean-Luc Nancy's Deconstruction of Christianity*," *Research in Phenomenology* 39 (2009), pp. 266–81.

36. Levinas, *Ethics and Infinity: Conversations with Philippe Nemo*, trans. R. A. Cohen (Pittsburgh: Duquesne University Press, 1985), p. 85; Marion, *BG*, p. 232.

37. Robert Bernasconi, "Who Is my Neighbor? Questioning the Generosity of Western Thought," in *Ethics and Responsibility in the Phenomenological Tradition* (Pittsburgh: Duquesne University, 1992), p. 22. For this question, see also Marion, "From the Other to the Individual," in *Transcendence: Philosophy, Literature, and Theology Approach the Beyond* (New York: Routledge, 2004), p. 49.

38. I am referring here to a rather perplexing statement of Levinas: "I often say, though it's a dangerous thing to say publicly, that humanity consists of the Bible and the Greeks: all the rest—all the exotic—is dance"; see Bernasconi, "Who Is My Neighbor?" p. 14.

39. Visker, *The Inhuman Condition*, p. 14.

40. Visker, *Truth and Singularity*, p. 349.

41. For this, one should ponder why in case of the first encounter with a stranger the first questions to be asked most often concern the other's name and his or her profession.

42. Alain Finkielkraut, *La humanité perdue: Essai sur le XXe siècle* (Paris, Seuil, 1996), p. 128, as cited in Visker, *The Inhuman Condition*, p. 160. The few instances in which Levinas gives a positive meaning to nonverbal language may not be able to counter these objections. For this nuance on the strict distinction between face and form, see both *TI*, p. 262, and *OB*, pp. 85, 192n. 27.

43. Heidegger, *Being and Time*, p. 158.

44. Ibid., p. 159.

45. Ibid.

46. See Marion, *Prolegomena to Charity*, pp. 90–101, and "From the Other to the Individual," pp. 50–52. Note that whereas the former text distinguishes between Kant and Levinas' ethics, the latter interprets Levinas' ethics in a Kantian fashion.

47. Marion, *Prolegomena to Charity*, pp. 92–93.

48. Ibid., p. 94, mod.

49. Cf. ibid., p. 95.

50. Marion, *EP*, p. 100, mod.

51. In this respect, I find Marion's somewhat gateway 'theory' of homosexuality most appalling; see *EP*, p. 165, where Marion discusses perversion and states the following: "I will play the nature of bodies against nature, without scruple or restraint [. . .]. Thus I will transgress the borderline between the sexes, I could almost end up—why not?—transgressing the borderline between species." Taken together with Marion's downplaying of successive monogamy, what is needed is perhaps not so much a treatise on the "divine form and essence of my [. . .] loves" (*EP*, 137) but rather a thorough phenomenological account of our finite, all-too-finite, loves: instead of hoping for an infinite, somewhat romantic, love, as Marion seems to do, the philosopher should dare to ask whether even love, that thing 'always sought and always missed,' might be finite.

52. This example is taken from Falque's "Phénoménologie de l'extraordinaire," p. 62.

53. For this critique, see Marion, "The Voice without Name: Homage to Levinas," in *The Face of the Other and the Trace of God: Essays on the Philosophy of Emmanuel Levinas*, ed. J. Bloechl (New York: Fordham University Press, 2000), pp. 224–42, esp. 226–28.

54. Ibid., p. 227.

55. See Heidegger, *The Metaphysical Foundations of Logic* (Bloomington: Indiana University Press, 1984), trans. M. Heim, p. 165n.

56. Heidegger, *Introduction to Metaphysics*, p. 7.

57. Ibid., pp. 7–8.

58. Levinas, "Un Dieu Homme?" in his *Entre Nous*, p. 72; my translation.

Chapter Eight. Marion and Levinas on Metaphysics

1. For Radical Orthodoxy's aversion to Duns Scotus, see J. K. A. Smith, *Introducing Radical Orthodoxy: Mapping a Post-secular Theology* (Grand Rapids: Baker Academic, 2004), pp. 96–100.

2. See Marion, *IeD*, p. 28, "La métaphysique pense l'Être, mais à sa guise." Note that, in French, the expression *à sa guise* has the connotation of doing something

in the manner one feels appropriate, so Marion retains here what one can call the "instrumental interpretation" of metaphysics, namely, that it reserves a place for God there where it is in need of protecting its system from incoherency.

3. Marion, "La science toujours recherchée et toujours manquante," in *La métaphysique: Son histoire, sa critique, ses enjeux*, ed. J.-M. Narbonne and L. Langlois (Paris: Vrin, 1999), p. 29. Compare Heidegger, "The Onto-Theo-logical Constitution of Metaphysics," p. 68.

4. See Smith, *Introducing Radical Orthodoxy*, pp. 92–93, "[Radical Orthodoxy] observes a deep continuity between the modern and the postmodern [but] contests the supposed continuity between the medieval and the modern, locating a decisive rupture in the late Middle Ages."

5. Marion quotes Heidegger's *Nietzsche*, vol. 1, trans. D. F. Krell (New York: Harper and Row, 1979), p. 106.

6. The reader is reminded that both Levinas and Heidegger entertain this definition of the subject. See *TI*, p. 36, and *Being and Time*, p. 150.

7. Note that 'ontotheology' concerns both the theologization of ontology (being understood from out of a supreme theological being) and the ontologization of theology (God or the Gods understood from out of being[s]). See Mabille, *Hegel, Heidegger et la métaphysique*, pp. 127–28.

8. Mabille, *Hegel, Heidegger et la métaphysique*, pp. 122, 130 *et passim*.

9. Ibid., p. 144.

10. Ibid., p. 142.

11. Marion is citing Heidegger, *Was ist metaphysik?* p. 21.

12. Mabille, *Hegel, Heidegger et la métaphysique*, p. 143.

13. Ibid., p. 149.

14. Heidegger, *The Fundamental Concepts of Metaphysics*, p. 42. Heidegger's italics, and *Die Frage nach dem Ding* (Tübingen: Niemeyer, 1962), pp. 50–53, 83–87, esp. p. 84.

15. Heidegger, *The Fundamental Concepts of Metaphysics*, p. 54; Heidegger's italics.

16. Ibid., p. 55; italicized in Heidegger's text.

17. Heidegger, *Die Frage nach dem Ding*, p. 77.

18. See Heidegger, *Parmenides* (Frankfurt am Main: Klostermann, 1992), pp. 72–79, esp. p. 76.

19. Heidegger, *The Fundamental Concepts of Metaphysics*, p. 55; Heidegger's italics.

20. Smith, *Speech and Theology*, p. 5.

21. Marion, "La science toujours recherchée et toujours manquante," p. 15.

22. Ibid., pp. 18–19.

23. Ibid., p. 21.

24. Ibid., p. 22.

25. Ibid.

26. Ibid.

27. Ibid., p. 23; my italics.

28. Ibid., p. 24, also for the references to Malebranche, Descartes, and Spinoza. On this univocal concept of beings, see also *IE*, p. 145.

29. Hemming, *Postmodernity's Transcending: Devaluing God* (London: SCM, 2005), p. 100.

30. Mabille, *Hegel, Heidegger et la métaphysique*, pp. 35, 368 *et passim*.

31. Ibid., pp. 35, 32 respectively; Mabille's emphasis. One should not underestimate the powers that are unleashed by such a noetization and the corresponding downplaying of the being itself. One might even argue for a retrieval of the *distinctio realis* between existence and essence to overcome the contemporary abundance of images and imagination. For, whereas the Middle Ages still knew the (qualitative) difference between essence and existence in that one might represent an essence that could not exist (for example: the concept of 'pink elephant' can be represented and held in thought clearly and distinctly but does not exist), in our days the danger seems to be that something can exist only insofar as it can be represented. If one can no longer tell the difference between the essence of a being (whether represented in the mind or virtually as an image on a screen) and its existence, one can divine what happens when one or the other empire or individual takes hold of such appearances that are no longer the appearance *of* something or someone. One might think here of recent phenomena such as photo-shopping or the Internet.

32. Ibid., p. 35.

33. Ibid., p. 36.

34. Marion, "La science toujours recherchée et toujours manquante," p. 26.

35. Ibid., p. 30.

36. See for this Marion, *DMP*, pp. 103–18.

37. See also Marion, *DMP*, p. 117: "[A]fter the insuffency of the *ego*, God comes along and fills the function of *causa sui*. This function is imposed on him only insofar as it precedes him in terms of the necessities proper to the onto-theology of *causa*." The logic of the *cause* thus precedes (the being of) God and *prescribes to God God's real being*.

38. See also Marion, *EP*, p. 221, which again indicates such univocity, stating that "God loves *like* we love, with the same love as us."

39. See also Marion, *DMP*, p. 68.

40. Marion, "The 'End of Metaphysics' as a Possibility," in *Religion after Metaphysics*, ed. M. A. Wrathall (Cambridge: Cambridge University Press, 2003), pp. 166–89.

41. Marion here refers to his study "La fin de la fin de la métaphysique," *Laval théologique et philosophique* 42 (1986), pp. 23–33.

42. Cf. Heidegger, *Was ist Metaphysik?* p. 21.

43. Levinas, "La souffrance inutile," in *Entre Nous*, p. 113.

44. See also Raffoul, *A chaque fois mien*, p. 229: "Je dois être proprement l'impropre."

45. Marion, "Notes on the Ontological Indifference," p. 28.

46. Kosky, *Levinas and the Philosophy of Religion* (Indianapolis: Indiana University Press, 2001), p. 50.

47. Ibid., quoting Levinas, *OB*, 42.

48. Or red to reddening, but since in "the verb of the apophansis, which is the verb properly so called, the verb to be, essence resounds and is heard" (OB, 41), one must conclude that "to be" is "the verb par excellence" (*OB*, 42).

49. See Levinas, *OB*, p. 134; *GDT*, p. 150.

50. For Heidegger's critique on language as mere designation, see his *Unterwegs zur Sprache* (Pfüllingen: Neske, 1975), p. 164, and *Introduction to Metaphysics*, p. 183.

51. See Levinas, *OB*, p. 42.

52. Kosky, *Levinas and the Philosophy of Religion*, p. 51.

53. Cf. Levinas, *OB*, p. 24, where "the question about the question" is posed from out of the fact that the intelligibility of ontology can itself be questioned in the sense of 'why ontology and knowledge at all?'

54. Levinas, *OB*, p. 150, mod.

55. See Heidegger, *Being and Time*, p. 56, and *The History of the Concept of Time*, trans. T. Kisiel (Bloomington: Indiana University Press, 1992), p. 85.

56. See for this, of course, Levinas, *OB*, pp. 45–48, 149, 150, 151.

57. Levinas' problem (and ours) is, of course, that that which 'is' 'otherwise than being' will 'be forever on the verge of becoming a noun' as well.

58. See for this also the section "The subject's self otherwise than being."

59. I use the word "*produce*" here in Levinas' sense. Recalling that "this book [*Totality and Infinity*] recounts how infinity is produced" Levinas' definition runs: "the term 'production' designates both the effectuation of being (the event 'is produced,' an automobile 'is produced') and its being brought to light or its exposition (an argument 'is produced,' an actor 'is produced')" Levinas, *TI*, p. 26.

60. Levinas, *OB*, p. 154/AqE, p. 197; emphasis added. When, therefore, Levinas asks on the same page whether "a face abide[s] at the same time [à la fois] in representation and in proximity; is it community and difference?," the answer is clearly affirmative. Confirmation for this interpretation might be delivered by Levinas himself, see OB, p. 158/AqE, p. 201, "the neighbor that obsesses me is already a face, both [à la fois] incomparable and incomparable, a unique face and in relationship with faces." It is thus no coincidence that this coincidentia oppositorum is produced with, precisely, the advent of the third party.

61. The French has significantly: "Il y a pesée, pensée, objectivation et, par là, un arrêt où se trahit ma relation anarchique à l'illéité." See AqE, p. 201.

62. Helpful are also Heidegger's remarks in Zeit und Sein, where he states that we do not say of being (as we do of beings) that 'being is . . .'; rather we say 'there is being' (es gibt Sein). See M. Heidegger, *On Time and Being*, trans. J. Stambaugh (New York: Harper and Row, 1972), pp. 4–5.

63. See also Marion, *DMP*, p. 333.

Conclusion: Toward a Phenomenology of the Invisible

1. Husserl, *Ideas Pertaining to a Pure Phenomenology and to a Phenomenological Philosophy*. Second Book, esp. pp. 100–01.

2. Lacoste, "Perception, Transcendence, and the Experience of God," in *Transcendence and Phenomenology*, ed. C. Cunningham and P. Candler (London: SCM, 2009), pp. 1–33.

3. See, Heidegger, *Vier Seminäre*, p. 137.

4. Heidegger, "On the Essence and Concept of Physis in Aristotle's Physics B, 1," p. 227.

5. One is tempted to add vocation (religious or otherwise) to this list not only because the grand story of vocation stemming from Jonah could be elucidated along these Levinasian lines but also because we perhaps still need a less violent account of religious vocation.

6. See, for instance, Heidegger, *Introduction to Metaphysics*, p. 111.

7. Levinas, "De L'Un à l'autre," in *Entre Nous*, pp. 155–56.

8. Ibid., p. 157.

9. Ibid., p. 155. Recall the equivalence between *term* and *terminus* I have described earlier.

10. Ibid., p. 171.

11. Although the 'nihil privativum' figures in Kant's *Critique of Pure Reason* as "the empty object of a concept," one should not forget that Ricoeur traces the origin of the concept to Augustine's conception of (original) sin. See Ricoeur, *Le mal: Un défi à la philosophie et à la théologie* (Genève: Labor et Fides, 1986), p. 24. This is so, of course, because, at least in Augustine's world, nothing can be said to exist outside God. This is why evil, which is seemingly without God, is nevertheless understood as a privatio boni: evil is not an instance distinct from God, but merely a lesser good. The reference to Kant can be found in *BG*, p. 195.

12. Visker, *The Inhuman Condition*, pp. 127–28.

13. Ibid., p. 130; Visker's italics.

14. See for instance, ibid., p. 172: "[I]nstead of their being an 'accord' between [the other and I] [. . .] there would rather be an unease, a discomfort between us—an affect—that is not eo ipso ethical. There would be between us an irresponsibility that is not the absence of an ethical responsibility—not a manco or lack of, but something sui generis that complicates ontology (i.e. this something is not a thing, an on, and it escapes logos) without giving ethics pride of place."

15. Ibid., p. 137; Visker's italics. For this question see especially Levinas, *OB*, pp. 153–54, where Levinas raises the question whether the election of the subject by the infinite "reduce[s] me to the status of an articulation of its divine economy." An affirmative answer might be intimated in the fact that for Levinas every contestation of the infinite is only possible if its pretension is already heard. Therefore, it is "by this contestation" that "is produced my entry into the designs of the infinite."

16. Heidegger, "On the Essence and Concept of Physis in Aristotle's Physics B, 1," p. 212; Heidegger's italics.

17. Ibid., p. 210. Heidegger's italics.

18. Ibid. For the German, see Heidegger, *Wegmarken* (Frankfürt a. Main: Klostermann, 2004), p. 275. In phenomenological terms: it concerns here the particular being in the how of its appearing as this or that being, in its mode of presencing. One might perhaps also think here of the Kantian category of 'quality.'

19. Ibid.

20. Ibid.

21. See on 'presencing,' also my "Anarchistic Tendencies in Contemporary Philosophy: Reiner Schürmann and the Hybris of Philosophy," *Research in Phenomenology* 37 (2007), pp. 417–39.

22. For Marion on the 'phenomenology of the invisible,' see Marion, BG, p. 157. See, however, also the retractatio in Marion, IE, pp. 109–11.

23. Marion describes the Levinasian other in like manner, in ID, p. 199.

24. Heidegger, "On the Essence and Concept of Physis in Aristotle's Physics B, 1," p. 227. Heidegger's italics.

25. Ibid., p. 226.

26. One should not pass over lightly Heidegger's preoccupation with the nothing ('das Nichts') in his later works. For it is intriguing to see that the endeavor to think the absolute Good suffers from precisely the same structural problems as an absolute Nothing. Indeed, as much as the absolute good loses its absoluteness because it always and already must show up by relation to the subject that thinks it, so the absolute nothing seems to turn into a *nihil privativum* (an absence of something appearing to someone) as soon as one starts to think it.

27. Heidegger, "On the Essence and Concept of Physis in Aristotle's Physics B, 1," p. 227.

28. Levinas, "Transcendence and Intelligibility," in BPW, p. 152.

29. Ibid., p. 153.

30. I owe the first formulation to Laurence Hemming; the second one comes from Nancy, *Le sens du monde* (Paris: Galilée, 1993), p. 62.

31. See, for this Richard Capobianco, "Heidegger and the Critique of the Understanding of Evil as Privatio Boni," *Philosophy and Theology* 5 (1991), p. 180. One should note some intriguing parallels in contemporary philosophy with regard to the question of total negation and (the) nothing. See for instance, Levinas, TI, p. 40, where he distinguishes between transcendence and negativity. For negation and its (im)possibility in contemporary philosophy, see H. Bergson, *Evolution créatrice: Creative Evolution* (New York: Holt, 1913), p. 278. For Levinas' discussion of this passage, see Levinas, *L'intrigue de l'infini*. Textes revues et présentés par M.-A. Lescourret (Paris: Flammarion, 1994), pp. 111–13. Marion criticises Bergson's account in *Being Given*, p. 338 n. 97. See also Husserl's thought experiment of the annihilation of the world in Husserl, *Ideen zu einer reinen Phänomenologie: Erstes Buch* (Hamburg: Felix Meiner

Verlag, 1992), pp. 103–06. All these authors seem to agree that a total negation is not possible, in that it always yields to some kind of presence (or affirmation). For Husserl as for Descartes, it leads to the immemorial presence of the ego, for the early Levinas to the less than generous presence of being as 'il y a,' for Marion to the privilege of givenness (which is already affirmed when denying it), for the later Levinas it leads to the 'presence' of otherness (since denying the primacy of the Other, is only possible on the basis of the prior affirmation), for Sartre negation is the very activity of consciousness as for Hegel it was the motor of the ascent and of the process of history. For Heidegger, finally, the nothing and angst again yields the possibility of a proper comportment to the world.

32. Mayz Vallenilla, *Le problème du néant chez Kant*, p. 69.

33. This is the hypothesis in ibid., p. 71: "Qu'arrive-t-il si la negation ne se conçoit non seulement come absence de qualities positives, mais au contraire, comme présence de qualité negatives."

34. Levinas, "Transcendence and Evil," in *Of God who Comes to Mind*, p. 128. One can understand this as a perfect reversal of the ontological argument: it is not God whose essence necessarily implies his existence; it is of the essence of evil that it exists, is present as an excess and not as a lack. When I burn myself on a stove, for instance, the presence of this pain is not merely the absence of something good, it is the presence of an excess that imposes its existence.

35. See for this the entry on original sin in *Dictionnaire de théologie catholique*, ed. A. Vacant, E. Mangenot and E. Aman (Paris: Letousey et Ané, 1930–1976), esp. pp. 439–44.

36. See for this ibid., pp. 323–27.

37. See for this esp. Marion, *ID*, pp. 185–95; *GWB*, pp. 186–97.

38. See Smith, *Who's Afraid of Postmodernism? Taking Derrida, Lyotard, and Foucault to Church* (Grand Rapids: Baker Academic, 2006). Citations are from Smith, *Introducing Radical Orthodoxy*, p. 151, 157.

39. Lacoste, *Carmel*, p. 581.

40. See for this remark, Pickstock, *After Writing*, p. 233.

41. Pickstock, *After Writing*, p. 234.

42. In a letter to the author of this text, dating 31st January 2001, ""mais pour aller plus loin [. . .] disons qu'il faut décrire une 'co-affection.'"" Note that the concept of co-affection, 'Mit-befindlichkeit' appears twice in *Being and Time*, on p. 181 and p. 205.

43. Marion, "Lacoste ou la correction de l'analytique existential," *Transversalités* 110 (2009), pp. 171–75.

44. The liturgical experience and the experiences of 'well-being there' seem to turn into an adversary of the existential analytic when "they themselves pretend to the most authentic experiences there are" (*PP*, 161).

45. It is noteworthy that a reflection on the shared fact of existing is not absent from Heidegger's later work. In his book on Plato's Sophist, for instance, Heidegger

traces what he calls the "commonality" of speech, see Heidegger *Platon: Sophistes* (Frankfurt am Main: Klostermann, 1992), esp. 593–610. What human beings have in common is that they speak about a shared world, or rather it is and through language that we participate in the world that is common to all: the world, as it were, happens in speech. In effect, for Heidegger as for Lacoste, with this speaking of the same things in and out of a shared world, it is a matter of something 'objective,' that is, it is a property of the things gathered in the world (see for this esp. p. 605).

46. Nancy, *The Experience of Freedom* (Stanford: Stanford University Press, 1993), trans. B. Mcdonald, p. 123. See also p. 126.

47. Smith, *Introducing Radical Orthodoxy*, p. 258. For Smith's critique, see pp. 157–66.

48. Smith, *Introducing Radical Orthodoxy*, pp. 157n. 40, 165–66.

49. See also Marion, *DMP*, pp. 293, 318.

50. Smith, *Introducing Radical Orthodoxy*, pp. 256, 166.

51. Hart, *The Tresspass of the Sign: Deconstruction, Theology, and Philosophy* (New York: Fordham University Press, 2000) p. xxxii.

Index

2513734R00144

Printed in Great Britain
by Amazon.co.uk, Ltd.,
Marston Gate.